Increase Your Web Traffic In a Weekend

Sixth Edition

Jerry Lee Ford, Jr.

and

William R. Stanek

Course Technology PTR

A part of Cengage Learning

COURSE TECHNOLOGY
CENGAGE Learning

Australia, Brazil, Japan, Korea, Mexico, Singapore, Spain, United Kingdom, United States

COURSE TECHNOLOGY
CENGAGE Learning™

Increase Your Web Traffic In a Weekend, Sixth Edition
Jerry Lee Ford, Jr. and William R. Stanek

Publisher and General Manager,
Course Technology PTR:
Stacy L. Hiquet

Associate Director of Marketing:
Sarah Panella

Manager of Editorial Services:
Heather Talbot

Marketing Manager:
Mark Hughes

Senior Acquisitions Editor:
Mitzi Koontz

Project Editor:
Jenny Davidson

Technical Reviewer:
Keith Davenport

Copy Editor:
Kim Benbow

Interior Layout:
Shawn Morningstar

Cover Designer:
Mike Tanamachi

Indexer:
Larry Sweazy

Proofreader:
Sandi Wilson

All trademarks are the property of their respective owners.
All images © Cengage Learning unless otherwise noted.
Library of Congress Control Number: 2010922096
ISBN-13: 978-1-4354-5666-2
ISBN-10: 1-4354-5666-1

Course Technology, a part of Cengage Learning
20 Channel Center Street
Boston, MA 02210
USA

Cengage Learning is a leading provider of customized learning solutions with office locations around the globe, including Singapore, the United Kingdom, Australia, Mexico, Brazil, and Japan. Locate your local office at:
international.cengage.com/region

Cengage Learning products are represented in Canada by Nelson Education, Ltd.

For your lifelong learning solutions, visit **courseptr.com**
Visit our corporate website at **cengage.com**

Printed in United States of America
1 2 3 4 5 6 7 12 11 10

Jerry Lee Ford, Jr.

To my wonderful children, Alexander, William, and Molly,
and my beautiful wife, Mary.

William R. Stanek

To my children, Jasmine, William Jr., and Jennifer.
Thanks for the joy, the laughter, and the light.
Always chase your dreams…

ACKNOWLEDGMENTS

There are a number of individuals who deserve credit for their work on the sixth edition of this book. Special thanks go out to Mitzi Koontz, senior acquisitions editor and Jenny Davidson, project editor. Thanks to everyone else at Course Technology PTR for all their hard work. Thanks also go out to those individuals who made significant contributions to the five previous editions of this book.

ABOUT THE AUTHORS

Jerry Lee Ford, Jr. is an author, educator, and an IT professional with over 21 years of experience in information technology, including roles as an automation analyst, technical manager, technical support analyst, automation engineer, and security analyst. He is the author of 35 books and co-author of two additional books. His published works include *Ajax Programming for the Absolute Beginner*; *HTML, XHTML, and CSS for the Absolute Beginner*; *XNA 3.1 Game Development for Teens*; *Scratch Programming for Teens*, and *Microsoft Visual Basic 2008 Express Programming for the Absolute Beginner*. Ford has a master's degree in business administration from Virginia Commonwealth University in Richmond, Virginia, and has over five years of experience as an adjunct instructor teaching networking courses in information technology.

William R. Stanek is a leading network technology expert and an award-winning author. Over the years, his practical advice has helped programmers, developers, and network engineers all over the world. He is also a regular contributor to leading publications like *PC Magazine*. He has written, co-authored, or contributed to numerous computer books, including *Microsoft Windows 2000 Administrator's Pocket Consultant, Microsoft SQL Server 7.0 Administrator's Pocket Consultant*, and *Windows 2000 Scripting Administrator's Guide*.

Mr. Stanek has a master's degree in information systems, with distinction, and a bachelor's degree in computer science, magna cum laude. Mr. Stanek has been involved in the commercial Internet community since 1991. He has experience in developing server technology, encryption, Internet development, and a strong understanding of e-commerce technology and its development.

CONTENTS

Sunday Morning
Attracting the Masses 155

Introduction

These days, everyone seems to have a home page or a Web site. However, just because you create and publish a Web site doesn't mean anyone will visit it. Competition to attract visitors is extreme. The reality is that of the millions of Web pages out there, only a handful actually attract a steady readership; and these same Web pages are the ones that attract advertisers. In order to compete, you need to develop and implement a Web site promotion plan.

What can you do when you build a home page that no one visits? What can you do to earn money on your Web site? Is there an easy way to attract readers and advertisers without spending a fortune? *Increase Your Web Traffic In a Weekend, Sixth Edition* answers these questions. It is designed to take the mystery out of Web promotion and to help you make your Web site stand out and get noticed.

What's This Book About?

With users from countries around the world, the Web has an extremely diverse audience. Trying to tap into the tremendous potential of the Web can be a daunting task. Enter *Increase Your Web Traffic In a Weekend, Sixth Edition*. The goal of this book is to lay out a cost-effective, comprehensive plan that both Web beginners and experts can use to build an audience for a home page or Web site.

This book has compiled low-cost Web promotion and advertising techniques collected from years of practical experience. These secrets could save you thousands of dollars. Now that's something to think about!

How Is This Book Organized?

This book is designed to be easy to follow and understand. Anyone, regardless of skill level or work schedule, will be able to learn the secrets of successful Web promotion and advertising.

This book is divided into five sessions. Session one begins with a Friday evening preview of what is ahead for the weekend. Saturday is broken down into morning and afternoon sessions designed to help you understand the following concepts:

- Where to publicize your home pages for free
- How to tailor your pages for search engines
- How to use <META> tags to increase Web traffic
- How to register with search engines
- How to submit your site to directories, guides, and lists
- How to use specialized directories, such as community guides
- How to use social networking Web sites to market your Web site
- How to use registration services

Sunday is also divided into morning and afternoon sessions designed to help you understand the following ideas:

- The right way to sell your site through e-mail
- Techniques that you can use to attract masses
- How to create, track, and manage banner advertising
- How to place ads on other sites without spending a dime
- How to find out who is currently visiting your home page

- ☐ How to track and analyze visitor statistics
- ☐ How to put those statistics to work
- ☐ How to direct visitors to popular areas of your Web site
- ☐ How to gain readers who otherwise would be lost because they used the wrong URL

Who Should Read This Book?

Anyone who wants to learn how to attract visitors to a home page or a Web site should read this book. Consider the following questions:

- ☐ Are you disappointed with the results that you've achieved through Web publishing?
- ☐ Have you created wonderful Web pages, yet receive only a few visitors?
- ☐ Do you think that the lack of visitors means that your ideas, interests, or products aren't interesting?
- ☐ Do you want to reach a larger audience?
- ☐ Do you want to learn how to attract a steady readership to your Web site?
- ☐ Do you want to learn the secrets of Web promotion and marketing?
- ☐ Do you want to attract advertisers to your Web site?
- ☐ Do you want to learn how to tap into the tremendous potential of the Web?
- ☐ Do you want to learn the secrets of marketing without spending a dime?

If you answered yes to any of these questions, this book is for you.

What Do You Need to Use This Book?

The most important ingredients for using this book are a connection to the Internet and a home page or Web site that you want to promote. You'll also need to set aside a little time to implement some of the Web site promotion techniques that you will learn about in this book. A major goal of this book is to present you with free and low-cost Web site promotion techniques. Depending on how eager you are to see increased Web traffic, you may want to set aside a small budget, anywhere from $50 to a few hundred dollars, to support your Web site promotion plan. However, 99 percent of the Web site promotion techniques that you will learn about as you go through this book can be implemented at no cost. So, setting aside a small budget is optional.

What Do You Need to Know?

Increase Your Web Traffic In a Weekend, Sixth Edition guides you through everything you need to successfully promote your Web site or home page. It is assumed that you already have a Web site that you are ready to promote. Although you certainly don't need to be an HTML expert, you should know at least the basics of HTML. If you don't know HTML, a good "how to" guide is Course Technology's *HTML, XHTML, and CSS for the Absolute Beginner* (ISBN: 1435454235). Finally, you should also know the basics of Web browsing. If this is all true, you're on the right track.

Conventions Used in This Book

This book uses a number of conventions to help make it easier for you to work with, including:

NOTE **Notes.** Enhance a discussion in the text by drawing your attention to a particular point that needs emphasis.

Tips. Offer helpful hints or additional information.

Italics. Used to highlight new terms and emphasize key pieces of information.

Promoting Your Web Site to the World

- ➤ Promoting Your Web Site without Spending a Fortune
- ➤ Making the Web Work for You
- ➤ Getting Your Web Site Noticed

Thousands of Web publishers have created home pages to sell products and services or to simply share ideas. Often they are disappointed with the results, receiving only a few visitors. These publishers might think that their ideas, interests, and products aren't interesting, but nothing could be further from the truth. The real problem is not the content of the Web site but a lack of visibility. You could have the best site in the world, but if no one knows about it, they can't visit it. Capitalizing on available resources and knowing how to promote your site are the keys to increasing your Web traffic. By the end of this weekend, you'll know a great deal more about how to do that and will be well on your way to having your site seen, visited, and explored.

So go ahead—get started. It's Friday evening (at least if you're following the schedule). This evening's session provides an overview of what you need to get started, and it gets you acquainted with crucial issues and resources you'll focus on to get your Web site noticed by the masses.

Increase Your Web Traffic In a Weekend, Sixth Edition is designed as a guide to everything you need to successfully promote your Web site or home page. In this book, promotion encompasses publicizing, marketing, advertising, and all the other techniques that help bring traffic to a Web site. Although promotion is 35 percent inspiration and 65 percent perspiration, promoting your Web site can be an awful lot of fun.

You Built It, but Will They Come?

As incredible as it might seem, cyberspace contains hundreds of millions of Web pages. As if this competition wasn't stiff enough, there are no Web maps—and there are relatively few signposts—to guide readers anywhere. So how can anyone find your Web site? Unfortunately, no easy answer to this question exists.

After you've spent hours of your time and possibly hundreds or thousands of dollars creating a home page, it is certainly disheartening when no one visits your site—or the traffic is so minimal that it might as well be non-existent. Usually, the next step for many Web publishers is to launch their own promotion campaign. They register with all the search engines they can find, blanket newsgroups and mailing lists with information about their home pages, tell everyone they know to visit their site—in other words, they explore all the promotion avenues they've heard and read about.

You could register with search engines till your fingers won't type any more, but unless you truly understand how search engines work and how to use their indexing features, you may not get the results you are looking for. You could send out tons of e-mail through mailing lists and news-groups, but unless you know what you are doing, you will get so much hate mail that you will truly wish you had never published a home page in the first place.

In the end, when the euphoria over getting a new Web page noticed wears off, many Web publishers wake up to the cruel reality that creating a Web page doesn't automatically draw visitors to it. Fortunately, there are reliable, low-cost and free ways to get your Web site noticed, as well as to sub-stantially increase traffic to your Web site. By the end of this book, you will have everything you need to successfully attract a following to your Web site, gain an audience for your ideas, and promote your Web site to the world.

Can You Really Promote Your Web Site without Spending a Fortune?

Invariably, people ask "How much will it cost?" If you've been publishing on the Web for a while, or if you have done some considerable browsing, you have probably come across sales pitches like these:

- Get 325 e-mail addresses for the top magazine, newspapers, and e-zines—only $325
- We'll submit your site everywhere for $275
- Send e-mail promotions to millions for pennies apiece!
- Get listed in 1,500+ search engines and directories for $99.95

Unfortunately, whether these types of pitches sell you on a pennies-apiece concept or a flat-fee-per-use concept, they are usually nothing more than cleverly designed ways to get you to open your pocketbook. For example, out of the list of 325 top magazines, newspapers, and e-zines, usually only a handful are really interested in the topic that your site covers, and you could get these e-mail addresses simply by visiting the related Web sites yourself. So why pay $325 for a few e-mail addresses that you could get yourself in less than an hour?

NOTE Most of the techniques or concepts presented in this book are cost-free. That said, the Web is constantly changing and what may be free or low-cost today may not be tomorrow.

Making the Web Work for You

Making the Web work for you means conducting your own Web promotion campaign. As with any campaign, your promotion efforts start with careful planning—such as Web site promotion through search engines. Few people truly understand how search engines do what they do. Now it is time to make these search engines work for you. Rather than visit

Google's Web site (www.google.com), shown in Figure 1.1, to find other Web sites, you will use Google to bring visitors to your Web site.

Figure 1.1

Google—one of the top search engines.

You start by learning to take advantage of the way search engines find and retrieve information. Although the inner workings of search engines aren't exactly state secrets, each search engine does things differently, which is why you should use many different techniques to make your Web pages friendlier to search engines. Web pages that are optimized for search engines using the techniques covered in the Saturday Morning session, "Capitalizing on Search Engine Fundamentals," will help put your Web site on the map. These techniques ease the burden of obtaining references to your Web pages.

After you gain a firm understanding of how search engines work, you should register your Web site with the search engines used by the majority of Web users. Although your promotion efforts begin with search engines, you don't stop there. Afterward, you move on to Web guides, lists, and directories, such as the Open Directory (**dmoz.org**), shown in Figure 1.2.

Figure 1.2

Open Directory—
one of the top
Web directories.

Just as few people understand how search engines work, few people take the time to plot out how to get the most out of Web guides, lists, and directories. You will create your own personal plan of attack in the Saturday Morning session, in the section called "Submitting Your Web Site to the Top Guides, Lists, and Directories."

The reason for targeting the best directories is to encourage you to use your time and resources wisely. Why waste your time registering with every single search engine and directory on the planet when 90 percent of Web users find what they are looking for by using the top 10 percent of the Web search and directory sites?

You will find many other search sites and directories that focus on specific types of information. These include Yellow Pages directories, category-specific directories, and specialty directories. Although these search and directory sites generally have narrow focuses, they are popular and frequently used to find information. For example, anyone looking for a business listing can use a Yellow Pages directory, such as yellowbook (www.yellowbook.com), as shown in Figure 1.3.

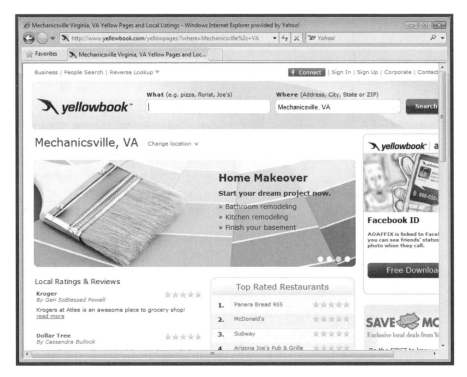

Figure 1.3

yellowbook—a
Yellow Pages
directory.

Including social media sites as part of your Web campaign is just as important as including search engines and directories. In recent years, social media sites have garnered the attention of hundreds of millions of people around the world, making them among the most frequented locations on the Web. Social media sites are different from traditional Web sites in that site members and visitors can directly interact with one another and are largely responsible for the content made available at those sites.

Social media sites form the basis of virtual communities that you are free to join and interact. By becoming a valued member of these sites, you can build up a loyal following and there is no end of the amount of traffic you can ultimately drive to your Web site. An example of one extremely popular social media Web site is Facebook, shown in Figure 1.4. You will learn all about Web marketing through social media based Web sites in Saturday Morning's session "Attracting Visitors Using Social Media."

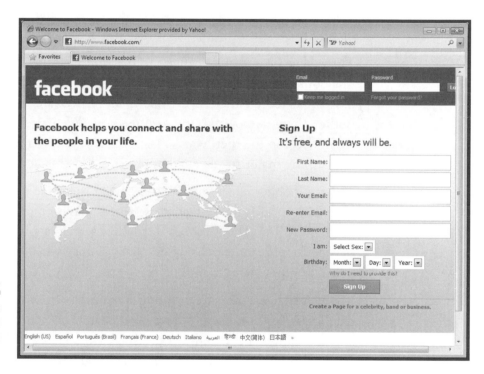

Figure 1.4

Facebook—one of the top social networking Web sites.

Leveraging Search Engines, Directories, and Social Media Web Sites

One of the major themes in any successful Web site promotion campaign is leveraging the search engines and directories to your advantage. However, because there are literally hundreds of search engines and directories out there, it is important that you choose wisely when selecting which search engines and directories to use. As you work your way through this book, you'll be introduced to the best search engines and directories.

Crawler-Based Search Engines

A search engine is a tool that assists people in locating Web sites on the Internet. Search engines seek out and locate new Web sites and then index their contents, storing the results in a search engine database. Search engine databases are repositories where search engines store information about the Web sites that they discover.

There have been many changes on the Internet since the first edition of this book was published. New search engines, such as Google and Bing have appeared on the scene while many others are no longer available. Rather than try to find and register your Web site with every search engine on the Internet, you will be better served by focusing your attention on the major search engines presented in this book.

Today, Google, Yahoo!, and Bing are by far the three most popular search engines on the Web. In fact, these three search engines handle over 90 percent of all searches. Beyond these three search engines, there are plenty of other significant search engines that you may wish to work with. These search engines include: AOL, Ask, Netscape, AltaVista, and Snap.

Many search engine sites no longer maintain their own search engine databases. Instead, they retrieve their search engine results from other search engines. For example, AltaVista is actually owned by Yahoo. Search results retrieved at AltaVista are actually pulled from the Yahoo! search engine database. So if you get your Web site registered with Yahoo, your Web site will also appear in the search results retrieved from AltaVista.

Part of the mission of this book is to help you wade through the complex set of interrelationships that have been established between search engines in order to identify the key search engines with which you will want to register your Web site.

Human-Powered Directories

Like search engines, there are many directories on the Web that people visit when looking for information. Human-powered directories are created and maintained by editors who manually review and add Web sites to the directory, as opposed to search engines, which use automated tools to locate and collect information about Web sites. Of the directories on the Web, Yahoo and Open Directory are the two biggest.

Yahoo! now operates its own search engine from which main results are retrieved when someone performs a search. However, Yahoo! still maintains its own Yahoo! Directory. The Open Directory, on the other hand, is a vast directory, created and maintained by a global community of volunteers.

Getting listed in a directory is important, because once listed there you'll find that some search engines will automatically discover your Web site and add you to their search engine database.

Hybrid Sites

The differences between search engines and directories have become blurred over the years. That's because many search sites pull information from search engines as well as directories. For example, AOL and Netscape retrieve their primary search results from Google. In addition, AOL and Netscape also pull results from the Open Directory.

In addition, another breed of search sites known as *meta search engines* retrieve their results by passing queries on to multiple search engines and then combining all the results that are returned back into a single listing. Examples of popular meta search engines include Mamma and Dogpile.

Paid Inclusion and Paid Placement

A primary focus of this book is to show you how to register for free with all the major search engines and directories. Generally speaking, it can take somewhere between 4 to 6 weeks for your Web site to appear in a search engine's listings once you initially register with it.

However, every major search engine on the Web also provides an option for *paid inclusion* and *paid placement*. These two options will cost you a few dollars but can be important when you are in a hurry to get your site noticed on the Web. Paid placement is a service in which you are guaranteed a high ranking for your Web site for certain search keywords. Paid inclusion is a service that guarantees you a place in a search engine's listings but does not guarantee you a high ranking. These two services can be very useful because they provide you with the ability to get your Web site registered and noticed within a few days.

Social Media Sites

Social media sites represent a new generation of Web sites based on new Web development and design techniques collectively referred to as Web 2.0. These Web sites are helping to transform the Web from a platform where Web site owners dictate content and discussion to one in which Web site visitors provide the content and interact directly with one another.

Social media sites comes in many different forms, including social networking sites like Facebook, Twitter, and MySpace, wikis like Wikipedia, video sharing like YouTube, as well as blog sites. These sites attract hundreds of millions of people. They facilitate the creation of virtual communities, allowing people with common interests to connect with one another.

By signing up with these sites and investing time joining and participating in communities and groups that attract and build relationships with the very same types of people your Web sites should interest, you can develop a reputation of knowledge and expertise. As a result, you'll drive high-quality traffic to your Web site.

Promoting Your Web Site to Joe Surfer

Joe Web Surfer is your average person browsing the Web. He's been there and done that. Now he's out looking for a bit of excitement or trying to find something—gasp!—useful. He's looking for a site like yours. He just doesn't know it yet. Well, to help Joe on his way, you have to give him a bit of prodding and grab his attention.

In the real world, you could grab Joe's attention by putting up a flashing neon sign that says, "Hey, Joe, over here!" In cyberspace, you grab Joe's attention using the tools of the Web promotion trade.

If Joe is looking for something cool, you grab his attention by getting your site listed as the Cool Site of the Day. Although Cool Site of the Day is one of the key awards that will get your Web site noticed, many other awards exist that will get him to notice your site as well. He may be looking for sites like those featured as Bizarre, Strange, Unusual, or Weird, such as the site shown in Figure 1.5 (www.webweirdness.com).

Figure 1.5

Definitely not a guide to the ordinary.

NOTE You'll find more information on these and other awards in the Saturday Afternoon session, under "Getting Your Site Listed as the Cool Site of the Day."

If Joe is looking to get something for nothing, you grab his attention with freebies, such as a giveaway. Then again, Joe may be interested in some other type of freebie, such as a contest, sweepstakes, or treasure hunt. Catching his eye when he's looking for freebies is covered on Sunday Morning under "Attracting the Masses with Giveaways, Contests, Sweepstakes, and More."

If Joe enjoys interacting with others, sharing information about himself and his interests, he may frequent Web sites like Facebook, MySpace, and Twitter. If Joe is interested in the same things you are, you can catch his attention by participating on these sites and providing information that will attract Joe. You can also get Joe to notice you by commenting on the content that he posts. Once you have his attention, you can encourage him to visit your Web site.

Other ways to grab Joe's attention include using straightforward Web advertising. Most Web users have a newsgroup or mailing list they like to follow, and Joe is no exception. So to get to Joe where he lives, you have to visit the discussion groups and forums where he hangs out. If Joe is interested in topics similar to those covered at your Web site, chances are good that you will find him hanging out in a like-minded newsgroup or mailing list. Web site promotion through newsgroups and mailing lists is featured on Sunday Morning under "Selling Your Web Site through E-mail."

Sometimes, the best way to get Joe's attention is to use good old-fashioned advertising. On the Web, this means using a banner advertisement. You have to admit that sometimes you do click on them, and so does Joe. If something grabs his eye, he's going to click on it, and when he does, you want it to be your site that he visits. To help Joe on his way, you can use the free advertising techniques that you'll explore on Sunday Morning under "Free Banner Advertising: No Joke."

Determining Who Is Visiting Your Web Site

Increasing your Web site traffic means taking a closer look at your Web site to understand the big picture—who is visiting your Web site and why.

Trying to promote your Web site without understanding the big picture is like trying to play baseball without a ball—you just can't do it.

To get your hands on the "big picture," you will need to collect and analyze statistical data regarding who is visiting your Web site, which you will learn how to do on Sunday Afternoon's session "Discovering Who's Visiting Your Site and Why." With this data in hand, you will be able to examine your Web site with an honest eye and take a look at problem areas within your Web site. By examining your Web site's statistical data, you will see firsthand the pages at your Web site that get the most visitors and those that don't get any visitors.

When you examine your site's traffic, you will move beyond tracking file accesses and zero in on the things that matter, such as page views and the actual number of visitors. When you look at page views and visitor counts, you can answer many of the following questions about your Web site.

- What are the busiest days of the week?
- What are the busiest hours of the day?
- What are the most requested pages?
- Where do visitors live and work?
- What is the average number of page views per day?
- What is the average number of visitors per day?
- What is the average number of page views per visitor?
- What is the length of the average visit?
- What is the total number of visitors?

You will use stats not only to understand who is visiting your Web site right now and why, but also to help put together a promotion campaign for your Web site. By digging deeper through the stats, you can find out whether people like what they see or are just racing through your Web site. You also can discover problem areas at your Web site that may cause you to lose visitors who otherwise might come back to your Web site repeatedly.

After you develop a clear understanding of your Web site, you will learn how to put your Web site's stats to work. The first step is to summarize the stats and transform them into meaningful data. Then you will use the stats to make your Web site a better place to visit by taking care of the following:

- Cleaning up unused pages
- Clearing out dead ends
- Fixing errors

You can use the stats to build cross-traffic to attract users to popular areas of your Web site.

Wrapping Up and Looking Ahead

Registering with search engines is a terrific way to build Web site traffic, especially when you consider that millions of people use search engines to find information every day. Social media sites are another integral component of any good Web marketing effort. As with search engines, you'll get more bang for your buck if you focus your time and attention on the most popular social media Web sites. Guides, lists, and directories can also help get your Web site noticed. Of course, to make the best use of your available time, make sure that you focus your attention on the best search engines, guides, lists, and directories. Although you aren't guaranteed a listing in a guide to the best of the Web, your time is still well spent when you consider that a single award could bring thousands of visitors to your site.

That's enough for this evening. It's time to put this book down and relax your mind and body. Tomorrow you'll learn how to start registering with search engines and how to submit your Web site for inclusion in the major guides, lists, and directories. You'll also learn about a number of specialty directories and how to get listed in What's New directories and what steps to take to get your Web site listed as Cool Site of the Day.

In addition, you will learn the basics of Web promotion using social media Web sites. So, watch a little TV and get a good night's sleep. Tomorrow will be a busy day.

Putting the Motion in Promotion

➤ Search Engine Fundamentals

➤ Registering with the Top Search Engines

➤ Submitting Your Web Site

Registering with search engines is a terrific way to build traffic to your Web site, especially when you consider that millions of people use search engines to find information every day. Guides, lists, and directories can also help your Web site get noticed. Although you aren't guaranteed a listing in a guide to the best of the Web, your time is still well spent when you consider that a single award could bring thousands of visitors to your site.

Capitalizing on Search Engine Fundamentals

Finding Web sites would be nearly impossible without sites that let you quickly and easily search for information. These so-called search engines provide a service that puts all the resources of the Web within reach. Search engines allow Web publishers to register their pages so that they will be added to the list of resources the search engine knows about. Search engines also allow Web users to find pages using keywords and keyword phrases that identify the information the users want to find.

Although search engines provide a great tool that you can use to get your Web site noticed by users around the world, few people truly understand how they work. That is, people rarely get the most out of search engines and often waste their time and resources when they register their site with search engines. In this session, you will learn how search engines work and how you can make the most of the techniques that search engines use to index and reference your Web site.

Millions of Users Are but a Search Away

Millions of people are just a click away from your Web site. They just need to follow the references that lead to you. The only problem is that your Web site probably doesn't show up in the results retrieved by the search engine they are using. Or on the rare occasion when the results show your site, users lack the information necessary to make the decision to visit your site. At that point, they head off to some other site. Day in and day out, this scenario plays out repeatedly at hundreds of search engines on the Web. The result is that your Web site doesn't get the level of traffic it deserves.

Because few people truly understand how search engines work, Web site publishers often get frustrated when they try to attract visitors using search engines. Usually, the Web site publisher will register the site with a few search engines, then sit back and wait for visitors to come. When visitors don't come, the Web site publisher registers with more search engines. Eventually, the Web site publisher might even turn to commercial services that promise to bring visitors to the Web site.

Search engines are one of the least understood Internet tools, and a lack of understanding can be a golden opportunity for someone to make a buck at your expense. You'll find services trying to sell you the Holy Grail for hundreds of dollars. These services tell you that they will register your site with every search engine available, get your site listed in the top 10 search results every time, or trick search engines into displaying your site more often. Don't buy whatever they're selling unless you've got money to burn. Instead, take the time to learn how search engines work, and use this information to get your site noticed by millions of Web users.

Indexers, Spiders, Crawlers, and Other Web Beasties

In the Web's early days, search engines were simply tools for finding information using indexes. Much like the index of your favorite computer book, the purpose of the index was to make finding information possible by using keywords. Rather than page references used in traditional indexes, Web indexes have hypertext links that you click on to access the information at Web sites around the world.

Over the years, search engines evolved. Today, the best search engines are complex applications that use advanced techniques to put millions of Web pages at the fingertips of Web users.

Working with Search Engines

No matter what label you use to identify a search engine, the fundamental purpose of a search engine is to index Web sites in a way that allows people to use keywords to find Web pages that interest them. To do this, search engines rely on a computer called an indexer, spider, or crawler to ferret out the pages at your site and then create indexed references to those pages in the search engine's database. After the pages are indexed, anyone can use the front-end search process to find the pages.

If you jaunt over to Excite at **www.excite.com**, you will find that the main page has an area called Search the Web. As shown in Figure 2.1, Search contains an input field for entering the keywords or keyword phrases on which you want to search. When you click on the Search button, the search engine uses the parameters you've entered to find matching references.

When you search using the keywords "central drive" and click on the Search button, you get a list of results like those shown in Figure 2.2. Typically, the results of a search are displayed according to their relevance to the search parameters that you entered. The first couple of results listed by the search engine will be sponsored results. The rest of the listing will consist of results that the search engine believes best match your search.

Most search engines display reference to the top 10 or 20 pages that match your search parameters. Successive groups of matching pages are also available, but you have to follow a link to another results page. At Excite, you can click on the Next link found at the bottom of the results page to see additional pages that might be matches for your search.

Figure 2.1

Using a search engine.

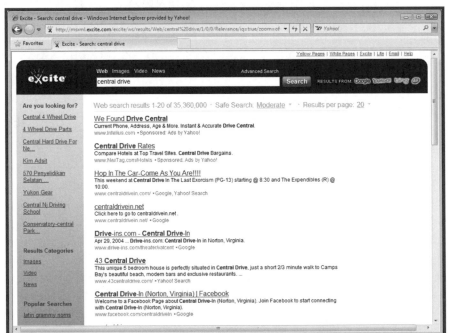

Figure 2.2

The results of a search.

Often, the matching pages are described using the page title and a brief description taken from the page itself. Most commercial search engines allow you to customize the search and results displayed. The search engine at Excite lets you customize the search in many different ways. For example, you can specify the number of results that are listed at a time or specify one of several safe search settings.

Comparing Search Engines and Directory Lists

Search engines and directory lists are very different. When you look for information with a search engine, you use keywords. When you look for information at a directory listing, you search by following links to pages within the directory site. You start your search by clicking on a broad category, such as entertainment, and eventually drill down to a very specific subject, such as movie reviews. One of the best-known directory lists is maintained by Yahoo! (**dir.yahoo.com**).

When you visit Yahoo's Directory page (shown in Figure 2.3), you are greeted by a listing of top-level categories of information available at the site. Under the top-level categories are more focused categories of information. If you select the News and Media category, you jump to the page shown in Figure 2.4. As you can see, this page shows many different broad categories of news. By selecting another link, you can get to a more narrowly focused category, such as business news or technology news.

Directory lists are covered extensively later in this session under the heading, "Submitting Your Web Site to the Top Guides, Lists, and Directories."

Who Powers Whom?

In order to make the best use of your time, it is important for you to know which search engines people use the most. This way you can target your efforts at the search engines that will help get your Web site noticed by the largest number of people.

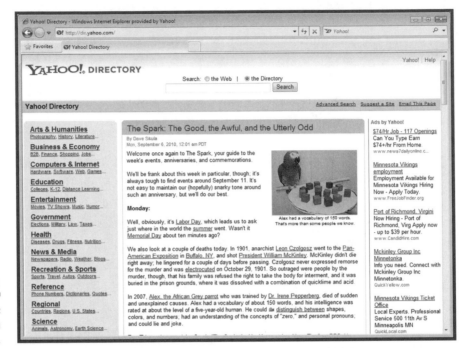

Figure 2.3

Directory sites are different from search sites.

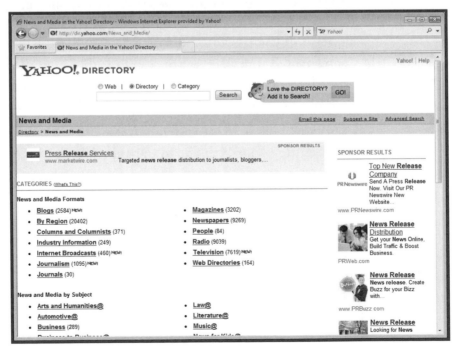

Figure 2.4

Accessing a broad range of information.

Today, the three most popular general-purpose search engines are Google (**www.google.com**), Yahoo! (**www.yahoo.com**), and Bing (**www.bing.com**). Bing is Microsoft's new search engine. Together these three search engines account for over 90 percent of all search engine queries. Perhaps even more importantly, many other search engines retrieve at least part of their results from these three search engines.

The search engine business is highly competitive, and things are constantly changing. As of the writing of the sixth edition of this book, Microsoft and Yahoo! had entered into a 10-year agreement, the result of which is that Bing will eventually serve as Yahoo!'s search engine. As of August 2010, all of Yahoo!'s U.S. and Canadian searches were being powered by Bing. By combining forces, Microsoft and Yahoo! hope to build an alliance that rivals Google's dominant position as a search provider.

In addition to providing its own search results, Yahoo! provides search results to AltaVista (**www.altavista.com**), which is owned by Yahoo!. Google is also a major source used by numerous search engines, including AOL (**www.aol.com**), Netscape (**www.netscape.com**), and Excite (**www.excite.com**). Excite also retrieves search results from Yahoo!, Bing, and Ask.

There are plenty of other good search engines of which you need to be aware. In addition, there are a number of special-purpose search engines, such as child-oriented search engines, that may also fit well into your Web promotion plan. You'll learn about these later in this session in the section named "Increasing Your Web Traffic with the Top Search Engines."

Search Engine Fundamentals

Before you run off and start registering your Web site with the different search engines, it is important that you understand exactly what search engines are and how they work. Although we've come to think of search engines as giant applications that find information, a search engine is really three different applications that work together to find and retrieve information.

The applications are as follows:

- **An indexer**. The back-end application that finds and indexes pages for inclusion in a database; other names for this type of application include *spider*, *crawler*, and *robot*.
- **A database**. The application that stores the index references to Web pages.
- **A query interface**. The application that handles the queries submitted by users.

Search engines can't find or index your Web site without a little help, which is why people register their sites. Another way for a search engine to find your Web site is through a link to one of your pages from someone else's site. After a search engine finds your Web site, it uses the links within your pages to find additional pages at your site. In this way, the search engine navigates its way through your Web site one link at a time and adds the information from your Web site into its database

What Do Search Engines Look For?

Search engines don't store all the data in your Web pages. Instead, they create indexed references to your pages. Most of the time, such an indexed reference contains the following information.

- **Page title**. From the `<title>` tag element of your Web page.
- **Page URL**. The absolute URL to your Web page.
- **Summary description**. A description taken from the Web page.
- **Keyword list**. A list of keywords taken from the Web page, accompanied by a relevancy index that explains how relevant each indexed word is to other indexed words and how relevant the indexed words are to the page title.

Most search engines create indexed references to your Web pages, although almost every search engine gathers this information from different areas of your Web page. Whereas one search engine might gather the summary description for your Web page from the first few hundred characters, another search engine might look for common words or phrases in the page to use in the summary description.

The various search engines use the summary information in different ways as well. Some search engines make all the information available to user queries. Other search engines store all the information categories, yet user queries are performed only against specific categories of data, such as the page title and keyword list.

What Does the Indexed Reference Look Like for a Real Page?

To get a better understanding of what indexers do, look at the code shown in Listing 2.1. As you examine the sample Web page, note the title and the use of the <meta> tag to describe the page and identify keywords. Also, note that the page contains lots of text.

Listing 2.1   A Sample Web Page

```
<html>

  <head>

    <title>Writer's Gallery: Resources for Writers and Readers</title>

    <meta name="description" content="Writer's Gallery is a place

      for anyone who loves the written word. You'll find links to

      hundreds of writing-related resources as well as new works of

      fiction published at our site. ">

    <meta name="keywords" content="writing, reading, write,

      read, book, author, story, fiction, nonfiction, literary,

      mythology, medieval, biblical, renaissance, library,

      Dante, Dickens, Faulkner, Shakespeare, news, world news,

      entertainment news, business news, current events,

      publishing, dictionary, encyclopedia, bookshelf">

  </head>

<body bgcolor="#000080" text="#ffff00" link="#fffbf0"

  vlink="#808000" alink="#ff0000">
```

```
<img src="wgtt12.jpg" alt="Writer's Gallery" border=0 align=left>
<center>
<h1>A place for anyone who loves the written word!</h1>
<h3>Over 250 New Resources!</h3>
</center>
<font size=-1><a href="vpspons.html">We're looking for
 sponsors.</a><br><br>
 Brought to you by the Original Virtual Press - - Fine
 Publications, Community Service and Much More Since March, 1994.
 If you'd like more information about <a href="vpbg.html">The
 Virtual Press</a> or would like to post information to the
 Writer's Gallery:  Send e-mail to
<a href="mailto:wg@tvpress.com">wg@tvpress.com</a><br><br>
</font>
<p><img src="bboard.gif" align="bottom" alt="* attn *">Put a
 bookmark here. Come back and visit!</p>
<br clear=all>
<h2><a href="vpwfeat.html">Writer's Gallery Features</a></h2>
<p>Find hundreds of zines, thousands of books and links to
 all good things related to writing!</p>
<h2><a href="vpwlite.html">Writer's Gallery Literary
 Resources</a></h2>
<p>If you need a literary reference look here. From Greek
 mythology to the Renaissance. From medieval to biblical.
 From the 9th century to the 19th century. This page covers
 it all.</p>
<h2><a href="vpwauth.html">Writer's Gallery Great Authors
 </a></h2>
<p>If you are looking for information on great writers from
 history, look here. You'll find information on writers from
```

```
Dante, Dickens, Faulkner, Shakespeare and more!</p>

<h2><a href="wcurrent.html">Writer's Gallery Guide to Current

 Events</a></h2>

<h3><a href="http://tvpress.comhttp://www..tvpress.com/idn/"

 Target="_parent">Internet Daily News</a> ||

 <a href="wcurrent.html#usnews">US News</a> ||

 <a href="wcurrent.html#worldnews">World News</a> ||

 <a href="wcurrent.html#busnews">Business News</a> ||

 <a href="wcurrent.html#entnews">Entertainment News</a> ||

 <a href="wcurrent.html#finnews">Finance News</a></h3>


<h2><a href="vpwcomp.html">Writer's Companions</a></h2>

<p>Dictionaries, encyclopedias & more! All the reference

 works you wish were on your bookshelf.</p>

<h2><a href="vpwresou.html">Writer's Resources</a></h2>

<p>A comprehensive resource list for writers! The Writer's

  Resource includes Virtual Libraries, Meta Indexes, Web

 Databases and more! Dozens of them . . . </p>

<h2><a href="vpncwgp.html">Newsgroups for Writers</a></h2>

<p>Looking for a great way to meet fellow writers?

 Join a discussion group!</p>

<h2><a href="vppubl.html">Who's in Publishing on the

 WWW</a></h2>

<p>Find publishers on the Web</p>

<h2><a href="vpwart.html#art">Art</a></h2>

<p>Interested in finding art resources?> Try these resources.</p>

<h2><a href="vpwart.html#movies">Movie &amp; Industry

 Information</a></h2>

<p>Movie reviews & great movie information</p>

<hr size=4>
```

```
<form method="post" action="mailto:wg@tvpress.com">
 <p>Help us grow; add a link to Writer's Gallery!</p>
 <p><textarea name="Writer's gallery links" cols="40" rows="1">
  </textarea></p>
 <p>Please describe the link.</p>
 <p><textarea name="Writer's gallery description" cols="40" Rows="1">
  </textarea></p>
 <p><input type="submit"> <input type="reset"></p>
</form>
<hr size=4>
<p>Questions or comments pertaining to the TVP Web site can be
 directed to <a href="mailto:webmaster@tvpress.com">
 <img src="mail.gif" align="middle" alt="*.e-mail*">
  </a></p>
<p>This page, and all contents, are <a href="vpcopy.html">
  Copyright © by The Virtual Press, USA.</a>
 </p>
 </body>
</html>
```

When retrieving results, search engines follow a set of rules known as an algorithm. Each search engine has its own unique algorithm, which is kept secret. As a result, when different search engines index this Web page, they will come up with different results. For search engine A, an indexed reference to the page could look like this:

- **Page title:** Writer's Gallery: Resources for Writers and Readers.
- **Page URL: http://www.tvpress.com/vpwg.html**
- **Summary description:** A place for anyone who loves the written word! Over 250 new resources. We're looking for sponsors.

- **Keyword list:** Author, biblical, books, bookshelf, business news, comment, community, companion, current events, database, entertainment news, events, finance news, gallery, Greek mythology, history, index, industry, information, library, literary, medieval, movie, mythology, news, newsgroup, press, publication, question, reference, renaissance, resource, service, sponsor, virtual, word, world news, writer, writer newsgroup, writing, written word.

Here, the search engine takes most of the information it needs directly from the body of the Web page. Because of this, each word in the page is weighed for relevancy and inclusion in the keyword list. You learn more about relevancy later in this session. Also, note that the summary description for this page is truncated at a preset number of characters, which means that the last sentence isn't complete in this case. For search engine B, an indexed reference to the page could look like this:

- **Page title:** Writer's Gallery: Resources for Writers and Readers.
- **Page URL: http://www.tvpress.com/vpwg.html**
- **Summary description:** Writer's Gallery is a place for anyone who loves the written word! You'll find links to hundreds of writing-related resources as well as new works of fiction published at our site.
- **Keyword list:** Author, biblical, book, bookshelf, business news, current events, Dante, Dickens, dictionary, encyclopedia, entertainment news, Faulkner, fiction, fiction works, library, literary, medieval, mythology, news, nonfiction, publishing, read, reader, reading, renaissance, resource, Shakespeare, story, world news, write, writer, writing, written word.

Here, the search engine obtains the page description from a <meta> tag, and then combines the keyword information provided in another <meta> tag with words used in the page to come up with a keyword list. Although this technique might seem unusual, many search engines that take advantage of meta-information combine the description and keywords that you provide with information taken from the body of the page.

NOTE   You will learn more about the <meta> tags and meta-information later in the session. Look for the heading, "Getting the Most from Keywords and Meta-Information."

For search engine C, an indexed reference to the page could look like this:

- **Page title:** Writer's Gallery: Resources for Writers and Readers.
- **Page URL: http://www.tvpress.com/vpwg.html**
- **Summary description:** A place for anyone who loves the written word! Over 250 new resources. We're looking for sponsors.

Here, the search engine only makes use of the page title and a summary description obtained from the first 100 characters of text found in the page. Although the streamlined entries in the database aren't desirable for the Web page publisher, the search engine designers probably chose this format because it drastically reduces the size of the database, which in turn reduces overhead and speeds up database queries.

What Happens After Your Web Site Is Indexed?

Indexing a Web site is not a one-time deal. After a search engine initially indexes your site, it is usually scheduled for reindexing at periodic intervals. By reindexing Web sites, search engines keep up with the ever-changing face of the Web. That said, not all search engines automatically reindex your site, and some search engines reindex your Web site so infrequently that you end up with outdated references.

Additionally, the way that a search engine reindexes your Web site might not be what you expect. Some search engines simply check to see whether the page still exists but don't update the actual reference to the Web page. Other search engines check the page header to see whether the page has changed, so if you changed text at the bottom of the page, the search engine won't reindex the page. Still other search engines use the modification date on the page to determine whether the page should be reindexed. The search engine then either reindexes the page immediately or schedules the page for reindexing at a later date.

Another problem with search engines is that Web pages you deleted months ago might still be listed. Although some search engines let you remove outdated references from the database, the best way to solve these and other problems you might encounter is to periodically resubmit your Web site to the search engine. For problems related to pages you've moved to different locations, you might also want to use placeholder documents and the redirection techniques examined in the Sunday Afternoon session under "Redirecting Lost Readers." In this way, you direct readers from the old page to the new page, and eventually the search engine will pick up on this and update the references to your Web site.

Determining Popular Keywords

Keyword selection is an important consideration in the preparation of your Web pages for search engine registration. People surfing the Web using search engines enter keywords or keyword phrases to generate lists of links to related topics. The better the keywords and keyword phrases on your Web pages match up against the keywords or keyword phrases entered by the people you are trying to attract, the more your Web site will get noticed.

Keyword Creation Tips

There are a number of different things that you need to think about when determining what keywords to use on your Web pages. For starters, think about the search words or phrases you think people will use when searching for the topic covered on your Web pages. These words and phrases should be your keywords and keyword phrases. For example, if you have a Web page that covers rock climbing, then "rock climbing" should be one of your keyword phrases.

TIP A good way to come up with keyword phrases is to think of magazine and newspaper headlines. A good headline helps attract your attention and guides you to articles that are of interest to you. A good headline is short, to the point, and descriptive.

In fact, it is better to use keyword phrases made up of two to three words than to specify single word keywords. For one thing, lots of sites specify single word keywords, making competition for these keywords intense. Instead, by creating phrases specific to your topic, you greatly increase the chances that your keyword phrases will be viewed by the search engines as being more relevant.

 TIP If your Web site covers a number of different topics, then you will want to generate different keywords and keyword phrases for each unique Web page.

Some search engines are case-sensitive. Therefore, searches on "Rock Climbing" and "rock climbing" may generate different results from the same search engine. One way around this is to specify different variations of capitalization when specifying your Web page keywords, such as "Rock Climbing," "Rock climbing," "rock Climbing," "rock climbing," or even "ROCK CLIMBING." However, since almost everybody searches the Web using lowercase typing, it is usually not worth the trouble trying to come up with every possible keyword variation. In addition, by attempting to anticipate every possible keyword capitalization variation, you run the risk of accidentally spamming search engines, as discussed in the next couple pages.

Researching Popular Search Engine Keywords

Another way to come up with good keywords is to take a few minutes to visit each of the major search engines to see what keywords are being used most often by people. Google provides a listing of top search engine queries on a daily basis at **www.google.com/trends/hottrends**, as shown in Figure 2.5.

Figure 2.5

Examining popular keywords used by people searching on Google.

The following list shows where you can go to research popular keywords for other major search engines.

- ▣ **Yahoo!: buzz.yahoo.com**
- ▣ **AOL: hot.aol.com**

Free Keyword Generation Tools

If you are still uncertain as to what keywords you want to create for your Web pages, you might want to try the keyword generator tool provided by Google. This tool is designed to help paying customers select keywords for ads. However, this service is free and you can use it to help generate your own keywords.

You can find the Google AdWords Keyword Tool at **adwords.google.com/ select/KeywordToolExternal** as shown in Figure 2.6.

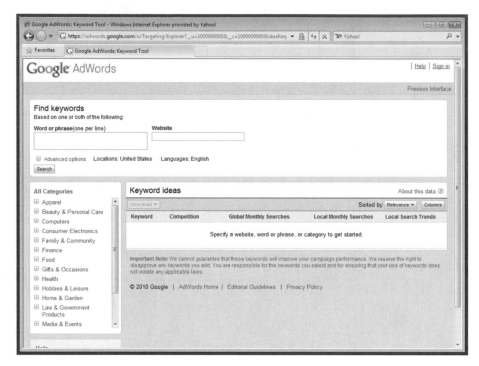

Figure 2.6

Using the Google AdWords Keyword Tool to generate your own keywords.

Be On Guard Against Accidental Spamming

Keywords are an important tool used to help attract visitors to your Web pages. However, it is important that you do not get too overzealous. If, for example, you repeat the same keywords, search engines may pick up on it and identify your Web page as attempting to spam the engines in an effort to achieve a high relevancy for certain keywords. If this happens, then either your Web page's ranking may be reduced or your Web page may even be removed from the search engine's index. So tread carefully in regards to how many times you repeat your keywords.

Boosting Visits with Ordinary Descriptions

To a search engine, text is the most important part of the page. Search engines use ordinary text to describe the page, build the keyword list, and determine the relevance of the page to particular subjects. Although search engines treat text in different ways, they share some common themes concerning how text is indexed and referenced.

Images are gaining importance with all of the major search engines. Search engines like Google, Yahoo!, Bing, Ask, and AOL all have added graphic search services to their search engine. Using these services, surfers can perform keyword search for images, and when they click on these images, they'll be transported directly to the Web site that displays them. You will learn more about graphic search services later in "Using Graphic Search Services to Increase Traffic."

Understanding Summary Descriptions

Whenever a search engine displays results, the main thing that sells your page to the reader is the summary description, which usually comes from the first 100 to 200 characters in the Web page. When you look at your Web page to see what the description might look like, be sure to include all text in headers, paragraphs, and other text elements on the page.

Search engines have very specific parameters for obtaining the summary description. Text at the top of the page is usually given more weight than text at the bottom of the page. Thus, if you have a short description at the top of your page followed by several graphic elements, tables, or linked lists, the search engine might not use text from later sections of the page. You can see why some page descriptions are short and others fill out the full 100 to 200 characters used by the search engine.

To help your Web site get noticed, create clear summary statements for your key Web pages, which include the home page and top-level pages at your Web site. The summary statement should be the first text element in the page, perhaps directly following your graphical banner. If you keep the summary statement short but descriptive, it will usually flow well with the rest of the page.

 TIP   Whenever possible, try to end your summary statement with proper punctuation. Believe it or not, a few search engines look for complete statements. Phrases without punctuation are considered ambiguous; phrases with punctuation are considered relevant.

Understanding Relevancy

The position of text in your Web page often determines its relevancy. Because of the variations in how search engines use text, relevancy is one of the hardest search engine terms to pin down. In general terms, the relevancy of text describes

- How a word relates to other words.
- The proximity of one word to another.
- The position of the word within the page.
- Whether the word is presented as part of a complete statement.
- How many times the word is used in the page.

The concept of relevancy explains why some of the techniques that publishers use to get their pages listed at the top of search results lists have little effect, as well as why a technique might work for one search engine and not for others. In the end, the varying definition of relevancy makes optimizing your Web pages for each and every search engine almost impossible. In fact, you'd probably be wasting your time if you tried to optimize your Web pages for all the search engines.

Have you ever come across a Web page that repeated a word over and over again? Well, the Web site publisher was probably trying to get the page listed as the top choice for searches using this keyword. Although this technique might work for a particular search engine, most other search engines will completely ignore the repeated use of the word, which causes the page to appear lower in their search results lists.

Have you ever come across a Web page that used phrases that didn't seem to fit in the Web page, yet the phrases were there just the same? Here, the Web site publisher was probably trying to get the page to show up when someone searched for a hot topic, such as news, entertainment, or sports. Again, this technique might work for a particular search engine, but other search engines will give the entire page lower relevancy because it's full of ambiguous phrases and doesn't seem to have a common thread.

Rather than haphazardly repeat keywords or use ambiguous phrases in your Web page, use sound organizational techniques that bolster the relevancy of your page's theme. Focus your attention on your home page and your top-level pages first. When you look at your home page or top-level page, ask yourself these questions:

- Is the subject of the page clear?
- Can I weave the main subject(s) of the page throughout the main text in such a way that it builds relevancy?
- Does the page build the relationship between the main subject and related topics?
- Can I add descriptions to lists of links to clearly define what the link points to?
- Are the statements made in the page clear and complete?
- Can I transform ambiguous phrases into clear statements that relate to the main theme on the page?

Using Page Titles to Your Advantage

A good Web page title will bring visitors to your Web site. Most search engines display Web pages according to their titles, making the page title one of the most important elements for bringing visitors to your Web site. Additionally, your browser displays the title at the top of its window, as demonstrated in Figure 2.7, and when you bookmark a Web page, the title is used to differentiate the Web page from other Web pages that you've marked, as shown in Figure 2.8.

Figure 2.7

A Web page's title is automatically displayed in the browser's titlebar.

Figure 2.8

A Web page's title is also used to label browser bookmarks.

Beyond its job of grabbing the reader's attention, the title also plays an important role in determining the relevancy of the Web page to the reader's search parameters. Specifically, the keywords in the title often receive greater emphasis than other keywords on the page.

The best titles describe the subject of the page in a clear and meaningful way. Instead of a title that says, "Welcome to my home page," use a title that says "Bill's Home Page: Find Sports Memorabilia, Sports Records, & Player Stats." In this way, search engines that use the page title to determine relevance will have a clear understanding of the page's subject and the most important keywords.

Getting Your Frame-Enhanced or Graphics-Intensive Page Noticed

Pages with frames, scripts, tables, and lots of graphics present special problems to Web site publishers and search engines. With frame-enhanced Web pages, the main document usually contains only references to the files that a browser loads into each frame. With scripts, the code is often located at the top of the code for the Web page in the place of the all-important descriptive text. With graphics-intensive pages, room for text on the page is limited.

Although some search engines are smart enough to understand and properly handle frame-enhanced pages, scripts, and graphics-intensive pages, such search engines are more the exception than the rule. Fortunately, you can get your Web page noticed without eliminating frames, scripts, or your wonderful graphics. One way for you to try to do this is through use of meta-information, which is discussed in a couple pages. However, there are a few element-specific tricks that you may want to consider as well, including:

- ☑ Dealing with frame issues
- ☑ Dealing with scripts
- ☑ Managing your tables
- ☑ Keeping graphics under control

NOTE Not every search engine provides the same level of support for meta-information. So while helpful, meta-information alone may not be enough to accommodate your frames, scripts, tables, and graphics on every search engine.

Handling Problems with Frames

Frames present a bit of a challenge for many search engines. When you create a Web site based on frames, you define a frameset and frames. The frameset specifies the location and dimension of each frame. However, some search engines are unable to see past the frameset page, meaning that they cannot locate the associate frame pages. At this point the rest of your Web site becomes effectively invisible to the search engine.

One way to deal with frames is to always remember to include a <noframes> tag. Using this tag, you can specify text that search engines and visitors with old browsers can see. The <noframes> tag allows browsers and search engines that can't understand frames to display other text so the page doesn't become a dead end. An example of how to apply the <noframes> tag is shown in Listing 2.2.

Listing 2.2   Using a <noframes> Area in a Web Page

```
<html>

  <head>

    <title>Las Vegas Virtual Tour Guide</title>

  </head>


  <frameset rows="25%,*" border=0>

    <frame src="side.htm" noresize>

    <frame src="main.htm" noresize>

  </frameset>

  <noframes>

    <body>

      Add text and links here for version of Web page without
frames.

    </body>

  </noframes>

</html>
```

If you include links along with the descriptive information, you can provide search engines with the ability to view the other pages in your Web site. Unfortunately, this approach opens up the possibility that a visitor may arrive at one of your frame pages, and because it is not presented within the overall context of your frameset, things begin to break down. However, you can easily fix this using just a few lines of JavaScript, as demonstrated here:

```
<script language= "JavaScript"
  <!—
    If (top == self) self.location.href = "frameset-url"
  //—>
</script>
```

Modify this code by replacing the frameset-url parameter with the name of your frameset page and then copy and paste the code into the head or body section of your HTML for each of your frame pages. If a visitor attempts to directly access any of your frame's pages, this code will automatically execute and load your frameset page as you intended.

Working Around Scripts

Embedding large scripts into your Web pages presents another problem for search engines. Since most people place their scripts at the top of their Web pages, the script pushes the content for the rest of the Web page down. Unfortunately, many search engines don't scan your entire page when indexing your Web site. This can result in the search engine missing out on most of your Web page's content.

One way to deal with this issue is to move your scripts, when possible, further down in your Web pages. Another option to consider is to externalize your scripts and call them from within your HTML Web pages.

Preventing Problems with Your Tables

Tables present search engines with a similar obstacle to that presented by scripts. For example, you may include a table about rock climbing equipment at the top of your Web page that visually displays like the one shown in Table 2.1.

TABLE 2.1 ESSENTIAL ROCK CLIMBING EQUIPMENT	
Equipment	**Description**
Boots	To protect your sore feet
Gloves	To prevent blisters and other injuries
Rope	To tie yourself down and prevent falling
Radio	To call for help in the event of an emergency
First Aid Kit	To deal with cuts, bruises, and other minor injuries

To a search engine, this table might look like

```
Equipment
Boots
Gloves
Rope
Radio
First Aid Kit

Description
To protect your sore feet
To prevent blisters and other injuries
To tie yourself down and prevent falling
To call for help in the event of an emergency
To deal with cuts, bruises, and other minor injuries
```

As you can see, any text on the Web page occurring after the table will be pushed much further down from a search engine's point of view, potentially pushing your content out of view.

As mentioned, the best way to deal with this situation is to try to move your tables further down in your pages and to make sure that, when possible, your tables include references to your keywords and phrases.

Working Around Your Graphics and Image Maps

As if frames, scripts, and tables weren't enough, search engines also have trouble with graphics. From a search engine's point of view, the only thing that matters on your Web pages is text. Graphics are ignored. You can create stunning Web pages that present all sorts of information in the form of graphics, and search engines won't see a bit of it.

Consider the importance of balancing presentation with content when you are designing your Web pages, because it's the text-based content that search engines see and use to rate the relevancy of your Web pages. One way to help mitigate the effectiveness of graphics is to always supply a descriptive <alt> tag that includes keyword phrases for every graphic on your Web pages. This way search engines will be able to read and index alternative information regarding the content of your Web pages.

If you make use of image maps as a navigation tool for providing access to your Web pages, you are presenting another problem for search engines. Once again, the search engine won't be able to view links that you've established via your image map and therefore will not be able to locate and index your other Web pages. One good way of working around this problem is to provide a text-based set of links to your Web pages at the bottom of each of your Web pages. As Figure 2.9 demonstrates, the text links don't need to be anything fancy. The important thing is to give search engines a way to find your other Web pages.

One other technique that you may want to consider is to create a site map for your Web site and to submit the site map to each search engine along with your main Web pages. A site map is a Web page that contains links to every Web page that makes up your Web site. By creating and submitting a site map, you ensure that the search engines will be able to locate every page on your Web site.

Text-based navigation links

Figure 2.9

Creating a text-based navigation link to each of your Web pages helps to ensure that search engines can properly navigate your Web site.

 TIP   Graphics take time to load. They take even longer for people that visit your Web site using a dial-up connection. Many visitors will leave your Web site if it takes too long for your graphics to load. To prevent this from happening, try keeping the total size of your main page and any other high-level pages below 50 KB.

Getting the Most from Keywords and Meta-Information

Meta-information is data that is included in a Web page header but is hidden from the reader. Usually, meta-information contains instructions or special notes for Web clients, such as your browser or the indexer used by a search engine. To provide meta-information to a Web client, you use the <meta> tag. The information that you can provide to search engines with the <meta> tag includes a very specific description of the page as well as additional keywords for the page.

<meta> tags alone are not enough to guarantee that your Web pages will get a top-10 ranking with any search engine. However, when used properly, they can help give you some control over the manner in which search engines describe your Web site.

Working with Meta-Information

Before you add meta-information to your Web pages, you should know that not all search engines make use of the <meta> tag. A search engine that doesn't use the meta-information simply ignores the information. For example, Google ignores the <meta> description tag and generates its own description of your Web page based on the content that it finds. Additionally, most of the search engines that use meta-information still index the entire contents of your Web page. Thus, you use the <meta> tag to give search engines additional information, not to replace the information that they've already gathered from the Web page.

You use the following two main attributes when you use the <meta> tag:

- **name**: Used to describe the type of meta-information that you are providing, such as name="description" or name="keywords".

- **content**: Used to supply the actual meta-information, such as the description of your Web page or a list of keywords for the Web page.

You can add a description to your page using meta-information as follows:

```
<meta name="description" content="Writer's Gallery is a place
  for anyone who loves the written word. You'll find links to
  hundreds of writing-related resources as well as new works of
  fiction published at our site. ">
```

You can add a keyword list to your page using meta-information as follows:

```
<meta name="keywords" content="writing, reading, write, read,
  book, author, story, fiction, nonfiction, literary,
  mythology, medieval, biblical, renaissance, library, Dante,
  dickens, Faulkner, Shakespeare, news, world news,
  entertainment news, business news, current events,
  publishing, dictionary, encyclopedia, bookshelf">
```

NOTE Most search engines ignore the `<meta>` keywords tag. However, some don't, so this tag is still worth including in your Web pages.

In a Web page, the meta-information is always added to the page header inside the `<head>` and `</head>` tags, as in this example:

```
<html>

  <head>


    <title>Writer's Gallery: Resources for Writers and Readers</title>
    <meta name="description" content="Writer's Gallery is a place
      for anyone who loves the written word. You'll find links to
      hundreds of writing-related resources as well as new works of
      fiction published at our site. ">
    <meta name="keywords" content="writing, reading, write,
    read, book, author, story, fiction, nonfiction, literary,
    mythology, medieval, biblical, renaissance, library,
    Dante, Dickens, Faulkner, Shakespeare, news, world news,
    Entertainment news, business news, current events,
    publishing, dictionary, encyclopedia, bookshelf">
```

```
    </head>
    <body>
        .  .  .
    </body>
</html>
```

NOTE If you do not use words located in your `<meta>` keywords tag elsewhere in your Web page, you won't see any boost in your search engine ranking, and if you repeat your keywords too many times in your `<meta>` keywords tag of your Web page, you run the risk of hurting your ranking or getting removed from the search engine's database.

Using Meta-Information in Your Web Page

The description of your page in the `<meta>` tag can be every bit as important as the summary description in the main text of the page. The advantage to describing a page in the `<meta>` tag is that you provide the exact description you want to use, rather than have the search engine extrapolate the description from the main text of the page. A good `<meta>` tag description summarizes the main selling points of the page in 200 characters or less. Because some search engines use page descriptions that are fewer than 200 characters, try to put the most relevant information first.

When it comes to finding your Web page in a search engine, a `<meta>` tag keywords list may give your Web page a definite edge over a page that doesn't use meta-information (for search engines that support it). The main thing to remember is that the `<meta>` tag keywords list is normally used in addition to the keywords that the search engine gathers from the main text of the page. Thus, rather than simply repeating keywords that appear in the main text, you might want to concentrate on related topics or variations of the primary keywords. For example, if the keyword is *writer*, you can use variations such as *write*, *writing*, and *written*.

TIP It is better to create keywords that are two or more words long. This makes them more relevant to your Web site.

You can also create various combinations of keywords or phrases in the keyword list. This doesn't mean that you should repeat the keyword several times. Instead, create working combinations, such as business news, entertainment news, and sports news. Keep in mind that some search engines penalize you for repeating specific keywords too many times. In fact, the search engine might disregard the keyword list entirely if you repeat keywords too many times, as in the following example

```
<meta name="keywords" content="news, news, news, news,
  news, news, news, news, news, news,
  business, business, business, business, business, business,
  business, entertainment, entertainment, entertainment,
  entertainment, entertainment, entertainment, sports, sports,
  sports, sports, sports, sports, sports">
```

The following example instead uses word combinations and variations of the topic for the keyword list.

```
<meta name="keywords" content="news, business, entertainment,
  sports, current events, business news, entertainments news,
  sports news">
```

Just as the length of your description is important, the length of your keyword list is important as well. Generally speaking, limit the keyword list to fewer than 1,000 characters. Further, try to restrict the number of times that you repeat any word in the keyword list. A good rule of thumb is to use a keyword or a word combination that uses the keyword no more than seven times. In the previous example, the keyword "news" was repeated four times.

After you update your home page and top-level pages with meta-information, consider adding meta-information to the rest of your Web pages. Although this might be a mammoth undertaking, the payoff makes the time investment worthwhile. Also, tailor your meta-information to each individual page rather than the site as a whole.

Meta Tag Generators

If you want a little help with the generation of your <meta> tags, to ensure that they have the correct syntax, help is just a few clicks away. There are a number of Web sites where you can go for assistance. You'll still have to supply the actual description and keywords that you wish to use for your Web site. These sites will take this information and generate <meta> tags, which you can then copy and insert into your Web pages. For example, look at the meta tag generator provided at **http://www.onlinemetatag.com**, as shown in Figure 2.10.

Figure 2.10

Use the free <META> tag generator at **www.onlinemeta tag.com** to create <META> tags for your Web pages.

There are plenty of other `<meta>` tag generator Web sites that you might also want to give a try, including:

- **AddMe! Meta-Tags Generator: www.addme.com/meta.htm**
- **KlickonUSA.COM FREE Meta Tags Builder: www.klickonusa.com/metatagbuilder/htm**

- **Submit Express Meta Tags Generator: www.submitexpress.com/metatags.html**

Analyzing Your Meta Tags

If you have already created your own `<meta>` tags, it might be worth taking a few extra seconds to get an impartial third party's opinion of how good your tags are. You can do this by visiting any number of Web sites that provide free `<meta>` tag analysis, such as the Meta Tag Analyzer provided at **www.submitexpress.com/analyzer/** (shown in Figure 2.11).

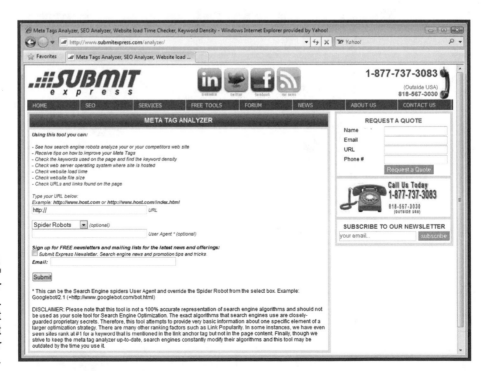

Figure 2.11

Just key in your Web page's URL and click on Submit for an instant analysis of your `<meta>` tags.

If you still want some additional feedback regarding the quality and construction of your <meta> tags, you can visit the following Web sites:

- ▣ **Hypergurl.com Meta tag Analyzer:**
  www.hypergurl.com/form.html
- ▣ **1 2 3 Submit Pro Free Meta Tag Analyzer:**
  websitesubmit.hypermart.net/metataganalysis.htm

Leveraging Your alt Tags and Comments

As has already been stated, search engines cannot read or gain information from graphics embedded in a Web page. Therefore, it is important to add an <alt> tag for each image. Obviously, each <alt> tag should provide a description of its associated image. Search engines read <alt> tags. Therefore, you can use them to help you increase your ranking for specific keywords and keyword phrases. To avoid accidental spamming, it's a good idea to limit the number of keywords used in your <alt> tags to 3-5 instances.

Search engines also read any HTML comments that you embed in your Web pages. HTML comments provide you with another opportunity to present your keywords and keyword phrases. Just don't go overboard and abuse them.

Inspecting Your Web Page's Body Text

Adding keywords and keyword phrases to your <title> and <meta> tags is an important step in your effort to achieve a high search engine ranking for your Web pages. However, in order for your keywords and keyword phrases to have their full effect, you must also include them in the text located in the body of your Web pages.

Many search engines add extra weight to keywords found at the beginning of a Web page over those found at the end of the Web page. Therefore, it's a good idea to make the integration of keywords and keyword phrases at the beginning of your Web page a primary objective.

TIP Some search engines build all or part of the description for your Web site from the text at the beginning of your Web pages. Therefore, it's a good idea to consider making the first sentence on your Web page match the text that you added to your `<meta>` tag description statement. This will increase the chances of you getting the description you want with some of the major search engines.

If the design of your Web page depends on the use of graphics at the beginning of your page, that's okay too. Just make sure that you find a way to include some text just above, below, or beside your graphics and that you remember to include keywords and keyword phrases.

A Last Look at Search Engine Fundamentals

As you have seen, you can do many things to improve the odds of someone finding your Web page through a search engine. The idea here is not to trick the search engine into displaying references to your pages. Instead, you are structuring your pages so the search engine can clearly identify the subjects your pages cover and index the appropriate keywords for those subjects. You are also using techniques that make it easier for your readers to identify the subjects covered in your pages. Figure 2.12 shows the main design concepts to follow when you optimize your Web pages for search engines.

If you haven't done so already, create descriptive blurbs for your Web site. Start by identifying the most popular areas at your Web site, and then use the subjects covered in these areas to come up with a brief description that identifies your site's niche. Next, create separate descriptions for each popular area at your Web site. When you finish this, take a few minutes to apply the concepts discussed in the search engine fundamentals section to your home page and other top-level pages at your Web site. This will prepare you to register with search engines of all types.

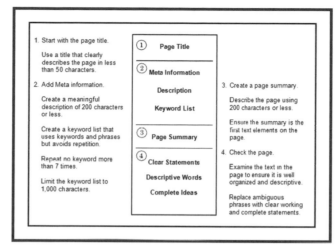

Figure 2.12

Optimizing your Web page for search engines, step-by-step.

Using Graphic Search Services to Increase Traffic

In recent years all of the major search engines have placed more and more importance on images, which makes perfect sense given that people are far more likely to be attracted to images than text. A good image may result in attracting a surfer that might otherwise pass on visiting a Web page based on its text description.

Recognizing the power of graphics, search engines have added image search services to their search engines. Google Images, shown in Figure 2.13 is by far the best known and most popular, servicing over a billion views every day.

Image search services allow surfers to perform keyword searches on image files, returning results as a thumbnail listing, as demonstrated in Figure 2.14. By clicking on a thumbnail, surfers are transferred to the Web page where the image is displayed. Obviously, this makes image search services an important source of Web traffic.

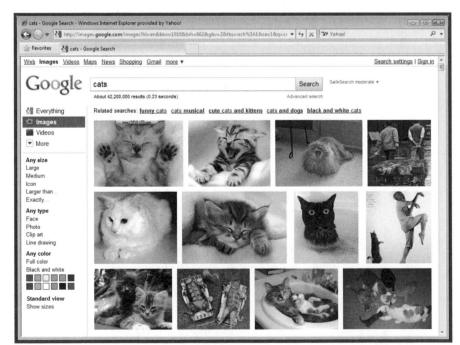

Here is a list of search engines and their associated image search service:

- **Google: images.google.com**
- **Yahoo!: http://images.search.yahoo.com**
- **Bing: http://www.bing.com/images**
- **ASK: http://www.ask.com/pictureslanding**
- **AOL: http://search.aol.com/aol/imagehome**

Keyword searches are based on image file names, the text included in links to the images, and the text that is published adjacent to those images. To take advantage of image search services to improve the traffic to your Web site, you must do several things. First, you must make sure that your images are worth viewing. They must have attractive subject matter and should be of good quality. Second, you should assign meaningful names to your image files. Avoid using names such as PCT12043.JGP and instead use names that include keywords that you think surfers are most likely to use when searching for an image like yours. To further strengthen the searchability of your images, make sure that the text in the links also contains keywords. Lastly, make sure that the text displayed adjacent to your Web page images also contain keywords.

As the old saying goes, a picture can speak a thousand words. By adding really interesting images to your Web pages and making them search engine friendly, you may be able to make them worth a thousand visits as well!

Take a Break

Okay, this is a good place to take a quick break. You've already accomplished a lot. Stretch. Relax for a moment and let things soak in. Go get a cup of coffee or tea and when you return you will review additional search engines and directories where you may also want to register your Web site.

Registering with the Top Search Engines on the Planet

Once you have optimized your Web pages for indexing, you are ready to submit them to search engines. Although hundreds of search engines are out there, trying to submit your Web site to every single one of them is not practical or worthwhile. Instead, you should start by registering your site with the major search engines. Because the search engines covered in this section index tens of millions of Web pages, they are the ones used most often to search the Web, and you can make the most of your time and resources by focusing your efforts on these search engines.

Submitting Your Site to a Search Engine

When you register with a search engine, you let the search engine know that your Web site exists. Many search engines take a preliminary look at your site immediately after you submit it and verify that the address you provided is valid. Afterward, the search engine schedules your site for indexing.

Although several days might pass before the indexing begins, the actual time you have to wait to get into the database depends on the backlog of new sites waiting to be entered and the efficiency of the indexer. Some search engines might index your Web site within hours, while others might not index your site for weeks.

How Does Indexing Work?

Most search engines use the URL you submit to find other pages at your Web site. Give the search engine the URL to your home page in this form: **http://www.your_isp.com/~you/**.

The indexer uses this page as a launching pad to all the other pages at your Web site. Generally, the indexer creates an indexed reference to the current page and then searches all the links on the page one by one. If the first link the indexer finds is to a page called background.html, the indexer accesses the background.html page, creates an indexed reference, and then searches all the links on this page one by one. Eventually, the indexer crawls through every page of your Web site.

NOTE If an area of your Web site is not linked to a main page that the indexer can find, that area will not be indexed. The solution is to add a link on a top-level page that the indexer can find or to register the area separately.

How Can You Exclude Directories and Pages?

Although indexing your site is a good thing, sometimes you might not want the search engine to index your entire site. There are a couple of different ways that you can control what pages are indexed and what pages aren't indexed. One option is to use a robot exclusion file. The exclusion file is a plain-text file placed in the top-level directory for your Web server. In the exclusion file, you specify the directories or pages that search engines are not allowed to index. The name of the exclusion file must be robots.txt.

Because you will generally want the exclusion to apply to all search engines, the first line of the file should read as follows:

```
User-agent: *
```

Here, user-agent refers to the search engine accessing the file, and the asterisk (*) is a commonly used symbol that means *all*. After telling the search engine to make the exclusions, you specify the directories or pages to exclude. Alternatively, you can exclude an entire directory as follows:

```
Disallow: /cgi-bin/
```

Or

```
Disallow: /images/
```

TIP You can use the free online robots.txt analysis tool located at **http://tools.seobook.com/ robots-txt/analyzer/** to scan and verify the contents of your Web server's robots.txt file.

If you prefer, you can exclude an individual single page as follows:

```
Disallow: /prg/webstat.html
```

You can put all these entries into an exclusion file as follows:

```
User-agent: *
Disallow: /cgi-bin/
Disallow: /images/
Disallow: /prg/webstat.html
```

TIP

If you publish a large Web site or publish your Web site as part of a larger domain, you should strongly consider using an exclusion list. With so many Web pages, search engines are finding it harder and harder to index everything at a Web site. For this reason, some search engines index only 500-700 pages per domain.

Another option available to you is the Robots `<meta>` tag. By placing an instance of this tag in the head section of a Web page, you can specify whether it should be indexed and whether the search engine should follow any links that it might find in the page. This option is particularly useful when you don't have access to the robots.txt file.

The Robots `<meta>` tag supports 4 different parameters (or directives), as listed below.

- **index:** Instructs the search engine to index the page.
- **noindex:** Instructs the search engine not to index the page.
- **follow:** Instructs the search engine to follow any links that it finds on the page.
- **nofollow:** Instructs the search engine not to follow any links that it finds on the page.

The following example shows a Robots `<meta>` tag that instructs the search engine not to index the Web page's content or follow any of its links.

```
<meta name="Robots" content="noindex,nofollow">
```

Similarly, the following example instructs the search engine to index the page but not to follow any of it links.

```
<meta name="Robots" content="index,nofollow">
```

How Often Is Your Site Reindexed?

Indexing your Web site is not a one-time deal. Most search engines periodically reindex your pages. By reindexing your pages, the search engine can verify that the pages still exist and update the database reference to your page if necessary.

In an ideal world, search engines would rapidly remove references to Web pages that no longer exist and just as rapidly create references to new Web pages that you build. In reality, search engines do not remove Web pages or find new Web pages as quickly as we would like. Whenever your site is busy, down, or can't respond to a request, the search engine simply marks the Web pages and moves on. If the server can't find the Web page on several occasions, the Web page is removed from the database.

Search engines don't add new Web pages as fast as one would like because they often don't reindex the entire site and all its contents. Instead, the search engine might check only for changes by comparing Web page headers or modification dates. The result is that the search engine might need several visits to find and index a new area of your Web site.

Why Won't This Search Engine List Your Site?

Sometimes you register with a search engine only to find, days or weeks later, that you can't locate your site anywhere in the search engine's database. A search engine might not list your site for several reasons, but the main reason is usually that the URL you provided couldn't be read or used. To avoid this problem, ensure that you type the complete URL to your Web site. Because URLs can be case-sensitive (depending on the Web server), make sure that your URL uses the proper case. For example, some Web servers might consider the URLs **http://www.tvpress.com/ HOME.htm** and **http://www.tvpress.com/Home.htm** as being different Web pages.

You should also watch the syntax of the URL. Some search engines will not use a URL that includes reserved characters, such as:

=   The equals sign

$ The dollar sign

?   The question mark

A search engine may not index your site if you use frames and the search engine doesn't know how to deal with them. To ensure that the search engine can find your page links, add a `<noframe>` tag that contains the text and links to the Web page.

Scripts and graphics-only pages can also present problems for search engines. Use the techniques discussed previously this morning under "Capitalizing on Search Engine Fundamentals" to make sure your Web page has a description and keywords.

Additionally, if you don't have your own domain, a robots.txt file might be the cause of your problems. As discussed previously, the robots.txt file can be used to keep search engines out of specific directories. To check the contents of the robots.txt file for your domain, use this URL:

http://www.your-domain.com/robots.txt

in which "your-domain" is your actual domain. If the robots.txt file excludes your directory or all public directories on the server, you've found the cause of the problem. If you find that your files are excluded in the robots.txt file, ask the Web server administrator whether this can be changed.

Search Engine Tricks to Avoid

One of the goals of this book is to show you proven techniques for improving your standing in the search engines. There are other unconventional tricks that you can also employ to try to dupe search engines into giving your Web site a better standing. You may have seen some of these tricks applied at other Web sites or read about them on the Web.

Use of these tricks is dubious at best and you should avoid using them.

Search engine developers consider these tricks to be a form of spam, and when you use spam, you have to expect a penalty. The penalty is often delisting from a search engine. Delisting means that none of your Web pages will be available in the search engine.

The next several sections point out some of these tricks (or traps) so that you won't fall prey to using them on your Web pages.

Title Tricks

Page titles are a very important means of improving your standing with search engines. Some Web site publishers try to get more oomph out of their titles using a technique called *keyword loading*. Using a form of keyword loading, you add multiple instances of the `<title>` tag to your Web pages and load them with keywords to try to improve keyword relevance. For example:

```
<title>Daily News: finance news, business news, current events</title>

<title>Sports Connection: baseball, football, basketball</title>

<title>Book Nook: rare book, collector book, first print book</title>
```

While it might be tempting to list lots of keywords in this manner, it is better to stick with the top 10 or so. This will give the keywords greater importance.

Having more than one `<title>` tag isn't considered proper HTML, but it doesn't cause any errors. Another trick that you may come across is `<title>` tag duplication. When you repeat a page title, you take a standard title (without keyword loading) and copy it several times. The thought here is that by repeating the same `<title>` tag statement, Web site publishers may be able to give their site better standing on some search engines.

For example, instead of

```
<head>
  <title>Daily News: Your news source</title>
</head>
```

You could use

```
<head>
  <title>Daily News: Your news source</title>
  <title>Daily News: Your news source</title>
  <title>Daily News: Your news source</title>
</head>
```

Modern browsers are smart enough to look only at the first instance of a `<title>` tag in a Web page and to skip over any duplicate tags that may follow. However, just because your visitors cannot tell the difference that does not mean the search engines won't identify the use of this trick and delist the offending Web site.

Hidden Text and Fields

Earlier, you read about adding descriptive summaries to your Web pages as a way of improving your standing. While this works in many cases, sometimes you don't want a summary paragraph in the midst of your polished page. Because of the importance of this text, you might be tempted to try to hide the text from visitors. You might also want to load up the page with additional descriptions or keywords that are all hidden from your visitors.

One way that some Web site publishers try to hide text from visitors is to add descriptions or keywords that use the same color as the background for the page. For example, if the background color is black, they might add hidden text by setting the font color to black. In addition, to give this text as small a footprint as possible on the page, the Web site publisher might set the font size to 1, as demonstrated here:

```
<font color ="#000000" size="1"> Writer's Gallery is a

   place for anyone who loves the written word. You'll find

   links to hundreds of writing-related resources as well as

   new works of fiction published at our site.</font>
```

TIP To avoid the watchful eye of search engines, some Web site publishers try to use a color that is close to the background color but doesn't match it exactly. However, most modern search engines now look for these types of tricks and may delist Web sites that use the same or similar color for both the font and background. Another technique to avoid a penalty is to use a background image with colors that your hidden text can blend into.

HTML comments also let you hide text from readers. With HTML comments, you can place text on the page that the search engine can see but your readers can't:

```
<!— Entertainment news, business news, current events —>
<!— Rare book, collector book, first print book —>
```

While it is perfectly acceptable to add keywords into your HTML comment statements, avoid loading them up. Otherwise, you'll run the risk that some search engines will view the comments as spam. Some search engines also read values associated with input fields. Some Web site publishers try to use hidden input fields to boost their standings, as demonstrated in the following example.

```
<input type="hidden" value="baseball, football, basketball, hockey">
```

Here, input type `hidden` and its associated `value` attribute were used to store additional descriptive text or keywords. Clearly, using hidden input fields in this manner puts any Web site that tries this at risk.

Setting Up Multiple Versions of Your Pages

Mirror sites have long been used to provide additional ways to access popular Web resources. What many Web site publishers have discovered is that if they mirror individual pages, they can drive additional traffic to their Web site. When you mirror a page, you create copies of a page.

To give the mirrored pages greater importance, the Web site publishers keep their mirrored pages short and stick with text descriptions and keywords. They use different descriptions and keywords to tailor the pages to specific audiences and search engines and then save the pages with unique names. For example, pages might be named sequentially, such as index1.htm, index2.htm, index3.htm, and so on. Once finished, each individual page is registered.

The idea here isn't to dazzle readers with these mirror pages, but rather to get the readers to visit the main Web site. Each of the mirrored Web pages contains links that directs them to the main page or will automatically redirect visitors to the main page via a <meta> tag. (Redirecting readers to a new page is discussed in the Sunday Afternoon session titled "Redirecting Lost Readers.")

Search engines and directories look unfavorably on any Web site that tries to manipulate things in this manner, and visitors often don't appreciate being redirected like this. The bottom line here is not to use this trick.

Increasing Your Web Traffic with the Top Search Engines

Registering with the major search engines is one of the best ways to increase traffic to your Web site. If you've followed the techniques for optimizing your Web site for search engines as discussed previously under "Capitalizing on Search Engine Fundamentals," you should see marked improvements in your Web traffic simply by registering with the search engines listed in this section. Don't expect a flood of traffic the day after you register your Web site; rather, you should see a steady increase in the level of traffic your Web site receives over time. The actual increase you see will depend on the subject of your site, its size and quality, and your use of search engine optimization techniques.

Although you could use the techniques discussed here to register with hundreds of other search engines, the reward for all your hard work usually isn't worth the effort. Millions of people use only the major search engines to find what they need. Every day, these search engines collectively handle about 95 percent of the searches performed by general search engines. Obviously, this means that the hundreds of other general search engines handle only 5 percent of the search transactions. Do you really want to spend countless hours registering with hundreds of other search engines when you can potentially reach the vast majority of users simply by registering with the most-used search engines? Probably not.

When you register with a search engine, you generally provide the URL to your top-level page. The search engine uses this single URL to find all the other resources at your site. You should also register the URLs of the top-level pages that cannot be reached from your home page.

The material that follows is designed as a quick reference resource that you can use time and again. The idea is to provide only the information you need. With this in mind, the sections are organized alphabetically based on the name of the search engine. You'll also find the URL to the main page and the relevant registration page (if available). If you find that the URL for the registration page is no longer valid, go to the main page and follow the submission link to the appropriate page. Usually, the submission link is labeled "Add URL," "Add a Page," or something similar.

NOTE Keep in mind that these are general search engines, not specialized or category-specific search engines. In upcoming sections, you will learn how to increase your traffic using other types of search engines. Note also that there are many popular alternatives to search engines, such as directories and guides, which are discussed later in the book as well.

The Big Three Search Engines

Google, Yahoo!, and Bing along account for over 90% of all searches.

Google

Main page: http://www.google.com

Submission page: http://www.google.com/addurl/?continue=/addurl

Instructions: Provide your URL and a comment about the content of your Web site before clicking on the Add URL button.

Figure 2.15

Google has become one of the most used and well-known search engines on the Web.

Yahoo!

Main page: http://www.yahoo.com

Submission page: http://search.yahoo.com/free/request

Instructions: Key in your top-level URL and click on the Submit URL button.

Figure 2.16

Yahoo! runs one of the two most popular general search engines on the Internet.

Bing

Main page: http://www.bing.com

Submission page: http://www.bing.com/webmaster/ SubmitSitePage.aspx

Instructions: Provide your URL and click on the Submit URL button to submit your site.

Figure 2.17

Bing is Microsoft's new search engine.

Other Popular Search Engines

AltaVista

Main page: http://www.altavista.com

Submission page:
http://www.bing.com/webmaster/SubmitSitePage.aspx

Instructions: Search results for AltaVista come from Yahoo!, which is getting its search results from Bing in the U.S. and Canada.

Figure 2.18

With millions of accesses every day, AltaVista is a major Internet search engine.

AOL Search

Main page: http://search.aol.com/aol.webhome

Submission page: http://www.google.com/addurl/?continue=/addurl

Instructions: Search results for AOL Search come from Google. New site submission must be made to Google.

Figure 2.19

AOL Search is a
search engine
owned by America
Online but
available to
everyone on
the Web.

Ask

Main page: http://www.ask.com

Instructions: Ask does not accept free URL submissions. Ask does
provide for paid advertising. However, chances are that over time the
search engine will eventually discover and add your Web site if you do a
good job of making your Web site search-engine friendly. You can access
information about paid advertising at Ask by clicking on the Advertise
link on its main page.

Figure 2.20

Ask used to be
Ask Jeeves, which
was known for
supporting searches
in the form of
questions.

Netscape

Main page: http://www.netscape.com

Submission page: http://www.google.com/addurl/?continue=/addurl

Instructions: Search results for Netscape come from Google. New site submission must be made to Google.

Figure 2.21

Netscape's search results include its own paid listings combined with search results retrieved from Google.

Metasearch Engines

In recent years, a new type of Internet search Web site has emerged called a metasearch engine. A metasearch engine doesn't crawl the Internet looking for content to maintain its own database. Instead, metasearch engines retrieve search results by passing search queries on to a number of search engines and directories and correlating the results returned from each source into a single, combined results listing.

Metasearch engines are generally best used when performing general searches because they return a broad set of results from different sources. Web surfers like metasearch engines because they can save time when looking for information.

The Mechanics Going on Behind the Scenes

Metasearch engines collect user queries and format them as appropriate for various search engines and directories. After submitting a query, the metasearch engine collects results from each source in a virtual database, from which it then removes duplicate results. Some metasearch engines display their results in one consolidated list while other metasearch engines display results by category or by source. Regardless of how a metasearch engine chooses to display its results, the results are ultimately sorted according to relevance.

Dogpile, Mamma, and Other Sites

Like search engines, not all metasearch engines are equal, some being more popular than others. In this section, you will find information about some of the most commonly used search engines.

Metasearch engines do not maintain their own databases. Therefore, they are not able to accept free URL submissions. However, most offer paid listings. To help ensure that your Web site is listed in the results returned by a metasearch engine, make sure that you get listed with at least one of the search engines or directories from which it retrieves results.

Dogpile

Dogpile (**www.dogpile.com**), shown in Figure 2.22, sends queries to a number of search engines and directories, including Google, Yahoo!, Bing, and Ask. The results returned from these sources are displayed in a single list according to relevancy. The name of the search engine or directory from which results were retrieved is also listed.

Figure 2.22

Dogpile combs numerous search engines and directories in an effort to collect results for user queries.

Mamma

Mamma (**www.mamma.com**), shown in Figure 2.23, sends queries to a number of search engines and directories, including Google, Yahoo!, Bing, LookSmart, and Open Directory. Search results retrieved from these and other sources are displayed in a single list according to relevancy, along with the name of the search engines and directories from which results originated. Mamma offers paid listings, which you can learn about by clicking on the Advertise with us link on the main page.

Dogpile and Mamma are just a couple of the many good metasearch engines available on the Web. The following list shows a number of other metasearch engines that you might consider.

- **Yippy: http://search.yippy.com**
- **WebCrawler: http://www.webcrawler.com**
- **SurfWax: http://www.surfwax.com**

Figure 2.23

Mamma is one of the older and best known of the metasearch engines.

Targeting Shoppers Using Comparison Shopping Engines and Directories

Today more and more people are using the Internet not just to find information or for personal amusement but for shopping. While there is no doubt that the majority of surfers on the Internet use the major search engines to find what they are looking for, a growing number of online shoppers are turning to a new type of specialized search engine, designed explicitly to assist shoppers find the best deal for their money. These new search engines retrieve product and pricing information from numerous vendors, allowing for product comparisons.

The *comparison shopping engines* or *CSEs* are focused exclusively on merchandising. The focus is on the sale of products. As a result, online shoppers only get what they are looking for, something to buy. If you have a product that you are selling from your Web site, comparison shopping engines may be exactly the tool you need to bring the people to your Web site.

Unlike regular search engines, you have a great deal of control over how the comparison shopping engines display the information retrieved from your Web pages. You can generally specify what you want presented and how it is displayed. Traditional search engines do not provide anything like this. Comparison shopping engines provide a lot of information besides just product names and prices. They typically provide detailed product descriptions, photos, product reviews, and tax and shipping information.

In order to get listed with a comparison shopping engine, your site must meet certain criteria. For starters, you'll need a shopping cart. If you do not have one, some comparison shopping engines, such as Google Product Search, will be happy to provide you with one. In addition, you must post the prices for all of the products that you are selling. If your Web site meets these basic criteria, it is a candidate for inclusion.

There are dozens of comparison shopping engines. However, just as with regular search engines, not all are equal. You'll get the best value out of your time and effort if you target the comparison shopping engines that people use most. Not all comparison search engines are the same. Some are free and others are not. Some charge an initial set up fee while others do not. Some make you pay based on the number of times visitors click on your links while others charge you based on a percentage of sales.

Comparison Shopping Engines

The following sections introduce you to a number of popular comparison shopping engines. The first two comparison shopping engines, Google Product Search and PriceScan, both accept free submissions. The remaining comparison shopping engines will charge you for their services. In addition, you'll be introduced to a number of comparison shopping directories as well, each of which accepts free submissions.

Google Product Search

Google Product Search, formally named Froogle, is a free shopping search engine located at **www.google.com/products**, as shown in Figure 2.24.

Google also uses Web sites registered with Google Product Search as a feed for its regular search engine results.

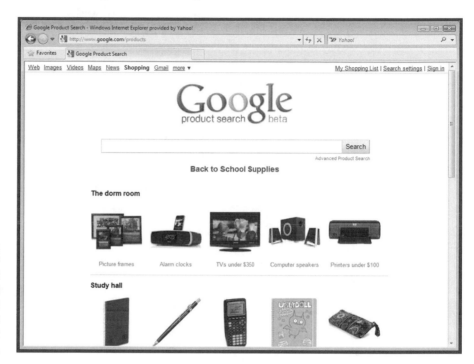

Figure 2.24

Google Product Search is a great comparison shopping engine with which to get started.

To register with Google Product Search you will have to sign up for a free Google account and for Google's merchant services, which is also free. If your Web site does not have the ability to make online sales, you can take advantage of Google's Checkout feature, which allows you to accept and process credit card sales for a low fee (2% of sales or 2 cents per transaction, as of the publishing of this book). To learn more about Google Product Search and to set up your Web site, visit **http://www.google.com/base/ help/sellongoogle.html**.

PriceScan

PriceScan (**www.priceScan.com**), shown in Figure 2.25, is another comparison shopping search engine that does not charge merchants for listings.

PriceScan makes its money through the sale of online advertising. In order to get your products listed on PriceScan, you must post your products online and have your own shopping card and payment system. PriceScan does not provide these services for you. To register with PriceScan, send an e-mail to **vendors@pricescan.com**.

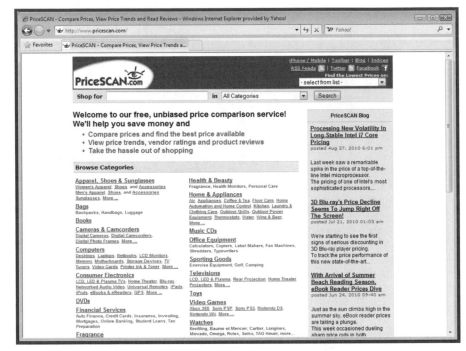

Figure 2.25

PriceScan is another excellent and free comparison shopping engine.

Other Comparison Shopping Engines

There are dozens of comparison shopping engines available on the Internet, a number of which are identified in the following list. Each of these comparison search engines involves some sort of set up fee or ongoing expense. Still, inclusion in their database can result in bringing masses of visitors to your Web sites, and since the people that will be brought in are looking for the types of products you sell, chances of making sales and generating return customers are very good.

- Yahoo! Shopping: http://shopping.yahoo.com
- shop.com: http://www.shop.com
- Shopping.com: http://www.shopping.com
- Shopzilla: http://www.shopzilla.com

Comparison Shopping Directories

In addition to comparison shopping engines, there are a number of comparison shopping directories available on the Internet. Some accept free listings and others do not. As with comparison shopping engines, comparison shopping directories require that you have a shopping cart in place and that you post your prices online. ShoppingSpot (**www.shoppingspot.com**), shown in Figure 2.26, is a small but growing comparison shopping directory that accepts free product listings. You can register your Web site and products here by visiting **www.shoppingspot.com/site/suggest.htm**.

Figure 2.26

ShoppingSpot provides buyers with the ability to compare an assortment of different types of products.

Submitting Your Web Site to the Top Guides, Lists, and Directories

The phenomenal popularity of resource directories such as Open Directory ushered in a whole new era of guides, lists, and directories designed to help people find things on the Web. Whereas the focus of Web guides is usually on the top or best sites, lists and directories focus on categorizing information found on the Web.

Just as hundreds of search engines are available, you can find hundreds of guides, lists, and directories on the Web as well. Unfortunately, trying to submit your site to every guide, list, and directory is a waste of your time and resources. Instead, you should focus on the top resources you find in this section.

Submitting Your Site to Lists and Directories

Guides, *lists*, and *directories* are all terms used to describe Web resources that provide links to Web pages. Web guides usually provide pointers to the best or top sites. Think of a guide as something you might buy at the bookstore to help you learn about a country you are visiting. Lists are exactly what the name implies: Lists of Web sites that are usually organized into several major categories. Think of a list as something you might put together before you go grocery shopping. Beyond lists, you will find directories, which usually have rather extensive listings of Web sites divided into many categories. When you think of a directory, think of the Yellow Pages directory, that huge yellow tome that lists tons of businesses.

Although size is usually the major factor that distinguishes a list from a directory, don't get hung up on the terminology. Generally speaking, lists and directories serve the same purpose and often the terms are used interchangeably.

Web site listings in guides and directories are very different from the results returned by a typical search engine. Guides and directories do not index your Web pages at all; they simply use the information you provide to create a listing for your Web site.

When you submit your Web site to a list or directory, you submit the URL for your home page or other top-level pages at your site. Along with the page URL, you usually are asked to submit the Web page title, a brief description of the Web page, and a specific category for the Web page. The Web page category should always be tailored to the specific directory to which you are submitting your page. Some directory sites have hundreds of narrowly focused categories, such as entertainment news for kids and computer book reviews. Other directory sites have only a few broadly focused categories such as entertainment and travel.

Most directory sites screen all new submissions rigorously. If the same page has been submitted previously, the site usually disregards the submission. The site might also disregard the submission if the page was submitted to the wrong category.

Rather than place your listing in a category that you think is popular, you should place your listing in a category that strongly relates to the topic your site covers. Placing your site in a category that fits your content ensures that readers who are looking for a site like yours will be able to find it.

Trying to submit the same Web page to multiple categories will usually get you in trouble. Rather than submit the same Web page to multiple categories, examine the type of content that you publish to see whether different areas of your Web site fall into different categories. For example, you could list your home page in one category, your writing area in another category, and your job center in yet another category. Whenever possible, list each of the major areas of your Web site separately in directories. This gives your Web site a better chance of getting noticed. And the more your Web site is noticed, the more your Web traffic will increase.

The Open Directory and Yahoo!

On the Internet, a directory is a human-edited collection of information about Web sites. People all over the world regularly visit the major Web directories to look for information regarding specific subjects. This makes getting listed in a Web directory very important to any Web site publisher.

Being listed in the major Web directories is even more important because just being listed in them is often all that it takes for your site to eventually get noticed by and then indexed by some major search engines.

While there are many Web directories out there, two are particularly well known and popular, the Open Directory and Yahoo!'s directory. As a result, they merit a little extra attention.

The Open Directory is the only major directory that is and always has been 100 percent free. Some directories only accept paid inclusion, whereas many others offer both free and paid inclusion. A global community of volunteer editors manages the Open Directory. One of the reasons that getting listed in the Open Directory is so important is because results from the Open Directory are retrieved by numerous search engines on the Internet, including Google, Netscape, and AOL. In addition, many search engines provide direct access to the Open Directory. For example, Google provides access to the open directory at **directory.google.com**.

Yahoo! is one of the Internet's largest search engines. Yahoo! also maintains its own directory (**search.yahoo.com/dir**). Yahoo! provides for free registration for non-commercial submission. Like the Open Directory, Yahoo!'s directory serves as a feed for numerous search engines, making it all the more attractive.

TIP   Before you run out and start registering with the various directories, it's best to do a little preparation. For starters, prepare a well written description of your Web site that is around 25 words long and be sure to include at least a few of your keywords or keyword phrases.

Submitting Your Site to Web Guides

The focus on the top or best sites puts Web guides in a league of their own. When you submit your site to a guide, you are betting that the guide's reviewers will find your site useful, informative, or well presented.

If the guide's reviewers count your site among the best, they will write a review of your site, and your site will show up in their database of the Web's top sites. If your guide's reviewers don't like your site for whatever reason, they will move on to the next site in their long list of sites to review.

Contrary to what you might think, the Web sites with the fancy graphics and multimedia don't always have the best ratings. In fact, some of the highest rated Web sites have mostly text.

You can improve your odds of getting your site reviewed by taking the time to learn what the guide looks for and what the guide's reviews look like. When you have gained a clear understanding of how the guide works, submit your site with descriptive information that will catch the eyes of the reviewers. Along with the summary information, you might want to include a rating for your Web site. If this rating is realistic, you might give the reviewer a reason to visit your Web site.

Another way to improve your odds with Web guides is to focus on the top-level areas of your Web site. For example, if your primary Web site publishes two key resources, Writers Gallery and Internet Job Center, you could submit entries for both of these areas rather than the Web site as a whole. The reason for this is that these areas have very different focuses—creative writing and jobs—and can't be realistically rated in the same review.

As a final note, remember that reviewers are real people. With thousands of Web sites to review, several weeks or even a month could elapse before a reviewer gets a chance to look at your Web site. If reviewers don't review your site, there isn't much point in inundating them with e-mail or repeated submissions. Instead, wait a few months and then try again.

How Do People Find Your Listing in a Guide or Directory?

Most guides and directories can be searched in two ways: by category or by keyword.

When you search by category, you follow links from a broad category to a progressively more focused category. In a category search, the categories themselves are the main elements driving users to your listing. Yet when users finally get to the detailed page that shows your listing, it is the page title and summary description that will influence their decision to visit your Web site.

A keyword search in a guide or directory is handled in a very different manner. Rather than follow links, you use a search interface to find categories and lists within the guide. If the keywords you enter lead to several categories, you see category headers. If the keywords you enter lead to a specific listing, you see either the listing itself or the page of which the listing is part.

How Often Is Your Site's Listing Updated?

Unlike search engines that periodically schedule your site for reindexing, most guides and directories rarely update their listings. The problem with updating listings is a logistical one. To update a list in a Web guide, a reviewer needs to take another look at the Web site. To update a listing in a directory, the directory site needs to have someone check the validity of the link and the description. Both actions require time and resources that could be directed at new listings.

Don't rely on someone from the guide or directory site to update your listing in six months or a year; take a proactive stance instead. If you move the furniture around a bit and add a new edition to your Web home, inform the folks who run the guide or directory site. Generally, you should send a message to the people who maintain the directory or guide. The key things to tell them are what the old information looked like and what the new information should look like.

Increasing Your Web Traffic with Guides and Directories

Getting your Web site listed in a popular guide or directory will definitely increase the traffic to your site. As with search engines, you will find that you get the most out of your time investment when you submit your site to the top guides and directories, which is why this session focuses on the best guides and directories.

Although you know that a Web page or area within your Web site will be listed in the directory, there is no assurance that you will get listed in a Web guide. Still, submitting your site to the guides listed in this section is worthwhile, especially when you consider that getting your site listed in any one of these guides could bring thousands of visitors to your Web site every single day. For many Web sites, an extra thousand visitors a day would effectively double or triple the site's traffic. Doubling or tripling your Web traffic from a single listing might seem like a pipe dream, but the reality is that people often seek out the best that the Web has to offer. After all, do you settle for bronze, when silver, gold, and platinum are waiting in the wings?

You should submit your Web site to the featured guides and directories. As discussed earlier, directories often ask for detailed information, which can include page URL, page title, keywords, description, contact information, and categories/topics. Before you submit your listing, you should have this information plotted out.

CANLinks

Main page: http://www.canlinks.net/

Submission page: http://www.canlinks.net/addalink/

Figure 2.27

CANLinks is a Web directory for Canada.

eiNET.net

Main page: http://www.einet.net/

Submission page: Click on the Add a Site link located on the main page.

Figure 2.28

eiNet.net has a lot to offer, although it might take a while to get listed.

Gimpsy

Main page: http://www.gimpsy.com

Submission page: Click on the Suggest a Site link on the main page.

Figure 2.29

Gimpsy is small but very well maintained directory offering free and paid URL submissions.

Illumirate

Main page: http://www.illumirate.com/

Submission page: Click on the Free Add URL link on the main page.

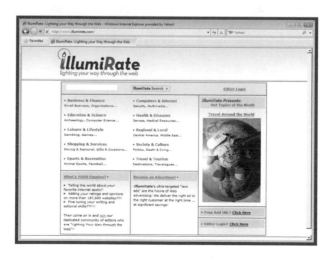

Figure 2.30

Illumirate is a small but well run Web directory.

Mavicanet

Main page: http://www.mavicanet.com

Submission page: Drill down into a subcategory and then click on the Add site link.

Figure 2.31

Mavicanet is a multilingual directory that spans more than 30 languages.

Open Directory

Main page: http://dmoz.org

Submission page: http://dmoz.org/docs/en/add.html

Figure 2.32

The Open Directory is the world's largest human-edited directory.

Skaffe

Main page: http://www.skaffe.com

Submission page: Click on the Suggest URL link on the main page.

Figure 2.33

Skaffe is a small but very good volunteer-edited Web directory.

Yahoo!

Main page: http://dir.yahoo.com/

Submission page: Visit the category where your site fits and the click on the Suggest a Site link.

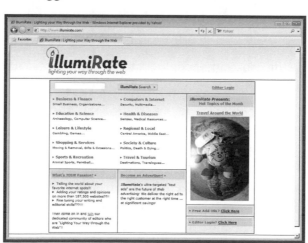

Figure 2.34

Yahoo! hosts one of the most popular Web directories on the planet; getting listed here can certainly bring visitors to your Web site.

Offline Marketing

Getting the most out of your marketing campaign also means going beyond the confines of the cyber world into the real world. As addictive as the Internet can be, people spend a lot more time moving about and interacting in the real world than they do online. So, to get to these people where they live, work, and play, you need to expand your promotional efforts.

Promoting Your URL Everywhere

You need to get the word out that you have created one of the Web's best and most useful sites. One of the best ways of accomplishing this goal is to get your URL out there for everyone to see. For starters, tell your friends and ask them to tell their friends. Tell your co-workers as well. If you are part of a sports club or social club, do your associates a favor and clue them in on the great Web site you have created. After all, if you don't spread the word, who will?

Updating Your Business Cards

If you use them, one of the easiest things that you can do to spread the word about your Web site is to add your URL to your business cards. The inclusion of your URL does not have to be anything fancy, just list it at the bottom of your card beneath your phone number and e-mail address and people will pick up on it easily enough.

Don't be like so many people that order a box of 250 business cards and a year later are still in possession of 240 of the cards. You took the time to design your card and have paid for it, now take advantage of them and pass them around. This doesn't mean standing out on the street corner and giving them away to complete strangers. Rather, anytime you are around people that you believe might be interested in your Web site, tell them about it and give them a copy of your card. Then ask them to visit and to provide you with their feedback. Many people like to be asked for their thoughts because it tells them that you value their opinion.

Modifying Your Letterhead

Never send out a personal letter or correspondence without writing it on your own letterhead, and make sure your letterhead includes your URL. This will not only let people know you have a Web site but it also gives you the chance to suggest they visit. For example, if your letter involves something related to what is on your Web site, you can reference your Web site as a place to go to get more information. Since most people know that Web sites generally provide information about contact site owners, including your URL on your Web site gives the recipient another means of getting in touch with you.

Integrating Offline Advertising

If you are currently involved in promoting your products or services offline, start including your Web site's URL in your promotional efforts. If you occasionally post fliers, start adding your URL to them. If you display information about your company on the side of your automobile, add your URL and turn your car, truck, or SUV into a rolling billboard that promotes your Web site. If you do radio, television, or newspaper advertising, don't forget to plug your URL every chance you get. Be creative in looking for different ways to integrate the promotion of your Web site with your offline advertising.

If you are running a contest on your Web site or giving something away, you might want to focus on promoting the contest or giveaway instead of your Web site. This lets you plug your Web site without actually plugging it.

Promoting Your URL Alongside Your Products and Services

If you sell anything, be it a product or a service, you should use a sale as an opportunity to plug your Web site. For example, if you have ever purchased a book from Amazon.com, you've probably noticed that when your book arrives, the book always includes one or more promotional fliers. You should do the same thing. Encourage your customers to learn more about whatever it is that you do from your Web site.

Put your URL on the package, on the invoice, and in any promotional materials that you include. If you provide services instead of a product, make sure that you leave a copy of your business card behind whenever you come into contact with your customers and include your URL on any invoices and receipts.

Wrapping Up and Looking Ahead

Millions of people use search engines to find information every day, and one of the best ways to build traffic to your Web site is to register with search engines. Guides, lists, and directories can also help your Web site get noticed. Keep in mind, you aren't guaranteed a listing in a guide to the best of the Web. Still, your time is well spent if you manage to garner one or more such listings for your site.

This afternoon, you'll examine many different types of search engines and Web directories. You'll learn about the best directories and search engines for business-oriented Web sites, industry- and category-specific directories, getting more mileage from What's New? directories, and a whole lot more.

The Coolest, the Hottest, and the Best

- ➤ Business Search Engines and Yellow Pages Directories
- ➤ What's New? Directories
- ➤ Getting Your Site Listed as the Cool Site of the Day
- ➤ Integrating Social Networking into Your Promotion Plan

Hundreds of business search and directory sites are currently available. The first part of this afternoon's coverage focuses on the best of these sites so that you can get the most exposure for your time investment. If you have time, make use of these resources as you learn about them; that is, proceed with the registration process as you go through this section. If you don't have time to get to them all now, come back when you do. It will be worth your while.

Later this afternoon, you'll find out how to vie for awards that will help your site get noticed by cyberspace travelers. Awards abound on the Web, and your site can sizzle as Hot Site of the Day or freeze out the competition as Cool Site of the Week. Some awards are more likely to increase your Web traffic than others, though, and this afternoon's session introduces you to some of the best. You will also learn how to leverage the popularity of social networking sites, using them to your advantage in your Web promotion plan.

The Best Business Search Engines and Yellow Pages Directories

Business search engines and Yellow Pages directories provide great resources for anyone who offers products, services, or business-related information on the Web. Most business-oriented search engines and directories provide much more detailed information than other search sites and directories. These detailed entries allow you to list your Web site and tout your products and services as well.

Submitting Your Site to Business Search and Directory Sites

Hundreds of thousands of businesses offer products and services on the Web. The sites that help Web users make sense of all these offerings are the business search engines and Yellow Pages directories. Because these search and directory sites are tailored for businesses, you can search for specific businesses by company name, location, and industry, as well as by the products and services that the companies offer. Although they are similar to traditional search engines, most business search engines do not index your Web site or the pages that you submit for listing at the search site. Instead, these search engines create an indexed reference to your site based solely on the information you submit, which doesn't necessarily include the URL to your Web site. In this respect, this type of business search engine is more like a directory listing than a traditional search engine.

Because business search engines don't actually index your site, many business search sites are called Yellow Pages directories. Although some Yellow Pages directories are modeled after the Yellow Pages of your phone book, most Web-based Yellow Pages directories have features of both traditional directory sites and traditional search engine sites.

Due to their very direct focus, business search sites and directories often want a great deal of information from anyone registering with the site. For this reason, before you register with these sites, you should have all the following information at hand:

- What subject category you want to be listed under
- How you want company contact information to read
- Who you will list as the contact name at the company
- What keywords you want associated with your site
- What Web pages' URLs you want listed
- What e-mail address you want to use for inquiries
- What description you will use for your company, products, and services

You should also know that, by their very nature, business search sites and directories are out to make a profit. The worst of these sites exist only to push paid services on unwitting souls who want to get listed at the site. However, there is no need to sign up for anything that will cost you money. Plenty of sites are happy just to have your listing and will list you without charge. These sites get their money from advertising rather than listings.

Increasing Your Web Traffic with Yellow Pages Directories

Just as the top search engines and directories receive millions of visitors every day, so do the top Yellow Pages directories. Accordingly, registering your Web site with Yellow Pages directories will increase the traffic to your Web site. That said, Yellow Pages directories generally don't drive thousands of visitors to a particular Web site; rather, you can reasonably expect relatively modest increases in your Web traffic over time.

The traffic depends, of course, on the types of products and services you offer. Right now you might be wondering if it's really worth the effort. The answer is yes—as long as you focus your efforts on the top Yellow Pages directories listed in this section.

Although Yellow Pages directories are popular and receive millions of visitors every day, they are business oriented. Visitors to these directories are usually looking for very specific types of information (for example, information on a management consulting service). Furthermore, because Yellow Pages listings contain addresses, phone numbers, and other contact information, people visiting the Yellow Pages directory might not visit your Web site at all. Instead, they might visit your physical storefront or contact you by phone, fax, or e-mail.

Whether visitors to a Yellow Pages directory go to your storefront, contact you, or visit your Web site, you have managed to bring in the all-important consumers who are actively looking for a business that offers products or services like yours. With a listing in a traditional search engine or directory site, you simply cannot bring in this type of visitor on a consistent basis.

Most businesses would much rather have 50 people browsing their aisles—virtual or otherwise—than have 500 people racing past the windows on their way to somewhere else.

NOTE　As you follow along with the discussion, submit your Web site to the search engines and directories found in this section. If you are in a hurry and don't have time to register with all the sites, simply start with the first site and register with as many sites as you can.

BizWeb

Main Page: http://www.bizweb.com/

Submission Page: http://www.bizweb.com/InfoForm/

Instructions: Click on the Submit Your Company link on the main page and supply the required information.

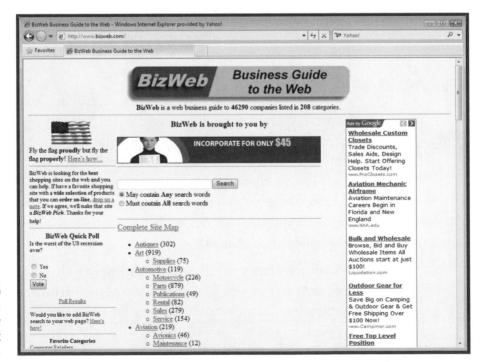

Figure 3.1

BizWeb is a popular directory for businesses that have Web sites.

Superpages.com

Main Page: http://www.superpages.com/

Submission Page: Click on the Add or Edit a Business link at the bottom of the main page.

Instructions: To create a listing, you'll need to enter your business phone number and then follow the submission guidelines.

Figure 3.2

Superpages.com provides free basic listings.

Where2Go

Main Page: http://www.where2go.com/

Submission Page: Click on the List Your Site link at the bottom of the main page.

Instructions: Enter your URL, read and accept the site's terms and conditions, and then follow the step-by-step submission process.

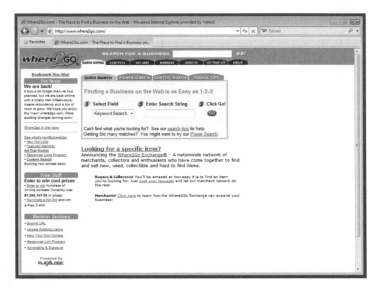

Figure 3.3

Where2Go is a Yellow Pages directory with listings for businesses throughout the world.

YellowPages.com

Main Page: http://www.yellowpages.com

Instructions: Click on the Advertise With Us link on the main page to register your Web site for free.

Figure 3.4

Yellowpages.com is one of the more popular Internet Yellow Pages directories.

Yellowbook

Main Page: http://www.yellowbook.com

Submission Page: http://www.yellowbook.com/ContactUs/?

Instructions: Select the option to Advertise with Yellowbook, and then supply the information required to complete the submission form.

Figure 3.5

Yellowbook provides the ability to search by company name or by keyword phrases.

Directories by Industry and Category

The major search engines and directories are great for getting your Web site noticed by the masses, but you also want your site to be accessible to people looking for specific types of information. This is where industry- and category-specific directories come into the picture. Whether your site covers fine dining in Seattle, outdoor sports activities in Australia, or one of thousands of other topics, there are directories devoted to your subject. This section will show you how to find and use them.

NOTE   Some of these directories have a fairly narrow focus. Be sure to read through the detailed descriptions before you submit a listing.

Getting the Most Out of Industry and Category Directories

Whereas industry directories focus on major industries, such as real estate or travel, category directories focus on specific topics, such as resources for writers or outdoor sports. People looking for specialized or tailored information seek out industry and category directories. This makes these directories the perfect place for your Web site to get noticed.

As with most directories, industry and category directories focus on pages rather than entire Web sites. Thus you generally submit the URL of a specific page or area that strongly relates to the topic of the directory. Along with the URL, you usually submit the page title and a summary description. Although the description of your page might not be published with your listing, the directory maintainer uses the description to determine whether the page is appropriate for the directory.

Because industry and category directories have a very specific focus, they are great for increasing the traffic to your Web site. In a way, getting listed in these directories is like conducting an advertising campaign that targets readers who are interested in the exact type of Web site you publish.

Before you submit your Web site to industry or category directories, you should take a few minutes to plot out the industries or categories that fit your Web site. Although the first industry or category you think of is probably the best, a typical Web site will fit into several categories or industries. Your collection of articles on Spain would probably fit in perfectly with a travel or tourism directory. But you could also look for metro or city guides that cover Spain. Additionally, your articles might cover the best restaurants in Madrid, making these pages suitable for a listing in a directory to restaurants, fine dining, or food.

Community Guides

Community guides are becoming increasingly popular. By focusing a directory on a specific city, state, or country, users can find information directly relating to an area of the world in which they are interested. If you want to find an Italian restaurant in Denver, you access a city guide featuring Denver. If you want to find a Web design firm in the Seattle area, you access a guide to the Seattle metropolitan area.

Every single Web site in cyberspace has a place in a community guide. After all, we all live somewhere. For this reason, you should register your site in a directory that covers your metro area, state, or country.

Unfortunately, only a few community guides actually let you submit listings. This section will highlight a number of excellent guides that accept submissions.

Creating a Listing in EscapeArtist

EscapeArtist (**www.escapeartist.com**) is a different kind of community guide. Instead of focusing on a particular city or state, EscapeArtist offers guides to a particular country or region.

EscapeArtist has hundreds of country- and region-specific guides. The easiest way to access these guides is to visit the main site and then follow the links to the guide with which you want to work. As shown in Figure 3.6, much of what you'll find at EscapeArtist is about travel and living in different countries.

To submit a listing to EscapeArtist, visit the guide for the appropriate category and click on the Add URL link at the bottom of the page. Provide the required information and submit the form. There is a $5 charge for new registrations.

Figure 3.6

EscapeArtist.com provides access to information on a regional or country-by-country basis.

Submitting a Listing to the MetroGuide Network

MetroGuide (**www.metroguide.com**), shown in Figure 3.7, is a community guide for Web sites located in the U.S. and around the world.

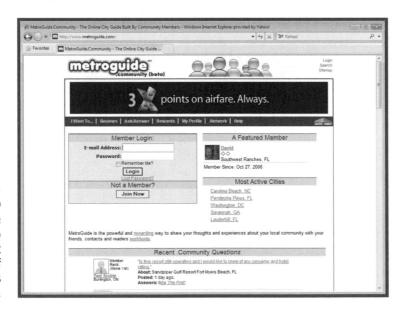

Figure 3.7

MetroGuide provides access to more than just a collection of metro guides around the world.

You'll find individual directories for each state in the U.S. In addition to providing access to metro guides, you'll find other guides for hotels, retail, dining, and so on. To get listed in MetroGuide, visit **login.metroguide.com/ join.asp** and join the MetroGuide community. As a member, you will be able to add your postings.

Yahoo! Country and Metro Guides

Millions of people are lost in the endless sea of the Web. They are looking for tailored information they can access easily and quickly, which is exactly what city guides provide. The growing trend to tailor information based on geographic boundaries is clearly evident when you visit the major search sites. Many of the major search engine sites have a city or metro guide. Yahoo! is no exception.

Yahoo! has set up separate areas for major metros and countries throughout the world. The Web site for Yahoo! Seattle (**seattle.yahoo.com**) is shown in Figure 3.8. If you want to register your Washington-based business or Web site in the Seattle metro guide, visit Yahoo! Seattle and go through the same submission process that you would for the main Yahoo! Directory. If you want to register your Web site in any other Yahoo! city guide, visit the city guide and go through its submission process as well.

The Seattle metro guide is only one of many other Yahoo! metro guides. Some of the other Yahoo! metro guides include

- **Yahoo! Atlanta: http://dir.yahoo.com/Regional/U_S__States/ Georgia/Metropolitan_Areas/Atlanta_metro/**
- **Yahoo! Boston: http://dir.yahoo.com/Regional/U_S__States/ Massachusetts/Metropolitan_Areas/Boston_metro/**
- **Yahoo! Chicago: http://dir.yahoo.com/Regional/U_S__States/ Illinois/Metropolitan_Areas/Chicago_metro/**
- **Yahoo! Miami: http://dir.yahoo.com/Regional/U_S__States/ Florida/Metropolitan_Areas/Miami_Metro/**

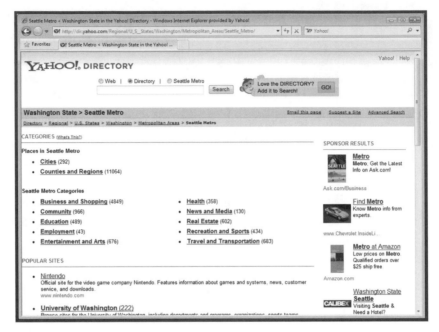

Figure 3.8

Yahoo! metro guides provide a lot of area-specific information.

Some of the Yahoo! country guides include

- ☐ **Yahoo! Austria: http://dir.yahoo.com/Regional/Countries/Austria/**

- ☐ **Yahoo! Denmark: http://dir.yahoo.com/Regional/Countries/Denmark/**

- ☐ Yahoo! France: http://dir.yahoo.com/Regional/Countries/France/

- ☐ **Yahoo! Germany: http://dir.yahoo.com/Regional/Countries/Germany/**

- ☐ Yahoo! Italy: http://dir.yahoo.com/Regional/Countries/Italy/

- ☐ Yahoo! Norway: http://dir.yahoo.com/Regional/Countries/Norway/

NOTE To find a complete list of Yahoo! city and country guides and their URLs, visit Yahoo!'s main Web site at **dir.yahoo.com**.

Real Estate Directories and Guides

When you think of real estate, you probably think of real estate agents and brokers. Although agents and brokers are the cornerstones of real estate, the real estate industry encompasses many other professions and organizations. At one end of the spectrum are the construction companies, developers, engineers, planners, workers, and service organizations whose efforts create the homes in which we live and the office buildings in which we work. At the other end of the spectrum are the property managers, asset managers, trust companies, and holding companies that manage the construction and the properties. In between are the financial institutions, the appraisers, the investors, and the property owners who make the construction possible.

With dozens of professions and organizations that make up the real estate industry, it is no surprise that this industry has a dominant presence in cyberspace. In fact, real estate directories are some of the best designed sites you'll find online. If your Web site or business covers any of the professions or organizations related to the real estate industry, you should add a listing to the directories in this section. Further, if you publish any information that relates to the real estate industry, you should consider adding a listing in the real estate directories as well.

Getting Listed at REALTOR.org

REALTOR.org (**www.realtor.org**), shown in Figure 3.9, is a real estate directory published by the National Association of Realtors. The directory covers many different aspects of the real estate industry. You'll find listings of real estate companies, retailers, products, and services. You'll also find listings of associations that are related to the industry.

REALTOR.org focuses on the U.S. real estate industry. It provides a built-in search capability for searching for real estate agents and offices. If your Web site has something to do with the real estate industry, you should consider registering with REALTOR.org.

Figure 3.9

REALTOR.org is one of the best known and most used real estate Web sites.

Getting Listed in Estates Today

Estates Today (**www.estatestoday.co.uk/i_site.html**), shown in Figure 3.10, is a terrific directory for the commercial real estate industry. Its primary focus is on real estate services for the UK and Europe. Unlike some real estate directories that focus only on providing listings to companies, agencies, and brokers, Estates Today provides specific Internet services to the commercial real estate industry. In addition, it maintains a directory named CityOffices.

The CityOffices directory provides links to information about commercial properties and is organized by major cities in the UK and Europe. Before you submit a listing to Estates Today, you should determine which directory best fits your Web site or company. Then submit an e-mail message to the e-mail address listed on the Web site's Contact Us page. The message should provide your company Web site title and the category in which you want your site listed.

Other Real Estate Directories

In addition to the real estate directories already discussed, many other real estate directories also exist. Some of the others you might want to consider include the Real Estate Cyberspace Society, Open House America, and Real-Estate-Agents.

The Real Estate Cyberspace Society (**www.recyber.com**) provides services for real estate professionals. You can become a member of the Real Estate Cyberspace Society by clicking on the SponsorLink link at the bottom of the page and then selecting the type of program you are interested in.

Real-Estate-Agents (**real-estate-agents.com**) maintains a comprehensive directory of commercial and residential real estate agents. Real estate agents can submit free listings by visiting the appropriate area within the directory and clicking on the Add Your Agency link.

Travel and Tourism: Guides and Directories

The travel industry covers many different professions and organizations. There are travel agents to book tickets and airlines, and cruise lines, train companies, and bus companies to provide transportation. Hotels offer a place to stay, and car rental agencies give you flexible mobility. Recreation and amusement businesses provide entertainment.

Because travel and tourism is a big business, the industry is well represented online. As with the real estate industry, many high-profile travel directories can help you build traffic to your Web site. If your Web site covers any of the professions or organizations related to the travel industry, you should consider adding a listing to the directories in this section. If you publish any information that relates to travel and tourism, you should consider adding a listing in the travel directories as well.

Getting Listed in HotelsTravel

HotelsTravel (**www.hotelstravel.com**) is an international directory for the travel and tourism industry. This comprehensive directory contains hundreds of thousands of listings.

You can search HotelsTravel by keyword or by following links to specific categories of information. Categories within the directory include hotels, airlines, airports, travel-related products, travel-related services, and travel references. Most of the major hotel chains have areas within the site as well.

Entries in HotelsTravel cluster around hotels, airports, and airlines. Figure 3.11 shows listings for hotels whose locations are identified graphically on a map of the Tampa area.

If your site features travel-related information, you can add a listing to HotelsTravel for a fee of $99. The URL for this page is **www.hotelstravel.com/ addsite.html**. Fill out only the information that pertains to your Web site. If you are submitting a travel-related site, be sure to specify the city or country that your site services.

Figure 3.11

HotelsTravel is a good choice for hotel and travel related listings.

Other Travel and Tourism Directories

After you submit listings to HotelsTravel, you might want to try other travel directories as well. After all, you want to build traffic to your travel-related Web site, and the best way to do this is to spread the word about your Web site through the key directories for the travel industry. Some of the other travel directories to which you might want to submit your site include WorldWeb and TravelHub.

WorldWeb (**www.usa.worldweb.com**) provides a search interface to thousands of hotel listings. To submit a listing to this site, click on the Add a Business link at the bottom of the page and provide the required information.

TravelHub (**www.travelhub.com**) is a directory of travel agencies. If you are a travel agent, TravelHub provides a number of free services that can help you build traffic and boost your company's bottom line. To find out how you can get listed in this directory, visit **www.travelhub.com/admin/listing/signup.html**.

More Guides and Directories by Category

Company-specific guides and directories are great ways to get your site noticed. The usefulness of category guides is apparent when you want to find specific types of information without having to wade through search engine results. Because category guides are so useful, they are also extremely popular. The Web contains thousands of category-specific guides covering every imaginable topic. If you are looking for a very specific category guide, one of the best places to find it is Yahoo! (**dir.yahoo.com/Business_ and_Economy/Directories/Companies/**), shown in Figure 3.12.

Figure 3.12

Yahoo! is the place to go to find additional directories. You'll find listings of specialty directories organized by category.

Before you go on to the next part in this section, look for additional directories that relate to topics or industries discussed at your site. Rather than try to submit your site in dozens of categories, focus on the top three. After you've identified these categories, submit your site to the best directories related to them.

Take a Break

Now that you've raced through most of Saturday afternoon, it is time to take a break. Crank up the radio. Grab an ice-cold drink and get something to eat. When you return, you'll learn how to hook up with a number of different specialty directories, including What's New? directories and Cool Site of the Day guides.

Children's Directories: Getting Noticed by One of the Web's Biggest Audiences

The Internet is as popular with young people as it is with adults. If your Web site in any way caters to children, then you ought to take advantage of the major kids' directories. These directories are different from other Web directories in that their content is filtered to weed out potentially objectionable sites. Their primary focus is to provide kids with a safe but still fun and interesting experience.

Unlike search engines, which provide tools that parents can use to attempt to block out objectionable material, kids directories are much safer places. One of the best known of the kids' directories is Yahoo! Kids (**kids.yahoo.com**), as shown in Figure 3.13.

Just like the regular Yahoo! Directory, Yahoo! Kids organizes everything into major high-level categories, which kids can drill down into to find Web sites with specific information. You can submit your Web site to Yahoo! Kids by clicking on the Suggest a Site link located at the bottom of the main page. You'll be asked to pick a category and then to supply a title, URL, and a 25 or less word description of your Web site.

There are a number of other online directories dedicated exclusively to kids that you might want to investigate further. These sites include:

- **AskKids—www.askkids.com**
- **KidsClick!—www.kidsclick.org**
- **Dibdabdoo—www.dibdabdoo.com**

Figure 3.13

Yahoo! Kids, formerly known as Yahooligans, is one of the oldest and best run kids' directories.

Getting More Mileage out of What's New? Directories

Announcement sites are an effort to capture the euphoria surrounding the exponential growth of the Web, and simultaneously tap into the usual excitement over things that are new and fresh. One of the first What's New? directories was maintained by NCSA (National Center for Super-computing Applications)—the same folks who gave the world the Mosaic browser. At its peak, the list received thousands of submissions for new Web sites every day. Today, it is no longer updated. However, many other sites publish extensive What's New? directories. When you visit the major What's New? directories, you will find that these Web sites are tremendously popular.

This popularity will help drive visitors to your Web site. What's New? directories are organized much like other directories, with specific broad categories, such as business and entertainment. Listings within a specific category are usually arranged alphabetically by title and often chronologically as well.

By nature, What's New? lists are guides to new sites. Still, if you've never submitted your site to a specific list before, your site is new to the list and therefore you can certainly submit a listing.

When you register with What's New? directories, you will generally see short-term increases in your Web traffic. The reason for this is that your site usually will be featured in the What's New? directory for only one or two days. Afterward, your listing will appear only in the site's archive files—provided that the site has archive files. If you are interested in short-term increases in Web traffic, What's New? directories are definitely for you. Considering that people often bookmark sites they like, a listing in a What's New? directory can provide a modest increase in traffic over the long haul as well.

Exploring the Starting Point Directory

Starting Point (**www.stpt.com**) is a directory service that has reinvented itself several times over the years. Whereas Starting Point once strove to become a major directory à la Yahoo!, the service now focuses on providing a guide to the best Web sites. Despite the change of focus, Starting Point still maintains one of the top guides to new sites. The Starting Point What's New? list is organized into 16 categories that range from business to health and fitness.

Within each category, listings are organized chronologically, with the most recent listings displayed first. Because Starting Point receives so many submissions, the directory displays only the most recent listings.

Figure 3.14 shows a partial directory listing at Starting Point. To get the most out of your listing, be sure to select a category that fits your Web site. You should also provide a descriptive title and a clear summary for the listing.

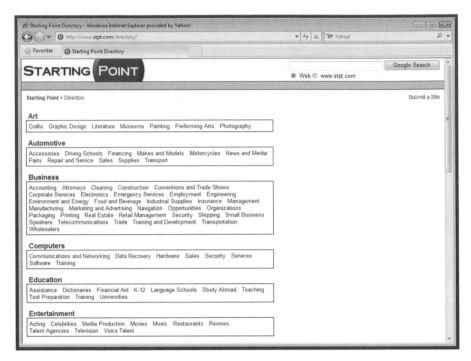

Figure 3.14

Starting Point maintains an extensive directory listing.

Starting Point charges a $99 fee. You can submit your site to Starting Point by clicking on the Add a Site link located on the Web site's main page.

Other What's New? Directories

Finding the new and the interesting is what announcement directories are all about. Two additional What's New? directories for you to consider are Yahoo!'s What's New? area and the New Web Directory. Yahoo!'s What's New? area (**dir.yahoo.com/new**) lists new Web sites that are added to Yahoo!'s Directory. Listings are organized into groups, as shown in Figure 3.15. To submit your Web site, click on the Suggest a Site link at the top of the page. To see if your site has been listed in the What's New? area, drill down into the category for which you submitted your Web site. If it is not there yet, come back later. Yahoo! always has a backlog of submissions.

Figure 3.15

Register your Web site with Yahoo!'s What's New? and get your Web site noticed fast.

NewWebDirectory (**www.newwebdirectory**) provides paid listings for a one time fee of $7.95. Site visitors can rate your site and even write a review of what they think of it. To submit your Web site, click on the Site Submission link and follow the submission instructions.

Getting Your Site Listed as the Cool Site of the Day

One of the most famous awards on the Web is the Cool Site of the Day award. Getting named the Cool Site of the Day is an accomplishment that gets your Web site noticed. But the Cool Site of the Day award is only the icing on the cake as far as awards go. There are dozens of other awards that range from the fleeting to the everlasting. Making sense of all these awards and finding the ones that truly make a difference is what this section is all about.

Nothing makes your Web site stand out from the crowd like an award. Awards are stamps of approval that tell the masses your site is worth their time. Not just any old award will do, though. The Web has more than a thousand different types of site awards. These awards range from somebody's individual Web site's Cool Site of the Day award to PC Magazine's annual Top 100 Web sites list. Bunches of small awards might do wonders for your ego but the actual awards themselves may do very little for your Web site's traffic. On the other hand, an award like making it onto PC Magazine's Top 100 list can dramatically increase traffic to your Web site.

Wandering in the Maze of Web Awards

Awards can work miracles when it comes to building traffic to your Web site, but they can also be mere self-serving trophies that you place in a glass case to brag about your achievements. The simple truth is that displaying your awards prominently doesn't build traffic to your Web site, no matter what the sites granting the awards want you to think.

TIP   When your Web site wins an award, you are usually required to display an icon representing the award somewhere on your Web site. This icon contains a link to the Web site that granted you the award. You might want to consider placing the icon for the award somewhere other than your main Web page because the icon is, after all, a link away from your Web site. If your Web site wins multiple awards, why not create an awards page?

The number of awards doesn't matter, either. You could have hundreds of small awards and it wouldn't make much of a difference as far as your Web site's traffic is concerned. The reality is that these days it seems everyone is offering a Web award of some type or another. There are dozens of variations of Cool Site of the Day awards. These awards are for Cool Site of the Moment, Cool Site of the Hour, Cool Site of the Week, Cool Site of the Month, and Cool Site of the Year as well. Beyond the cool site awards, there are the Hot Site of the Day, Hour, Week, Month, and Year awards.

Next comes the Crazy Site of the Day, Hour, Week, Month, and Year awards. There are so many awards that Web neophytes have started offering backward awards, such as the Mediocre Site of the Day, Ugly Site of the Day, and the Bottom 95 Percent of the Web.

NOTE   Another way to get your Web site noticed is to create your own award. That way, the more sites that you give your award to, the more links there will be pointing back to your Web site and the higher your Web site's ranking will become. However, creating and managing an awards site is a lot of work. You have to come up with formal criteria for judging Web sites and add supporting Web pages to your Web site to manage the award process. In addition, you have to be prepared to handle all of the entries that you may receive. In the event that the entries don't measure up, you may need to be prepared to set aside time to go surfing and looking for sites that you can offer the award to.

If displaying your awards or the number of awards doesn't matter, you are probably wondering what does matter. Well, the true equalizers are the underlying meaning of the award and the strength of the award giver's announcement medium. When an organization, such as *PC Magazine*, recognizes your Web site as one of the Top 100 of the year, you can expect your traffic to skyrocket. Again, the reason for this isn't so much the award itself as the significance of the award and the channels through which it is announced.

PC Magazine is well respected in the industry. The Top 100 of the Year award (**http://www.pcmag.com/top-web-sites-2010/**) is bestowed upon sites only after thorough research and extensive review. The list of recipients of the Top 100 is published in *PC Magazine*, which has several million readers. After publishing the list in its print edition, *PC Magazine* publishes the list in its online edition (see Figure 3.16), where it is available to the Web community throughout the year. The longevity of the print edition coupled with the continued traffic to *PC Magazine*'s Web site and Top 100 list itself are what drives traffic to the Web sites of the recipients.

Figure 3.16

PC Magazine
Top 100 award can
place your Web site
in front of millions
of potential visitors.

Finding the Right Award

The right award can make all the difference in the world when it comes
to increasing traffic to your Web site. To find the right award, you really
need to visit the home of the organization or person granting the award.
When you get to the Web site, spend some time reviewing the site and
the techniques used to display awards.

Ideally, current awards are showcased at the site for at least a day and then
later put into an archive that can be searched. Because the popularity of
the award site is also important, you should try to gauge the level of traffic
at the Web site. The busier the award site, the better the chances that it
will increase traffic to your Web site.

All this talk of finding the right award might seem strange. After all, these
sites are giving away an award! Unfortunately, with more than a thousand

different organizations offering awards of one type or another, you really do need to make sure the award is meaningful and worthwhile before you take the time to submit your Web site. Fortunately, you don't have to look too far; this section already identifies some of the best awards sites.

Submitting Your Site

Receiving an award depends largely upon the personal tastes of the reviewer and the philosophy of the award site as a whole. Some award sites look for truly cool sites based on graphic design or coverage of zany issues. Other award sites look for great resources, with no consideration going to whether the site uses mostly text or a cutting-edge graphic design. Because personal opinion weighs heavily in the decision, truly great sites are sometimes passed by.

To improve your odds of being selected, take the time to get to know the types of sites that the reviewers prefer. If they review mostly entertainment sites and you have a business-oriented site, the odds are high that you will get passed by. So rather than submit the URL of your main business page, submit the URL for that fun area where you let customers interact with your products online, or highlight this area in the summary description you supply with the submission.

You can also improve your odds of winning by submitting each of the key areas within your Web site separately. If your site has three different areas, you might submit each of these areas. Ideally, these areas would cover unrelated topics, such as sports memorabilia, music singles from the '50s, and multi-media DVDs for the Mac. In this way, you are truly submitting something different.

The adage, "If at first you don't succeed, try, try again," certainly applies to awards. Don't abuse the submission process by submitting your site every few days or weeks, though. Instead, wait a few months before submitting your site again. In the interim, you might also want to work on the design, flow, and content of your Web site.

Cool Site of the Day

Cool Site of the Day is one of the most popular awards. To help you make sense of the many offerings, you will find the top Cool Site of the Day awards in this section. These sites are the best of the best when it comes to the Cool Site of the Day award because they follow guidelines for a good award, discussed previously. For the most part, the awards are showcased for at least a day. Then, because they are archived, the awards can continue to generate traffic to your site over the long haul. The sites are also popular, which will help to improve your chances of increasing your Web traffic.

One of the best Cool Site of the Day awards is the original award at **www.coolsiteoftheday.com**. Along with the Cool Site of the Day award, this site has many other features that make the site a great destination (see Figure 3.17). All sites that receive the Cool Site of the Day award are showcased on the day of the award. Afterward, they move the reference to the Web site to an archive featuring all past awards.

You can submit your Web site by clicking on the Submit Your Site! link at the top of the site's main page.

Figure 3.17

If you are looking to get noticed, Cool Site of the Day can help.

Arguably the best cool site of the day recognition you can get comes from **www.komando.com**. This Web site belongs to Kim Komando, host of the nationally syndicated radio talk show, "The Kim Komando Show." In addition to sharing a wealth of experience and knowledge, America's Digital Goddess, as she is affectionately known by her legions of fans, selects a new cool site of the day every day at **www.komando.com/coolsites**, as shown in Figure 3.18.

Figure 3.18

Kim Komando's three-hour radio talk show is heard on over 450 radio stations, reaching out to millions of loyal listeners.

To suggest your site, click on the Contact link located at the bottom of the page and send Kim an e-mail. If Kim's selects your Web site, not only will your URL get listed on **www.komando.com** for the day, but a nice little introduction of your Web site will be provided as well. Be warned, however, that after a mention on **www.komando.com,** some sites are actually unable to handle the barrage of new traffic. So make sure your Web site is ready.

Best of the Web

Many Web guides offer insights into the best sites on the Web. Two in particular are worth taking a look at: World Best Websites and the Webby Awards.

The World Best Websites Award

The World Best Websites award (**www.worldbestwebsites.com**) is presented to Web sites that implement "best practices" in their design and communications. Particular emphasis is placed on Web sites that are on the leading edge of design and technology. See Figure 3.19.

Sites that are submitted as candidates compete for a number of different awards starting with Merit, and then advancing to Bronze, Silver, and Gold. Once nominated, a Web site is visited repeatedly over a 12-week period.

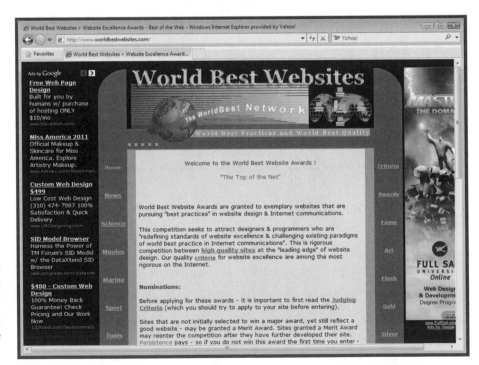

Figure 3.19

The World Best Websites award evaluates Web sites based on an extensive set of criteria.

Web sites are judged on a 100-point scoring system based on the following five (equally weighted) major categories:

- Functionality
- Design
- Content
- Originality
- Professionalism and effectiveness

Winners of the Gold award are eligible to enter an even more strenuous "Level Two" award contest. The criteria used in evaluating Web sites for this award include:

- Significance
- Exemplary innovation
- Quality standards
- Site performance analysis
- Search engine visibility
- Search engine rankings
- URL clarity
- Differentiation and branding strategy
- Business analysis
- Server security checks
- Hosting efficiency
- Surfer votes and customer endorsements

To submit your Web site as a candidate for the World Best Website award, you can send an email to **webcoms04@worldbest.net** that includes:

- Your name
- Your e-mail address
- Your Web site's title
- Your Web site's URL
- A brief description of your Web site

Alternatively, you can submit your Web site by filling out the form found at **www.worldbest.com/submit.htm**, as shown in Figure 3.20.

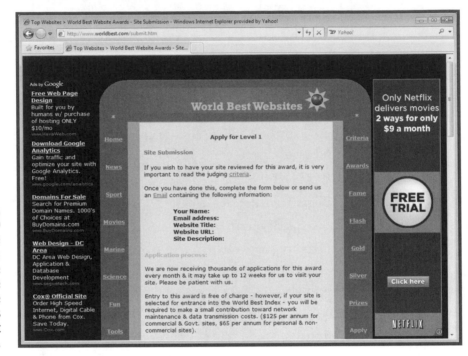

Figure 3.20

If your Web site doesn't garner an award the first time you submit it, take some time to make improvements and then submit it again.

The Webby Awards

Perhaps the most prestigious award any Web site publisher can get is a Webby Award (**www.webbyawards.com**), as shown in Figure 3.21. This award is to be taken very seriously. It is awarded to the best Web site in 60 different categories and operates very much like the Academy Awards, including a once-a-year gala celebration event.

The Webby Awards are presented by the International Academy of Digital Arts and Sciences in order to honor Web sites that excel in design, functionality, usability, and creativity. Five Web sites are selected for each category judged by the academy.

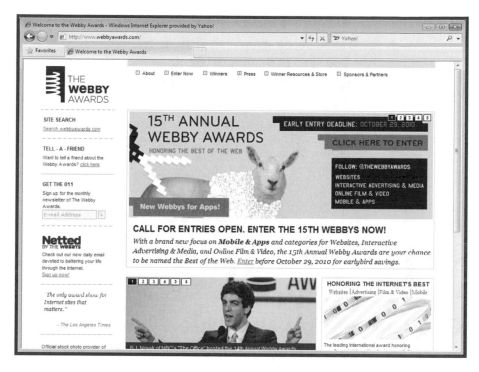

Figure 3.21

Without a doubt, the Webby Awards are among the Web's most prestigious honors.

The following six criteria are used in making Web site selections:

- Content
- Structure and navigation
- Visual design
- Functionality
- Interactivity
- Overall experience

Candidate Web sites are eligible to win two honors. One is the Webby Award, which is judged by the International Academy of Digital Arts and Sciences. The other is called the People's Award, and it is judged by popular vote. In addition, the Academy also designates some Web sites that don't win an award but still show excellence as being Webby Worthy.

The Webby Awards is an annual event. There is a nomination period, followed by an evaluation period. To nominate your Web site for a Webby Award or to find out when the nomination period opens up, click on the Enter Now link at the top of the Webby Awards main page. If nominations are not being accepted yet, you will be presented with a form that allows you to sign up for a notification message.

Nominating your Web site for a Webby Award is not cheap. As of the writing of the sixth edition of this book, the entry fee for a Web site was $255. The entry fee goes down if you want to enter additional Web sites. If you really think that your Web site is good enough to win a Webby Award, you should seriously consider taking a chance and submit your Web site. If you win, or even if you garner a "Webby Worthy" designation, your Web traffic could sky rocket.

Getting Social to Drive More Web Traffic

In Chapter 2 you learned all about search engine optimization. This included learning how to formulate your Web pages to make them as search-engine friendly as possible. In addition, you learned how to register with many of the most popular search engines and directories on the Web. In recent years, online social networking has grown to great prominence on the Web, so much so that that Social Media Marketing, or Social Media Optimization (SMO) as it is often referred, has become an important component of most Web marketing campaigns. Therefore, including social media sites as part of your Web campaign is just as important as including search engines and directories.

Over the last several years social networking sites have grown from small Web sites where teenagers and young adults liked to hang into global communities made up of hundreds of millions of people of all ages and interests. Today, social media sites are among the most frequented locations on the Web.

Social media sites are different from traditional Web sites in that visitors are able to interact with one another and are largely responsible for the content that is provided. This differs significantly from traditional one-way communication that has always been the hallmark, where Web site owners exercised total control over what was provided on their sites.

Social media sites are made possible through a new generation of Web development and design techniques collectively referred to as Web 2.0. Social media Web sites come in many different forms, including social networking sites like Facebook, Twitter, and MySpace, as well as photo and video sharing sites like Flickr and YouTube.

If you invest a little time participating in social communities, you can develop a reputation of knowledge and expertise and ultimately drive high-quality traffic to your Web site. Therefore, social media sites are an important part of any good Web marketing effort. As with search engines and directories, your time will be better spent if you focus your efforts on the most popular social Web sites. The rest of this chapter will focus on introducing you to the major categories of social Web sites and provide advice and instruction on how to best go about working with them.

NOTE Participation in a social community takes time and effort, and while a lot of social sites will be explored here, don't think that you have to join and participate in all of them. As you make your way through the rest of this chapter, consider which social Web sites will work best for you. Think about which ones are most likely to put you in touch with the people you are trying to reach and put your efforts into those sites. If, as time goes on, you like the results you are getting and have a little extra time, you can always pick an additional social community or two in which to participate and promote your Web site.

Social Networking Sites

The fifth edition of this book talked about how to promote Web sites using MySpace, which at the time was a leading player in social Web sites.

A lot has changed over the last several years. MySpace is still a major social network. However, it has been supplanted by Facebook in terms of overall size and prominence. In addition, Twitter has emerged as a rival to both of these sites and is rapidly building large communities.

Given that these three sites are among the most popular of all social networking sites, let's begin with them.

Generating Traffic Using MySpace

At the time of this writing, MySpace (**www.myspace.com**) is the eighth most popular Web site in the world. MySpace members intermingle by developing networks of friends. In the process, they post and share information using blogs, video, photos, and private messaging. Musicians were among the first to realize the viral marketing capabilities of MySpace, quickly finding groups of friends interested in their music. Authors, amateur movie and video creators, and artists have all found MySpace to be an incredibly powerful tool for sharing their work and collaborating with others. There is no reason that you cannot leverage MySpace as a means of putting the word out about your Web site and using it to deliver new Web traffic made up of people interested in what you have to share or sell.

MySpace, shown in Figure 3.22, is totally free to join, which you can do by going to **www.myspace.com** and clicking on the Sign Up link. The first thing that you will want to do is create your profile. Keep things fun, perky, and interesting. Next, you can begin adding content to your MySpace page. Adding an interesting background or a cool piece of music will help to set the mood. While you are at it, consider adding a banner that links back to your real Web page. Of course, you want to add content that others will find interesting. You also want to add information about your Web site and encourage people to visit. Include a picture of yourself or your logo. This will help you to begin to develop your own brand. MySpace also provides you with access to your own blog. Use it to provide regular updates to your MySpace page. Give people a reason to return and read it.

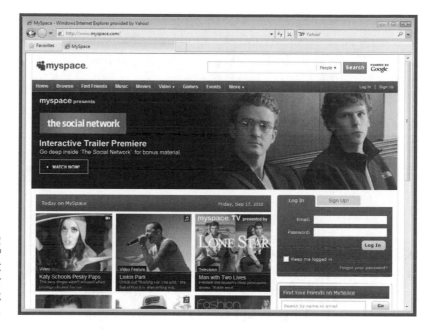

Figure 3.22

MySpace is a great place to begin your social network marketing.

Once you have set up your profile and added whatever content you want to share, you need to begin building your list of friends. For starters, add everyone you know at MySpace to your list of friends. Next, examine the profiles of your friends to see who they have added to their friend's lists and send those people messages asking for permission to add them to your list. After all, MySpace is about social networking and a never-ending quest to meet new friends. After a while, once you have met plenty of people, you'll find that people will start soliciting you as a friend.

With your profile in place, your MySpace page created, and your list of friends increasing, your next step should be to search MySpace for people with interests similar to the content that you are providing on your Web site. If these people have blogs, look for opportunities to post an interesting comment. Everyone who visits that page will see your posting and your link. Don't do anything commercial or just blatantly start plugging your Web page. If you make this mistake, you'll lose friends faster than you can make them. Instead, when you post a comment, keep it interesting and on point. Most of all, make sure it provides value or at the very least is entertaining. If people like what you have to say, they'll look up your profile to find out about your Web site and where more information can be attained. As you look for blogs on which to post comments, focus on finding the most popular people that you can because this will result in more people reading what you have to say.

Generating Traffic Using Facebook

The largest and most popular social networking site on the Web is Facebook (**www.facebook.com**), shown in Figure 3.23. As of the writing of the sixth edition of this book, Facebook has more than 500 million users.

The first thing you should do after signing up for a free Facebook account is to make sure you fill out your profile because the data you enter into your Facebook profile is made available to search engines. Complete profiles are more interesting than sparsely filled in profiles. When adding your URL, make sure that you include http:// as part of the URL name. This will turn it into a clickable link. Also upload your picture or your Web page logo to help you build up your brand.

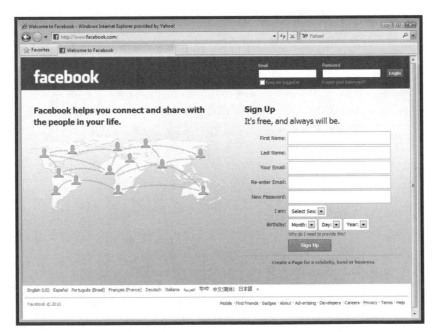

Figure 3.23

Facebook is the world's largest social networking Web site.

Once your profile is complete, you have a couple of options: create a face group, a page, or both. Both have value and are worth doing. Groups focus more on bringing people together who have common interests. Groups work sort of like mini-forums. To help get your group page off to a good start, consider setting up a contest and giving a prize away.

However, between the two choices, pages are generally more important to your marketing efforts. Facebook pages are where most people go to interact. One advantage of Facebook pages is that they are indexed by the major search engines, whereas groups are not indexed. To gain further benefit from your Facebook pages, make them more search-engine friendly by including keywords in your page name.

As you get started, make sure that you add valuable and entertaining content to your Facebook pages. Take advantage of Facebook's free applications. You can use them to share your Flickr pictures and YouTube videos, as well as to display your blog feed.

Be careful not to jump right into Web site promotion. If you do so, you'll drive your friends away and get nowhere really fast. Instead, focus on providing something that people will find beneficial. Once you have established yourself as an expert and a trusted friend, you can start publishing links to pages on your Web site that your Facebook friends might also find useful. Just don't overdo it.

Once you have your profile defined and have created your Facebook group page, you need to find yourself some friends. Begin by inviting everyone that you already know on Facebook to become your friend. Next, join a few groups related to the same types of topics covered on your Web site. Ask people that you meet in these groups to be your friend. You can also have Facebook suggest new friends to you. When you ask people to become your friend, make sure you give them a good reason to do so, referring to the value of information that you've placed on your group or page. But in your zest to add new friends, don't get carried away trying to add hundreds of friends every day. If you do so, you run the risk of being seen as a spammer. If your Facebook page or group is good, it should not take long for you to amass a considerable group of friends.

Also, regularly visit other people's groups and pages, and whenever you have something of value to share, do so by posting a comment. This will make group and page owners want to be your friend. Once you have a good following of friends, you need to make sure you regularly update your Facebook page or group so that your friends will continue to visit you and ultimately your Web site.

Generating Traffic Using Twitter

Twitter (**www.twitter.com**) is a fast rising up-and-comer in the world of social Web sites. At the time of writing the sixth edition of this book, Twitter had over 145 million members. Twitter, shown in Figure 3.24, supports what is known as *micro-blogging*, where member post short messages, referred to as *tweets*, that are 140 characters or less. A big part of Twitter's success is its support for mobile users, which allows them to tweet anytime and anywhere using mobile devices like their cell phone. Your tweets are sent to other Twitter members who subscribe to them. These members are referred to as your followers. One of your goals is to get as many people as you can to follow you.

Today, most major companies around the world, like Apple and Microsoft, use Twitter as a means for quickly getting the word out about new products, promotions, and so on. You can do the same. Another advantage of using Twitter is that search engines index the site. As a result, your Twitter page may show up in search engine results, even if your Web page does not.

You can join Twitter by signing up for a free account at **www.twitter.com**. Here again, the first thing you should do after joining is to fully fill out your profile information. Include your picture or Web site logo as well as your URL, prefixed with http:// so that it will be clickable. Spend some time looking for other members who you think will be interested in what you have to share and follow them. Odds are they will follow you back. You can find these people by searching Twitter directories or by searching member profiles.

Figure 3.24

Twitter is the Web's most popular micro-blogging Web site.

Remember, Twitter is a social networking site and not a marketing site, so don't start blatantly marketing your Web site. Make sure you are a good community member and that you follow other members and stay active in the community. When you post, make sure that your postings are useful or entertaining. Each time you make a posting, include an invitation at the end inviting people to follow you. When you provide postings that are especially useful, you can direct your followers back to your Web site.

Social Bookmarking Sites

Social bookmarking is an online community service in which members create, describe, organize, and search for bookmarks online that they wish to share with others. Unless explicitly marked as private, social bookmarks are publically searchable. There's an important distinction between bookmarking sites and other sites that allow people to share resources—social bookmarking sites don't share resources, they only link to them.

Social bookmarking sites allow members to do more than simply create links to Web sites. Social bookmarks also include detailed descriptions of the sites to which they are linked. Descriptions may consist of text or votes in support of or against the target Web page's quality. Bookmarks can also include tags (keywords) collaboratively generated by the bookmark's creator as well as comments later added by others through a process known as *social tagging*.

Social bookmarks can be searched via social networking sites. They can be searched chronologically by tag or browsed via category. Because the major search engines index social bookmarks, they also appear inside search results. Social bookmark sites also track bookmark popularity and usually display the number of people who have bookmarked the same URL.

Social bookmarking can be used to help promote your Web pages. You should generate social bookmarks for your Web site's landing page as well as for each of the major topic pages. Do not create more than one bookmark for the same page, and do not create bookmarks for every page in your Web site. If you do, you run the risk of being labeled as a spammer and having all of your bookmarks removed.

In addition to creating your own bookmarks, make sure that you spend time writing comments on other people's bookmarks. This will increase the likelihood that they will reciprocate and add comments to your bookmarks, including the bookmarks you've added for you own site. If your bookmarks are compelling enough, people will be motivated to click on them and visit your Web pages.

Social bookmarks represent links to Web sites, so any links that you add to your Web pages will increase your Web page's search engine ranking. Since people must decide to click on the social bookmarks to your Web pages, the traffic you get from these will be of higher quality because the people who click on them are obviously interested.

If you want to make social bookmarking a part of your Web marketing campaign, a good place to start is **www.delicious.com**, as shown in Figure 3.25. Delicious is a social bookmarking site owned by Yahoo!.

Figure 3.25

Delicious is a social bookmarking Web site where members share and comment on bookmarks to their favorite sites.

Social Review Sites

Social review sites are Web sites where members and users post their opinions about products and services covering pretty much any topic they wish. The primary objective of social review sites is to provide visitors with feedback on products and services they may be considering purchasing. Examples of the kind of reviews you may come across include television shows, movies, restaurants, toys, cars, and so on.

One of the most popular social review sites is Epinions.com. Shown in Figure 3.26, Epinions.com is a general consumer review site owned by Ebay.

At Epinions.com, members can post reviews on any product or service they wish. Visitors can then read these reviews and use them as input on their purchasing decisions. Members provide these reviews for free. In return, they have the opportunity to earn money and recognition of their expertise.

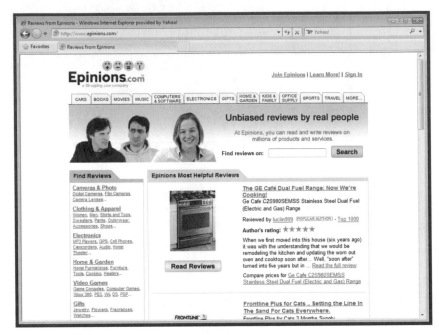

Figure 3.26

Epinions.com is a
social review site
where members
share their opinions
on just about
everything.

Epinions.com allows members to submit two types of reviews: express and regular. An express review consists of 20-199 words, whereas regular reviews are 200 words or more. Members can also rate opinions, thus adding additional value to them. When rating a regular review, members can rate their opinions using any of the following:

- VH—Very Helpful
- H—Helpful
- SH—Somewhat Helpful
- NH—Not Helpful
- OT—Off Topic

When rating an express review, members can rate opinions using either of the following:

- S—Show
- DS—Don't Show

The first thing you should do after joining Epinions.com is to completely fill out your profile. This includes supplying a photo and your Web site's logo. Make sure you specify your URL, as this is important in generating referral traffic back to your Web site.

Once your profile has been established, you should begin writing reviews about products and services with which you have experience and expertise. Include some reviews about your own Web pages and the content provided there. Once you have written some reviews, the next thing you should work on is to gain the trust of other members.

At Epinions.com, members can decide to trust or block one another. The accumulation of trust and block relationships form what is called a Web of Trust, or WOT. Your WOT, along with the ratings assigned to your reviews, will determine the order in which reviews are displayed to visitors. Reviewers who write a lot of reviews and whose reviews are well rated may be assigned Top Reviewer or Category Lead status, in which case their reviews are placed at the top of review listings.

By becoming a member of Epinions.com, you can write reviews about the information available on your Web pages and, as a result, generate referral traffic back to your Web site. By building a large Web of Trust, you can generate more referrals. Another advantage of participating at Epinions.com is that their review pages are indexed by the major search engines, so this can also improve your search engine ranking.

Social News Sites

Social news sites are Web sites where members submit and then vote on news stories and related content. Voter results impact the order in which news sites are displayed in searches. Social news site reviews are generally indexed by the major search engines, and any links to your pages that you add at these sites will help increase your Web site's popularity. There are numerous social news Web sites out there, but two of the very best are Digg and StumbleUpon.

Getting Your Web Pages Dugg at Digg

Digg allows members to submit news stories (videos, pictures, and so on), which other members can then vote up or down through a process known as *digging* or *burying*. Submissions include a custom description of the material being submitted. The most "dugg" stories end up on the front page of **www.digg.com**, as demonstrated in Figure 3.27. People visit Digg to read up on the most interesting news stories of the day, generally focusing their time and attention only on the must dugg stories.

Membership at Digg is free. The first thing you must do when signing up is establish your profile, after which you should add anybody you know at Digg to your list of friends. You can find additional friends quickly by examining your friends' friends and making those people your friends as well. Next, add a few entries for the most interesting pages on your Web site and "digg" them. Hopefully, other people will review and "digg" your pages as well, driving lots of traffic back to your Web site. Whenever you update content on your Web pages, make sure you log into Digg and send out "shouts" to all your friends. And don't forget to ask your friends to tell others if they like what they find.

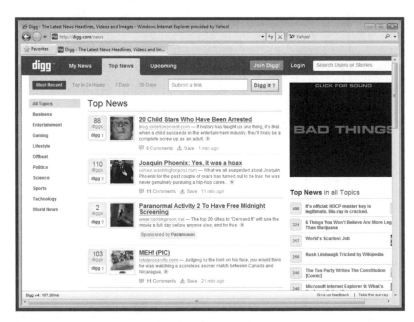

Figure 3.27

Digg is a social news site where members vote up (digg) or vote down (bury) content.

Ensuring Web Surfers Stumble Upon Your Web Pages

StumbleUpon (**www.stumbleupon.com**), shown in Figure 3.28, puts a slightly different twist on things by using its personalized recommendation engine to present members with Web pages to view based on information retrieved from their profiles, previous ratings of other news stories, and ratings assigned by their friends. All members need do is download and install a free StumbleUpon toolbar and click on the Stumble! button located in the StumbleUpon toolbar to begin. As they review stories, members are encourages to share their opinions.

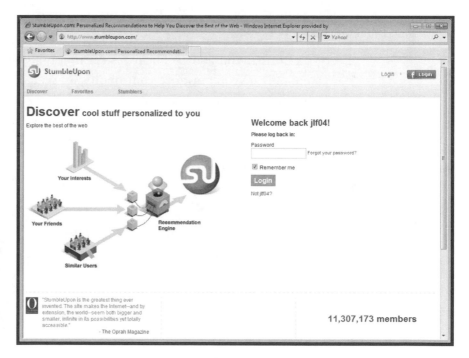

Figure 3.28

StumbleUpon is a social news site where members vote on Web pages that are selected for them.

Like Digg, you can submit your own Web pages for review, knowing that people of similar interest will stumble upon them as well. If your pages are good, you should see plenty of new traffic at your Web site.

Social Photo and Video Sharing Sites

Also incredibly popular are Web sites built around communities of people who share their photos and videos, made possible through the advent of broadband technologies. For example, one of the most popular photo sharing social media sites is Flickr, where people can upload and share pictures with their friends, relatives, and people around the world. When it comes to video sharing, YouTube remains the top dog.

Publishing Your Photos at Flickr

At Flickr (**www.flickr.com**), shown in Figure 3.29, photos are shared with Flickr members and are also made available through search engines like Google and Yahoo!.

Every photo that you add to Flickr results in a link back to your Flickr page so make sure you optimize your photos for search engines, assigning them relevant keywords that will help people find them. People who admire your photos and follow these links will be able to view your Flickr profile and use it to locate your Web site, thus driving more traffic to it.

Figure 3.29

Flickr is a photo sharing site where members showcase and share their photographs.

Flickr provides both free and Pro accounts (a Pro account costs $29.95 a year), the difference being that free accounts have a 100MB per month bandwidth limit. Begin by signing up for a free account and see if the results merit later converting to a Pro account. When you sign up, be sure to completely fill out your profile and to upload your picture or Web site logo. Every user has to define a screen name for his picture and you may want to include your Web site URL in that name. Don't forget to link back to your Web site. Lastly, you get to create your own Flickr URL, which you can customize just about any way you want. Consider including your Web site's URL into your Flick URL. For example, if your Web site's URL is www.photofanatic.com then you might make your Flickr URL www.flickr.com/photos/photofanatic/.

Also, don't forget that Flickr is a social community. To get as much benefit from it as you can, you need to participate. To do so, join a couple of groups, submit your photos to them, and take time to comment on other people's photos. Even better, create your own group and allow others to join you.

Using Video to Promote Your Web Site and Products

In recent years, video has exploded all over the Internet. People just cannot seem to get enough of it. If you know how to create and edit your own videos using your computer, then you can take advantage of this new communication medium and use it to increase your own Web traffic.

Without a doubt, one of the best places to post your videos and get attention is on YouTube (**www.youtube.com**), as shown in Figure 3.30. YouTube is a video sharing Web site where visitors can view and comment on video clips uploaded by anyone who is a member of YouTube. Anyone can register and join YouTube.

YouTube was created in 2005 and within one year was purchased by Google for 1.65 billion dollars. YouTube's astoundingly rapid growth was due in no small part to viral marketing. By uploading videos of your own, you can tap into YouTube's viral marketing and draw people to your own Web site.

To upload a video to YouTube, you must first register, after which you can click on the Upload link located on **www.youtube.com** and start uploading your videos. For each video that you upload, you get to supply a title, description, and category. Make sure you include keywords that will help people find your video. By adding credits to the end of your video, including your Web site's URL, you can encourage people to visit your Web site to find other videos and related content. You can also display information about your Web site, including its URL, so that anyone watching your video can learn more about where it came from. Make sure you leave your URL visible for at least five seconds. YouTube likes to transition quickly between videos, so unless you build in a long pause, people won't have time to see it.

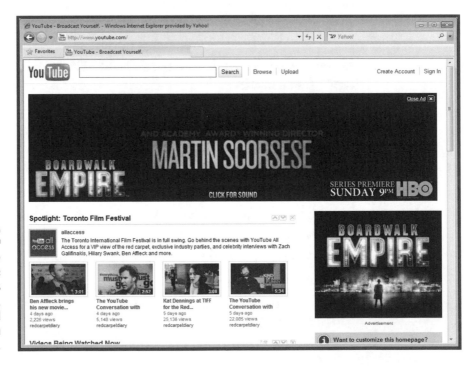

Figure 3.30

YouTube is a video sharing Web site where members and visitors upload, watch, and comment on each other's videos.

NOTE People go to YouTube and other similar video sharing sites to have fun. Do not submit videos that are nothing more than commercials and marketing hype. Instead, make sure that your videos are entertaining. This doesn't mean that you cannot mention your Web site in your video or work it in somehow. As a general rule, try to keep your video under five minutes long and focus on making it as funny or entertaining as possible.

Social Question-and-Answer Sites

Community-driven question-and-answer (Q&A) Web sites are yet another new type of social networking Web site gaining rapid popularity. These sites allow members to submit questions and answers posed by others. Two of the most popular Q&A sites are Yahoo! Answers and Answers.com.

Figure 3.31 shows the Yahoo! Answers main page. At the time of writing the sixth edition of this book, Yahoo! Answers boasts a membership of over 200 million users with more than 15 million visits per day.

Figure 3.31

Yahoo! Answers is an online question-and-answer site.

To participate, you must have a Yahoo! account. When you set up your account, take advantage of the ability to upload your photo or Web logo in order to promote your brand. Although you can, you do not have to use your login account as your user name. Instead, give yourself a user name that sounds real. It will add credibility.

As soon as you sign up, you can begin answering questions posted by other community members. Just go to **http://answers.yahoo.com/** and browse or search for questions that you can answer. Make sure your answers are of the highest quality. Each time you answer a question, make sure you include a link back to your Web site. Note, however, that your link will not be posted until you have earned 200 points.

By default, questions are left open for four days, although the person who posts the question can elect to close the answer period sooner or extend it for an additional period of time. In order to ask questions, you must have a balance of at least five points. Yahoo! Answers uses a point system that is designed to encourage members to answers questions. Once a member has demonstrated expertise in an area and has answered a sufficient number of questions, a label of Top Contributor is displayed under their avatar. Yahoo! does not publish the formula used to determine Top Contributor status. It does, however, publish information about its point system, which is shown here.

- Begin participating (100 points [one time only])
- Ask a question (–5 points)
- Choose best answer (3 points)
- No best answer was selected by voters (–5 points)
- Answer a question (2 points)
- Delete an answer (–2 points)
- Log in to Yahoo! Answers (1 point per day)
- Vote for an answer (1 point)
- Vote for no best answer (0 points)

- ⊡ Have an answer that is selected as best answer (10 points)
- ⊡ Receive a thumbs-up rating on one of your best answers (1 per thumbs up [up to 50])

Your goal is to provide the best answer and to gain recognition of your knowledge and expertise. As you do so, you'll begin generating quality traffic for your Web site.

Blogging Sites

The term *blog* is short for Web log. It is a Web site or a part of a Web site where the owner is able to post entries that others can read. Blog entries may consist of text and graphics, and are typically displayed in reverse chronological order. Most blogs are interactive, allowing visitors to comment on the entries.

If you have a Facebook or MySpace account, then you already have access to your own blog. Your Web site provider may also give you access to a free blogging service. In addition, there are plenty of online blogging services you can try, including Blogger (**www.blogger.com**) shown in Figure 3.32.

Blogs are frequently indexed by the major search engines. Blogs can help you build your reputation and brand as well as drive traffic back to your Web site. You can also draw traffic to your Web site by visiting other people's blogs and posting comments, along with your URL. Obviously, to get the most out of this approach, your comments will need to show that you have something interesting or useful to share; otherwise, people won't click on your URL.

Not all blogs are equal. Finding and commenting on the most popular blogs will drive more traffic your way than commenting on less popular blogs. Blogging provides you with the opportunity to interact directly with your visitors and to adapt how you do things based on their comments.

Figure 3.32

Blogger will provide you with a free blog.

Another way of effectively using blogs to help bring traffic to your Web site is to guest blog. In guest blogging, you submit blog entries on someone else's blog. This gives you the opportunity to reach out to new readers and to further increase your link popularity when you include your URL as part of your blog entry.

As a slight variation of traditional blogging, you should also join and participate at Squidoo (**www.squidoo.com**), shown in Figure 3.33. Squidoo is a social community where members create Web pages known as *lenses*. Lenses are very similar to blog posts, except they are focused on a single topic. When you join Squidoo and start creating lenses, you become a Lensmaster. Lenses are indexed by all the major search engines, so when you create new lenses make sure that you use appropriate keywords.

Squidoo is a good place for finding people with interests similar to your own. By posting high-quality lenses, you can generate a reputation of expertise. Each lens you make can be linked back to your Web site, increasing your link popularity and Web traffic. Squidoo also supports the formulation of community groups. By joining groups and making useful comments on other people's lenses, you can drive even more traffic, especially if you target groups that are popular.

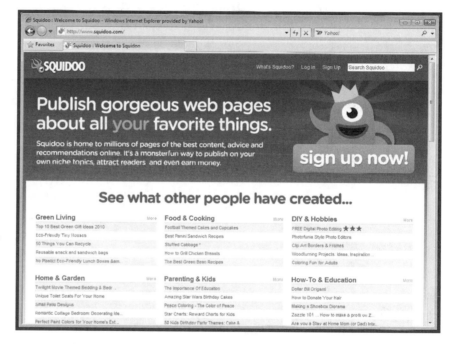

Figure 3.33

Squidoo is a blog-like Web site where members create pages called lenses that work very much like blogs.

Demonstrating Expertise through Wikis and Article Sites

Another final category of social networking Web sites that merit attention are wikis and articles. Wikis and related sites allow you to submit and contribute to online articles. Article directories, on the other hand, accept your published articles, which are then made available for free for posting on other Web sites. Both wikis and article sites provide you with the opportunity to demonstrate expertise and develop name recognition. At the same time, you can increase your link popularity and improve your search engine results position.

Sharing Authoritive Information through Wikipedia

If you believe that your Web site is truly an authoritative source of information on a particular topic, you may want to consider sharing some of this information with the rest of the world using Wikipedia (**www.wikipedia.org**). Wikipedia, shown in Figure 3.34, is an online collaborative encyclopedia. Anyone is welcome to add content to Wikipedia, provided they follow Wikipedia's editing policies and rules.

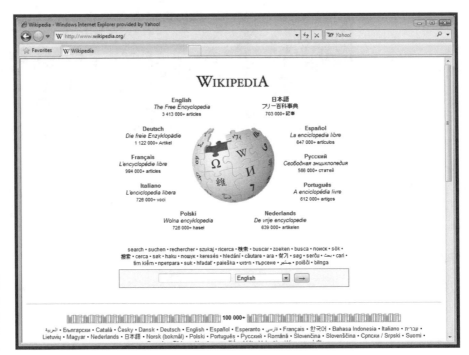

Figure 3.34

Wikipedia is an online community-driven encyclopedia.

For starters, begin by searching Wikipedia to see if the topic that your Web site covers already exists. If it does not, then you can create a new Wikipedia page on that topic. In doing so, you can even provide a link to your Web site. But you must do so carefully. If the information you provide comes across as commercial, it will quickly be pulled. It is absolutely critical that you provide content that is totally objective and factual. In addition, it is expected that you reference other resources as part of your topic, including other related topics already in Wikipedia.

By being objective and providing material that is factual and informative, your topic should pass editorial scrutiny. Of course, you can use your Web site as an external reference. However, if your Web site is too commercial, you should avoid listing your site's main page's URL and instead list the URL of a page that is not designed to plug your Web site and its products and services. If Wikipedia readers find your topic interesting, they will follow the link to your Web site, and once there, they will almost certainly look around.

Reaching Out to Users through Online E-zines

Another way of bringing new traffic to your Web sites is to leverage the power of e-zines. An *e-zine* is an electronic publication or newsletter distributed over the Internet. To receive an e-zine, readers must sign up for it. Most e-zines are distributed via e-mail. However, some are posted on Web sites or in blogs, and an e-mail is sent to notify subscribers when new editions are available.

Finding e-zines is easy. All you have to do is perform a quick search using "e-zine" as the keyword in any search engine. Alternatively, you can search for e-zines of interest using The Ezine Directory (**www.ezine-dir.com**). This directory, shown in Figure 3.35, provides access to hundreds of different e-zines.

You can leverage the marketing power of e-zines by contacting those that cover topics closely related to the material on your Web site, and then pay to place an advertisement. Alternatively, you can contact an e-zine and submit your own articles to them for publication. Two other good directories to which you can submit your articles include Recent Articles (**www.recent-articles.com**) and ArticleTrader (**www.articletrader.com**).

When you write and submit articles, you do so with the hope that people will visit the article directory with which you register, and then display a copy of your article on their own Web site. This will help increase your link popularity and help drive high-quality traffic directly to your Web site when readers click on the link that you include with your articles.

Figure 3.35

The Ezine Directory provides links to a host of Web sites that would be happy to host your online articles.

Wrapping Up and Looking Ahead

If you offer products, services, or business information at your Web site, you should definitely list your site with business search sites and directories. Business search engines and Yellow Pages directories offer unique places to get your business and your business-oriented Web site noticed. After submitting your site to these search engines, you should go on to submit your site to search engines and directories that focus on specific industries. These guides can also help your Web site stand out from the crowd, especially when you consider that the major category guides attract millions of visitors, yet have considerably fewer listings than mainstream directories, such as Yahoo!.

Kids' directories and award sites are also important. Kids represent a significant segment of the Internet community. Thousands of organizations are offering Web awards. Web awards range from daily awards, such as the Cool Site of the Day award, to yearly awards, such as *PC Magazine*'s Top 100. Lastly, let's not forget about social networking. The incorporation of promotion aimed at taking advantage of social networking Web sites is also essential to any Web promotion.

Now, put this book down and relax a bit. First thing tomorrow morning you'll learn how to submit your site to many search engines and directories simultaneously. As always, the focus will be on using resources that are low-cost or free.

Attracting the Masses

➤ Selling Your Web Site through E-mail

➤ Attracting the Masses with Giveaways, Contests, Sweepstakes, and More

➤ Free Banner Advertising

Many companies offer services that allow you to register with multiple search engines and directories. These so-called registration services are great if you want to quickly spread the word about many different Web page URLs. You'll spend this morning learning about these and other valuable means of promoting your Web site.

Registering with Many Search Engines and Directories Simultaneously

Like search engines and directories, registration services have different submission processes. This session covers registration services: how they operate, what to watch out for, and how to use these services without paying a dime.

Introducing Web Registration Services

Registration services are one of the most innovative types of Web services to come along. The idea is that instead of having to register with search engines and directories one by one, you can use the service to register with many different search engines and directories at once. Although one central interface for registering your Web site is wonderful, you still sometimes have to go through a rather lengthy submission process.

While registration services can certainly save you some time, it's best if you go through each search engine or directory site's submission process yourself. When you work hands-on with a search engine or directory site, you get a clear idea of how the site works. When you work with a registration service, you rely on the service to take advantage of how a site works.

Using Registration Services

The registration process usually starts with you entering information into a form. This information may include all the elements you would normally enter into the submission form of a search engine or directory, such as the page title, page description, and personal contract information. Next, you select the search engines and directories to which you want to submit your site. Afterward, you begin the submission process, which often involves having to register each site separately by clicking on individual submission buttons that will send your information to a specific search engine or directory.

Because most search engines and directories use unique categories or require you to fill out other information, you usually enter this additional information during the submission process. For example, before you can submit your page to the Yahoo! Web directory, you need to select a category.

All these intermediate stops along the road mean that the registration process isn't always as easy as the registration services would like for you to believe. Still, the process is an improvement over manual submission if you are in a rush.

Working with Registration Services

Like any service-oriented business, registration services are for-profit enterprises. You can't blame these services for trying to make a buck off their hard work. The cost of registering your site can jump to hundreds of dollars, however, and most registration services base their charges on the number of URLs that you want to register and the number of places to which you submit your URLs. For example, a registration service might charge $30 to submit a single URL to 50 search engines, $60 to submit two URLs to 50 search engines, or $100 to submit one URL to 150 search engines.

But before you shell out your hard-earned cash or corporate money, you should know what you are buying. The first thing you might notice when you examine the resources provided by a registration service is that you've probably never heard of most of these sites. Some of the sites are small and receive very little Web traffic at all. Worse, you might find that some of the sites don't even function.

Additionally, you should note that resource sites are frequently for restricted types of search engines and directories. You will find Yellow Pages directories that take only business listings. You will find directories for Web sites covering specific geographic areas, such as Canada, Europe, or Asia. You will also find specialty directories, such as What's New? directories, award sites, and guides to the best of the Web.

In the end, whether you can register with 50 or 500 search engines doesn't really matter. What matters is the number of search engines that you can use out of those available. Fortunately, the best sites are usually those included in the first 50. Because of this, you get more bang for your buck if you stick to the basics—and the free services covered in this chapter are the ultimate in getting your money's worth.

The most important thing to consider when you use registration services is the type of site with which you are registering. As you learned in previous chapters, there is a huge difference between a search engine and a Web directory.

Search engines use the URL that you specify to crawl through your entire site and will usually schedule your site for periodic reindexing. Because search engines reindex your site, you only need to register with a search engine once. And because search engines crawl through your entire site, you only need to register the URL to your top-level home page. That said, it is still a good idea to register your Web site with search engines once every six months. This protects your site from being dropped or not being reindexed automatically.

On the other hand, Web directories create a listing only for the page you specify, and they rarely update the listing. Because Web directories focus on pages rather than entire sites, you can register multiple URLs for the same site. The URLs that you submit should be for separate areas that cover different topics.

Because Web directories rarely update listings, you are responsible for updating your listing in the directory if you move the furniture around at your Web site, which doesn't necessarily mean that you should reregister with the directory. Instead, you should check the directory to see whether it has an update or change process. To make life easier on yourself and to avoid having to submit changes for your listings, you can use the redirection techniques discussed in the Sunday Afternoon session under "Gaining Lost Readers from Error Analysis."

 NOTE While this chapter focuses on providing you with a list of online registration services, there are also a number of software products that you can purchase and install on your computer in order to set up your own registration process. However, unlike the free services listed in this chapter, these software products will cost you a few dollars. If you are interested in learning more about these software products, check out Appendix A, "Additional Resources on the Web."

In the end, if you use a registration service, don't waste your time reregistering with search engines and directories you've already signed up with. Concentrate on the search engines and directories with which you haven't registered.

AddMe.com

Main Page: http://www.addme.com

Sites: Submits to 20 search engines and directories for free. The submission process takes 5 to 10 minutes. Your information is saved for resubmission.

Details: Before you can submit your site using AddMe, you need to fill out the listing information shown in Figure 4.1. In exchange for using its submission services, AddMe requests that you add a link to it on your Web site by cutting and pasting a supplied piece of HTML code.

Figure 4.1

AddMe.com is a comprehensive registration service.

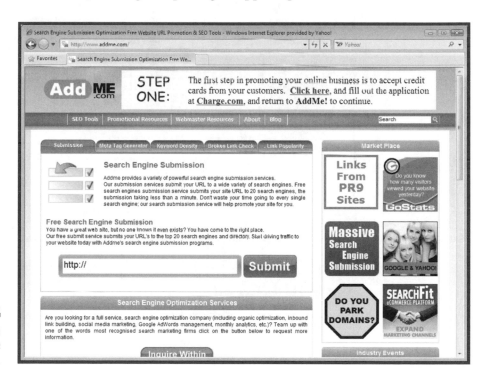

Easy Submit

Main Page: http://www.scrubtheweb.com/abs/submit

Sites: Submits to 10 search engines.

Details: The registration process is broken into three steps. Non-members can use Free Easy Submit to register with 10 preselected search engines. People who sign up for a paid membership can submit to many more search engines.

Figure 4.2

Easy Submit provides a simple and straightforward submission process.

Submit Express

Main Page: http://www.submitexpress.com/free-submission.html

Sites: Submits to 70 plus search engines. The entire submission process only takes 1 to 2 minutes.

Details: Submit Express provides one of the fastest ways to submit your site to search engines. Enter your URL, e-mail address, name, phone number, and country, then click on Submit Now. That's all there is to it. A small report is then displayed at the bottom of the submission page showing the results of each submission attempt.

Figure 4.3

Submit Express is fast and easy, but you can't add detailed information about your Web site.

Checking on Your Listings

Once you have finished submitting your Web site to the search engines on your list, you are going to want to keep tabs on how each search engine is managing its links to your Web pages. You'll want to know when your Web site is listed and if anyone is linking to it. This way, if something goes wrong and a particular search engine doesn't add your Web pages to its database within 4 to 6 weeks, you'll know about it and can submit your Web site again.

NOTE If your Web site doesn't get listed in a particular search engine's database, it may be the result of a simple oversight. Or it could be that you mistyped your URL during the submission process, and the search engine couldn't find your Web site. However, it could also be that the search engine found something objectionable at your Web site. Before resubmitting, review your Web pages and make sure that you haven't added any content that might be interpreted as spam.

Determining Whether Your Web Site Has Been Listed

There are a number of ways that you can go about checking on the status of your Web pages at various search engines. At a minimum, you will want to keep tabs on things at Google, Yahoo!, and Bing, since they are the three most popular search engines.

Perhaps the most simple and obvious option is to visit each search engine and enter the URL of your Web site's main page and any other Web pages that you wish to check on. You can also use this option to find out if any of your competitors are listed in a given search engine's database. For example, to see if the Bing engine has listed any Web pages for **www.tvpress.com**, you would do a search as shown in Figure 4.4.

 NOTE   If only your URL is listed in the search engine's output results, then the search engine has most likely added an entry for your Web site to its index, but it hasn't crawled your Web site yet. In this case, be patient but keep checking.

Figure 4.4

Checking to see if the Bing search engine has added pages from www.tvpress.com to its database.

Finding Out Which of Your Web Pages Are Listed

Once you know that your Web site has been added to a search engine's database, you'll want to check and see which of your pages have been indexed. You can do this by using your browser to open the search engine's Web page and entering the `site:` command, as demonstrated in Figure 4.5.

As Figure 4.5 demonstrates, you execute the `site:` command by keying it into the search engine's search field. Take note that there is no blank space between the `site:` command and the specified URL.

NOTE Google, Yahoo!, and Bing all support the `site:` command. Other search engines may support this command or provide a different command to produce the same results. You can usually find out specific information regarding the search commands for a given search engine by consulting the search engine's Help area.

Figure 4.5

Use the `site:` command to determine which of your Web pages have been added to a search engine's index.

After verifying that your Web site is listed in each of the big three search engines and checking to see which of your Web pages were added to each search engine's database, it is a good idea to check and see if anybody else's Web pages have links to your Web site. After all, the number of good links to your Web pages has a lot to do with how close your Web pages come to making the top 10 search results. Hopefully, you will find that the number of links will grow over time. Otherwise, you may want to investigate different ways of improving the situation, such as by signing up with a link exchange service, as will be discussed later this morning.

To check on links to your Web site using Google and Bing, you can use the `link:` command. For example, to check on the number of links to **www.tvpress.com**, you would enter **link:www.tvpress.com** into either search engine's search field as demonstrated in Figure 4.6.

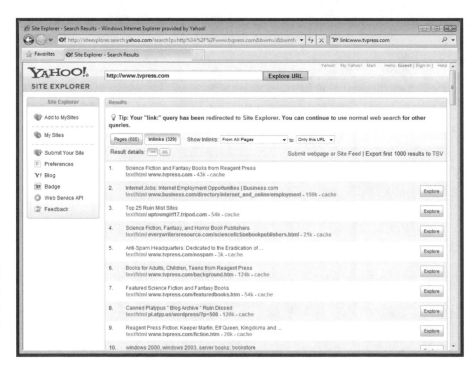

Figure 4.6

Researching the number of links from other Web pages to your Web site.

In addition to directly querying specific searches regarding the link popularity of your Web site, there are a number of Web sites that provide free link checking. For example, at AddMe.com (**www.addme.com/popularity.htm**) you can submit your URL and e-mail address and generate a report showing how popular your Web site is in terms of how many links there are to it. As Figure 4.7 shows, results are retrieved from Ask, Google, Yahoo!, AltaVista, and AllTheWeb. By clicking on the Details link associated with each search engine, you can view additional information about your links.

Figure 4.7

Using the Link Popularity service at AddMe.com to examine the number and quality of links to your Web site.

Selling Your Web Site through E-mail

Plain old e-mail is an extraordinary means of promoting your Web site. Every day, people send more messages by e-mail than by standard mail, and why not? Messages sent by e-mail are usually free. The millions of daily e-mail messages bounce around the globe in one of three forms: messages sent from person to person, messages posted to a newsgroup, and messages submitted to a mailing list.

In your promotional efforts, you can use all three ways of distributing e-mail to promote your Web site. However, nothing will get you into hot water quicker than sending unsolicited or unwanted e-mail. To help you steer clear of the pitfalls of e-mail promotion and get the most out of your efforts, this section shows you the right ways to sell your Web sites through e-mail.

Web Site Promotion through Direct E-mail, Newsgroups, and Mailing Lists

E-mail has been around since the earliest days of the Internet. The widespread popularity of e-mail comes from the fact that it is so compulsively usable. Unlike standard mail, you can use e-mail to quickly and easily send the same message to hundreds, thousands, or millions of recipients. Unlike limitations presented by using a telephone, you can send e-mail at any time of the day or night without fear of waking the recipient. Unlike using a fax machine, you can send a message without having to worry whether the recipient has stocked the fax machine with paper or whether the fax line will be busy.

Just as most people don't want to receive calls from telemarketers, unsolicited faxes, or junk mail, most people don't want to receive unsolicited e-mail either. In the world of electronic mail, no four-letter word is more odious than *spam*. Spamming is the electronic equivalent of junk mail. Any time you send unsolicited or unwanted messages, you are guilty of spamming. Sure, Web advertising agencies will try to sell you on the concept of bulk e-mail by telling you that the word spam applies only to unsolicited messages sent to multiple recipients, multiple discussion groups, or multiple mailing lists. In the end, however, an unsolicited message is an unsolicited message, whether it is sent to one or a thousand recipients.

As anyone who has ever sent unsolicited e-mail will tell you, the consequences can be severe. Your e-mail box might be bombarded with hate mail. Your Internet service provider (ISP) might pull your account. You might even run into legal difficulties. Despite these potential pitfalls, people all over the world continue to spam the electronic byways. The reason is the tremendous value of being able to send messages to anyone, anywhere, at any time.

Although you can certainly take a haphazard approach to Web site promotion through e-mail, there are ways to work within the system and current guidelines for newsgroups and mailing lists without rocking the boat. Working within the guidelines allows you to tap into the wonderful potential of e-mail, newsgroups, and mailing lists while minimizing the risk of backlash.

 NOTE You can do your best to work within the system while minimizing the risk, but you won't be able to please all the people all of the time. The simple truth is that some people like to huff and puff. When you encounter someone who cries foul for no apparent reason, you should do one of two things: simply ignore the person or send a brief apology and move on.

The following section offers a look at how you can effectively promote your Web site through direct communications, newsgroups, and mailing lists.

Establishing a Privacy Policy

Before you begin soliciting visitors to your Web site for permission to send them e-mail, you need to earn their trust. After all, very few people are going to give you their name and e-mail address if they think you might abuse their information. In the context of this discussion, abuse refers to spamming visitors with unexpected or unsolicited e-mail or sharing their personal information with other parties. To alleviate these types of concerns and to make your visitors feel comfortable giving you their contact information, it is essential that you develop a privacy policy and that you display it prominently in a location where visitors can easily find it. For example, most Web sites put a link to their privacy policy right at the bottom of their Web pages.

When you formulate your privacy policy, make sure that you tell your visitors exactly what type of information you are collecting about them and exactly how this information will be used. Also, it is a good idea to mention that you respect each individual's right to privacy and will conform to and respect anti-spam laws.

One way to begin putting together your own privacy policy is to take a look at how somebody else has already done it. For example, Figure 4.8 shows the beginning of Amazon.com's privacy notice.

Figure 4.8

Amazon.com's privacy notice is extensive and goes into detail regarding how customer information is handled.

If you want a little help in putting together your own privacy policy, you can get it from **www.privacyaffiliates.com**. All you do is answer a few multiple-choice questions about your customers and your Web site, and a custom privacy policy will be created for you. However, this service is not free. At the time the sixth edition of this book was written, the fee for creating a privacy policy was $19.95.

Promoting Your Web Site Directly

When you send a message to people using their e-mail address, you are using the most direct e-mail method: person to person. As a rule, you should never send e-mail to anyone who doesn't want it. Instead, you should put together a promotional campaign that is responsive rather than proactive. Don't send unsolicited e-mail; instead, ask your visitors—and anyone else who contacts you—whether they want to receive promotional material.

Sending Promotional Material

Promotional material that you send to subscribers can take many different forms. For a straightforward marketing approach, you can use advertisements and press releases pertaining to your organization as well as your products and services. You can also use an approach that focuses less on marketing and more on information. With this approach, you send subscribers information on what's new at the Web site, clips from recently published pages, or highlights of interesting places within the Web site.

The best way to invite participation is to add a subscription field to the HTML forms that are already at your Web site. In previous chapters, you saw that many forms used by search sites and directories have subscription fields. These fields ask whether you want to receive information or other promotional material by e-mail.

Subscription fields are often selected by default, which in itself isn't a bad thing, but some search sites go out of their way to ensure that most people who submit their forms join the subscription service. It is a deceptive practice to try and hide the subscription field or to blur the wording so that it is isn't clear.

Tips for Direct Mailings

To ensure that you receive subscriptions only from people who are truly interested in what you have to offer, place the subscription field so that it can be clearly seen, use clear wording, and deselect the field by default. Doing so makes subscribing an active process that requires a conscious effort from the reader.

Consider adding a subscription field if you use forms at your Web site that allow visitors to submit comments, sign a guest log, or enter any other type of data. The subscription field can be as simple as the option buttons shown in Figure 4.9. Here, the subscription field asks visitors whether they want to sign up for various mailing lists.

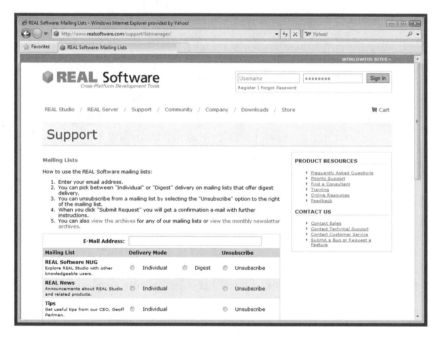

Figure 4.9

Soliciting permission to send e-mail to your visitors.

Some other more general subscription field questions that might be useful include these:

- ⊡ Can we send you press releases related to our company?
- ⊡ Would you like to receive advertisements and promotional material from our sponsors?
- ⊡ Do you want to receive notification when this page is updated?
- ⊡ Would you like to receive weekly updates on what's new at our Web site?
- ⊡ Can we send you weekly highlights of interesting areas within our Web site?

The important thing here is to keep things short and sweet. The more information that you ask for, the less likely your visitors will take the time to provide it. Also, you want to make it as easy as possible for your visitors to sign up.

Examine your Web site and look for opportunities to offer email to your visitors. For example, if you run a regular contest, you might want to offer to send your visitors an e-mail each time the contest deadline approaches. Or you might offer to send an e-mail to announce who won the contest or what the next contest prize might be. Likewise, if you give away freebies or downloads, you should consider each of these events as opportunities to remind your visitors of your newsletters and e-mail lists.

Another way to encourage your visitors to sign up for your newsletters and e-mail is to create a Members Only area on your Web site where additional content is available. You could provide free access to this area to any visitor who signs up for your mailing list. Think of these types of opportunities as giving you the chance to build a relationship with your visitors and to encourage repeat traffic and loyalty.

 TIP Always make sure that any e-mail or newsletters you send out include a link back to your Web site and that you give your visitors a reason to visit. For example, you might mention that more information is available back on your Web site about a particular product, service, or topic. In addition, consider encouraging the recipients of your e-mail to pass them on to their friends and colleagues. This will allow you to reach out to new visitors without risking being seen as sending out spam.

Promoting Your Web Site through Newsgroups

Newsgroups are popular places for people with common interests. When you send a message to a newsgroup, you submit the message to a discussion area where everyone who follows the newsgroup can see it. Newsgroups, like Web sites, cover just about every imaginable subject, and whether your Web site discusses cats or conspiracy theories, a newsgroup relating to your Web site topic exists.

Finding Newsgroups You Can Use to Promote Your Web Site

With thousands of newsgroups available, trying to find one without a little help is very time consuming. Rather than browse newsgroups individually, you should visit a newsgroup archive site such as Google Groups (see Figure 4.10). Google Groups is a Web service provided by Google.

Figure 4.10

Finding newsgroups at Google Groups.

At Google Groups (**groups.google.com**), you can search through millions of current postings to newsgroups by keyword. You can also browse your way through the hierarchy of existing groups. If you don't see a group that fits your Web site topic, you can create a new newsgroup to get things started.

As shown in Figure 4.11, if you did a search on cats, you would find thousands of messages featuring this keyword. By clicking on the message subject line, you could access the most recent messages posted to the specified newsgroup. You'll also find a list of groups related to cats at the top of the page. If you find discussion groups related to topics you want to promote or participate in, write down the name of the groups.

Figure 4.11

Messages using
the keyword
are shown.

Posting Tips for Newsgroups

After you have compiled a list of all the newsgroups that might be of interest, you should familiarize yourself with the groups by reading some of the recent postings. Nothing enrages newsgroup participants more than a promotional message that doesn't relate to the topic at hand. Going a step further, some newsgroup participants loathe all advertisements.

For this reason, you should do the following:

- Spend some time getting to know the group.
- Ensure that your promotional message strongly relates to the subject at hand.
- Use a conversational style without a lot of hype.
- Keep the promotional message short—a few paragraphs at most.
- Post a message to a specific group one time and one time only; if people are interested, they'll respond.

As with direct promotion to individual users, you might want to focus less on marketing and more on information. For example, if a newsgroup participant asks about feline pneumonia and you have a terrific article on this very subject at your Web site, you might want to reply with a message like this one:

> Feline pneumonia is a serious illness that affects thousands of cats every year. Because my own cat nearly died from pneumonia, I put together an article detailing the symptoms pet owners can look for and the treatments that my veterinarian discussed with me. You can find this article at. . .

Promoting Your Web Site through Mailing Lists

Mailing lists are similar to newsgroups, but they are organized in a different manner. Whereas a message sent to a newsgroup goes to a central discussion area, mailing list messages are sent via e-mail directly to all the people who join the list. Because of the way lists work, you must subscribe to a list before you can participate in it. After you subscribe, you can read messages posted to the list and post your own messages.

The simple act of posting a message to a mailing list doesn't ensure that it will be sent to list members. Many mailing lists have moderators who review messages before they are actually distributed to the list members. If the message contains anything inappropriate, the moderator might cut out the questionable parts or remove the message entirely.

Finding Mailing Lists You Can Use to Promote Your Web Site

You can find mailing lists by visiting one of the many mailing list archive or index sites. One of the best mailing list directories is available at Tile.net. You can search through the directory using keywords or browse the lists alphabetically (see Figure 4.12).

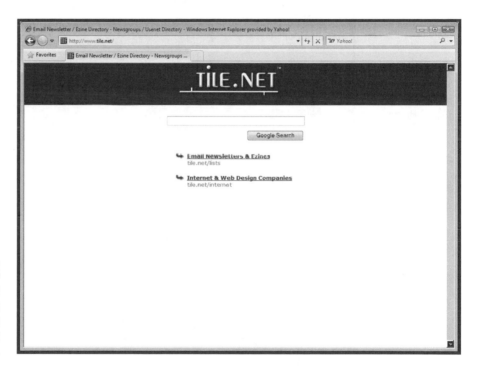

Figure 4.12

You can perform a keyword search in order to locate interesting mailing lists.

When you search through the mailing list directory, you will notice that mailing lists aren't organized into hierarchies. In place of hierarchies, mailing lists use a naming system based loosely on the topic of the list or the name of the organization sponsoring the list.

When you find a mailing list in Tile.net, you will see a brief description of the list (see Figure 4.13) as well as the information you need to subscribe to the list.

Figure 4.13

All entries include a brief summary of the mailing list along with instructions on how to join.

Mailing lists are one of the most fluid resources on the Internet. Every day, dozens of new mailing lists are born, and dozens of old mailing lists fade away into oblivion. Keeping up with this constant change is a chore made possible only with help from the list creators and moderators. Because of the constant changeover in mailing lists, it is a good idea to check several different mailing list directories before making a decision about which you would like to participate in and possibly use to promote your Web site.

Posting Tips for Mailing Lists

As with newsgroups, you should read some of the postings to a mailing list before you submit anything. With thousands of people on the receiving end of your promotional message, you have to be very careful about the marketing approach you use. Nothing will generate hate mail faster than a blatant advertisement posted to a mailing list.

Rather than post an advertisement, you might want to focus more on information. Ideally, your posting should be helpful and useful to those who read it. For specific tips on creating your posting, refer back to the posting tips for newsgroups.

Almost every mailing list out there has a set of rules. Usually, these rules are outlined in a set of FAQs (Frequently Asked Questions) for the list. Definitely try to find and read the FAQs before you participate in a mailing list. To make it easier to know and follow the rules, most mailing lists send out a confirmation message after you subscribe. In this message, you will usually find a list of the rules and lots of other good information. Save this message; you might need it later.

"Tell a Friend" Marketing

Direct mail, newsgroups, and mailing lists all provide you with powerful marketing tools. However, *viral marketing* or word-of-mouth marketing can be even more powerful because it leverages the opinions and efforts of your most important resources—your visitors. Let's face it, there are very few marketing techniques that are more powerful than the advice of a friend. By encouraging your visitors to pass on information about your Web site, product, or service, you increase the odds of bringing in new Web traffic.

Whether you realize it or not, you see viral marketing techniques implemented all over the Web. For example, Amazon.com implements this referral technique extensively, as demonstrated in Figure 4.14. Somewhere on every page where a book (or product) is displayed at Amazon.com is a Tell a Friend button.

You can implement your own word-of-mouth promotion by placing a link or button next to a product, service description, or on a Web page that you want more people to know about. Make sure your link or button stands out prominently and uses an active voice to encourage visitors to act upon your request. When clicked, you can open up the visitor's e-mail application and fill out the subject title and main body fields with information about your Web site, product, or service. Alternately, you could look to a free service on the Internet to set up and run your referral efforts for you. For example, 1-Hit.com (**www.1-hit.com**) provides a free Tell-a-Friend service at **www.1-hit.com/all-in-one/tell-a-friend.htm**, as shown in Figure 4.15. All you have to do is sign up and add a little customizable HTML to your Web pages, and you'll be ready to go.

Figure 4.14

Amazon.com takes viral marketing to a whole new level.

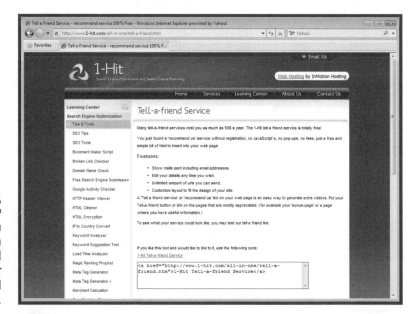

Figure 4.15

1-Hit.com can assist you in setting up and administering your Tell-a-Friend marketing efforts.

Announcing Your Web Site, Products, and Services by E-mail

Promoting your Web site through topical discussions is a terrific way to build traffic over the long term. Another way to build traffic is to announce your Web site, products, and services through e-mail. Although you can certainly announce your Web site in newsgroups that discuss topics similar to those at your Web site, you can use several additional avenues for making announcements. These avenues include:

- Using newsgroups specifically for announcements.
- Using business-oriented newsgroups.
- Using marketplace, commerce, and for-sale newsgroups.

You can browse current postings to any of the newsgroups discussed in this section by visiting Google Groups (**groups.google.com**). After you read some of the postings and are sure that the list is right for you, you can post your announcement. The key is to style your message in a manner that is appropriate for the discussion group.

When you make an announcement, you might want to organize your message like a press release that covers your Web site or the products and services that you discuss at your Web site. Ideally, your message will only be a few paragraphs long and fewer than 500 words. Brevity is important because most readers won't spend more than a few seconds glancing at your message.

In the body of the message, you should include the URL to your Web site or the particular area within your Web site that you are promoting. It's a good idea to repeat a URL at the top and bottom of the message, or to direct readers to different URLs within the Web site. This way, anyone scanning the message can zero in on the all-important URLs.

Announcement Newsgroups

Just as you can list your Web site in a What's New? directory, you can also list your Web site in discussion groups that are devoted to Web announcements. Although most announcement groups focus on announcements for new Web sites, some discussion groups focus on products and services.

Newsgroups that you can use to announce your Web site include:

alt.biz.misc
biz.marketplace
comp.infosystems.www.announce
comp.internet.net-happenings
misc.news.internet.announce

Business Newsgroups for Making Announcements

If you have ever wondered whether a place exists where blatant advertising and capitalism rule the day, look no further than the biz.* newsgroup hierarchy. In the biz.* newsgroup hierarchy, you will find dozens of newsgroups devoted to announcements for products and services. Although many of the announcements in biz.* newsgroups are filled with hype, the most successful announcements are the ones that focus less on marketing and more on information.

The primary newsgroups in the biz.* hierarchy that might be of interest in your promotion efforts include:

alt.biz
alt.biz.misc
biz.books.technical
biz.general
biz.digital.announce
biz.marketplace.computers.discussion
bis.marketplace.discussion

More Newsgroups for Announcements

With thousands of discussion groups available, the listings in this chapter are only the tip of the iceberg. If you know what to look for, you can find dozens of other places to post announcements.

With newsgroups, searching the hierarchy listings for keywords is usually the best way to find what you are looking for. You can do this at **groups.google.com**.

To find business-related newsgroups that might accept your announcements, try using some of these keywords in your search:

> **announce**
> **biz**
> **business**
> **commerce**
> **forsale**
> **marketplace**
> **www**

Setting Up Autoresponders

Communication is an important component of any Web campaign. After all, if you do not effectively get the word out and communicate your message about your Web site, no one will visit. E-mail can certainly be an important component of your overall Web campaign. Depending on how you use it, you may find yourself the recipient of quite a bit of e-mail as well.

People like to feel that when they take the time to say something, they are being heard. With e-mail, this means getting a message back. Depending on the amount of incoming e-mail you find yourself faced with, this may become a challenging task. One way to help you deal with this challenge is to employ an *autoresponder*. Autoresponders automatically send out predefined e-mails in response to incoming mail. Using an autoresponder, you could for example, thank the person for sending you the e-mail and perhaps provide them with some additional information about your Web site.

One of the nice features of autoresponders is that they work all the time, allowing you to provide a quick response to any e-mail, no matter what time of day it arrives. Using an autoresponder can also help to give you a more professional image. There are a number of autoresponder services available on the Internet. For example, FreeAutobot (**www.freeautobot.com**) provides a free autoresponder service that allows you to set up both plain text and HTML-based e-mail. Each time the service sends out an automated response on your behalf, it tacks a small line onto the end of your e-mail that provides a link back to FreeAutobot.

Other autoresponder services that you may want to check out include GetResponse E-mail Marketing and SendFree. GetResponse E-mail Marketing (**www.getresponse.com**) is free for the first 30 days. SendFree (**www.sendfree.com**) is also free for the first month.

Creating a Professional Image Using Multiple E-mail Accounts

One way of generating a more professional image is to set up and use multiple e-mail addresses for your Web site. Using this approach, you can set up e-mail addresses for different topics. For example, you might set up an e-mail account to respond to all inquiries for more information, a second e-mail account to deal with contests, and a third e-mail account to handle all other issues.

NOTE Consider setting up an autoresponder for each of the e-mail accounts that you set up. This will make it easy to automatically send out customized e-mail to people requesting more information or entering a contest.

By defining multiple e-mail addresses, you will give your Web site the same professional look and feel as larger Web sites, like Amazon.com. Setting up multiple e-mail accounts shouldn't cost you anything. Most Web site hosts provide you with the ability to set up and manage any number of e-mail accounts.

NOTE   Using e-mail forwarding, a service provided by most Web site hosts, you can forward all the e-mail from your various e-mail accounts to a single account, making it easier for you to view and manage all incoming e-mail.

Creative Signature Files

An e-mail signature is an extra you can add to the end of all your e-mail messages. This trailer can help you promote your Web site as well as your products and services each time you send an e-mail message. Your signature can be styled as a mini-promotion for your Web site or anything else that you want to highlight.

Although you might see e-mail signatures that run 10 to 20 lines, most signatures are fewer than 5 lines. As a rule of thumb, 3 to 5 lines are usually a good length. Because your e-mail signature will go out with all your mail unless you delete the signature, it's a good idea to limit the hype.

Listing 4.1 demonstrates how you might want to format your own e-mail signatures. This should give you an idea of how you can create a signature that is effective yet doesn't look like an advertisement. If your e-mail application allows you to create a signature using fancy fonts or special formatting, keep in mind that this formatting is created with HTML and may not be displayed with any special formatting in another e-mail application. Additionally, you can improve readability in compliant e-mail applications by using simple font types and readable font sizes.

Listing 4.1   Sample E-mail Signatures

```
Jerry Lee Ford, Jr.

Information Security Professional and author of computer books

http://www.tech-publishing.com
```

Most e-mail applications allow you to create a signature file. In some cases you do so using an ordinary text file. After you create and save the signature file, you can use the standard features of your favorite e-mail applications to add the e-mail signature to all your outgoing messages. Most modern e-mail applications also provide you with a built-in editor to assist you in creating your custom signature. For example, if you used an online e-mail service such as Yahoo! mail, you would set up your signature as outlined here:

1. Open you browser and log in to **mail.yahoo.com**.
2. Click on the Options link located in the upper-right corner of the screen, and then click on More Options.
3. Next, click on the Signature link in the left side panel.
4. Type in the text for your signature file in the space provided.
5. Select the Show a Signature on All Outgoing Messages option.
6. Click on Save Changes to save your signature.

If you use a desktop e-mail application, such as Windows Live Mail, the process is pretty much the same.

Developing an Online Business Card

In addition to communicating with Web surfers through e-mail and promoting your Web site through a signature file, you may also want to consider creating and distributing an online business card. An online business card is simply the electronic equivalent of a traditional business card, only instead of giving away a paper card, you give away the URL of your business card, allowing anyone with whom you share it to look it up and get your contact information and Web site URL.

If an online business card sounds like something that you can use as part of your Web marketing campaign, you can set one up for free by visiting Triumph PC at **www.triumphpc.com/netcard**, as shown in Figure 4.16.

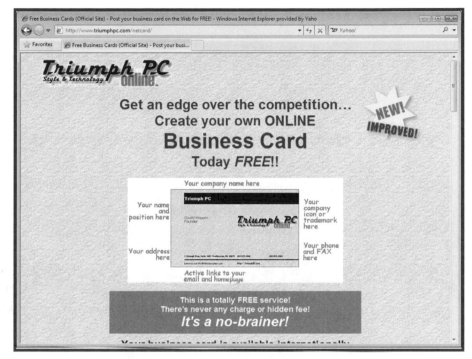

Figure 4.16

At Triumph PC, you can create your online business card in a just a few seconds.

By filling in a simple form, you can create a business card that displays your name, company name, job title, phone numbers, e-mail addresses, and your URL. Best of all, your URL will show up as an active link that when clicked will open your Web page.

Take a Break

Congratulations! You are halfway through the Sunday Morning session. It is time to take a break. Crank up the radio. Grab a drink and get something to eat. When you return you will learn about a number of different and exciting ways to bring more traffic to your Web site.

Advertising on eBay

There is no doubt that eBay has become a major force on the Web. It provides a Web service that facilitates the buying and selling of products all over the world. For individuals and companies with something to sell, eBay provides a service known as an eBay store, as shown in Figure 4.17.

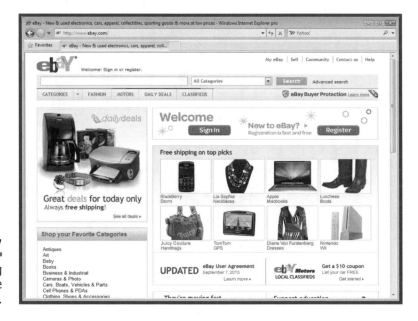

Figure 4.17

eBay makes setting up an online store a snap.

If your Web site has something to sell or if you plan on selling something, eBay may be your ticket to success. At the time that the sixth edition of this book was written, you could set up a new eBay store starting at just $15.95 a month. This automatically puts you in front of millions of eBay shoppers. You'll have total control over how your online store looks. You decide on the content, graphics, and colors. Your store will get its own URL, and your customers will even be able to pay online via credit card.

In order to open a store, you must open an eBay account and place your credit card on file. You can then open up a new store by logging in to eBay, going to **stores.ebay.com**, and clicking on the Open a Store link.

Once opened, you can set up your store as demonstrated in Figure 4.18. As you can see, the store shown belongs to Midwest Sports Tennis and Sandals.

Figure 4.18

Midwest Sports is an online tennis store.

As you can see in the figure, Midwest Sports has a considerable inventory of tennis products for sale. You can click on any of the items shown in the store to learn more information, purchase it, or place a bid on it, as demonstrated in Figure 4.19.

If you return to the Midwest Sports store and click on the Me link, a page with information about the store is displayed. Scroll down further on this page, and you will see a section labeled Favorite Links. If you click on the Midwest Sports Supply link, you will be taken to the store owner's real Web site (**www.midwestsports.com**). This will encourage customers to visit them on the Web (see Figure 4.20) and potentially make purchases directly from this Web site, thus bypassing eBay completely.

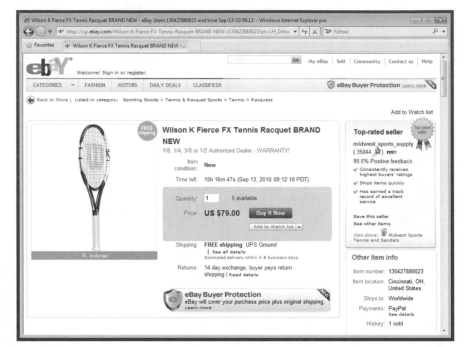

Figure 4.19

Examining a tennis racket being sold at the Midwest Sports' eBay store.

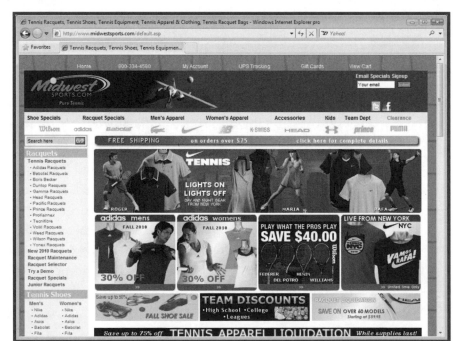

Figure 4.20

By setting up an eBay store, an online business can drive even more traffic to its Web site.

Get Noticed on Craigslist

Another amazingly popular Web site is Craigslist. At Craigslist, people from all over the world gather to buy and sell things through an enormous collection of classified ads. As shown in Figure 4.21, Craigslist is organized into sections that are devoted to community matters, housing, jobs, personals, for sale, and services. Discussion forums are also hosted.

Figure 4.21

When used effectively, Craigslist can drive a lot of traffic to your Web site.

Within the Community section, there is a link labeled General. This is a good place to advertise whatever you want to give away or sell. Make sure you add a URL back to one of your Web site. However, if you have anything that properly fits into any of the more specific community categories, then place your ad there instead.

You can also generate quality Web traffic by participating in discussion forums that address the same topics covered on your Web site. When you add postings, make sure that they are relevant to the discussion topic and have plenty of value. This is not the place to make an obvious sales pitch, but do mention that your URL is a good place where additional relevant information can be found.

If you have items to sell, the categories listed in the For Sale section are the place to market them. Here you can freely promote your stuff and provide your URL without worrying about breaking any rules. Similarly, if your Web site promotes a specific service, you can advertise it and your URL in the in the appropriate Services category.

Craigslist looks for duplicate adds, preventing you from posting the same add in several different categories. However, by making slightly different versions of your ads, you can avoid being labeled as a spammer if you want to post ads in different categories. In order to get the most out of Craigslist, it's a good idea to generate several versions of your ads and to rotate them regularly. Make small changes to each ad each time you post it. This way you'll keep things fresh and avoid being viewed as a spammer. As long as you play by the rules and don't try to oversell your stuff or your URL, you can drive some high-quality traffic back to your Web site.

Setting Up a Cybermall Shop

If you have products to sell, another way to reach out to online customers is to add your Web site store front to a cybermall. A *cybermall* is an online virtual shopping center that brings together the home pages of multiple storefronts from across the Internet to provide buyers with a unified shopping experience. The idea behind cybermalls is very much the same as the idea behind traditional shopping malls, namely that by grouping stores together and providing shoppers with a convenient way of moving from store to store, you can attract more customers than member stores could do on their own.

Benefits

Cybermalls provide an obvious convenience for shoppers by providing everything that they need in one place. Cybermalls also make shopping easier by providing buyers with a single shopping cart that allows them to visit different stores and to put everything into a single cart. Later, when the buyer is done shopping and ready to pay for his purchases, he can do so in a single transaction managed by the cybermall. This is a lot more convenient than having to purchase products from each store individually.

Finding the Right Place for Your Web Site

Cybermalls are becoming very popular. There are a number of very large cybermalls, like buy.com (**www.buy.com**). Getting your Web store into one of these cybermalls may be quite challenging if you are just starting out. You may instead want to start by targeting a smaller cybermall, such as the Slowtowne Market Place (**www.slowtownemarketplace.com**) as shown in Figure 4.22.

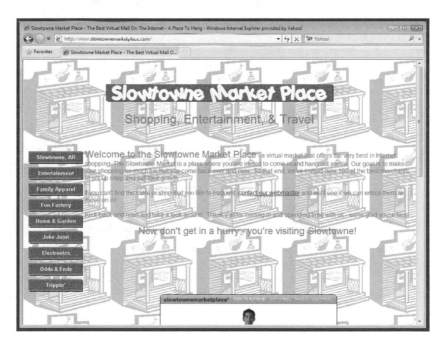

Figure 4.22

The Slowtowne Market Place organizes its members' stores into different shopping categories.

Begin by spending a little time browsing the other stores at the cybermall, and if you think that your Web store is a good fit, click on the Contact Our Webmaster link on the main page. This will open your default e-mail application and create a new e-mail with a subject line of "add retailer" addressed to **webmaster@slowtownemarketplace.com**.

Getting Access to Millions of Customers Working with Amazon.com

Amazon.com is one of the most popular destinations on the Internet with tens of millions of customers. Even Web surfers who are not comfortable with making online purchases often shop Amazon.com because of its strong reputation. Amazon.com provides a number of different ways in which you can align your Web site with Amazon.com and access its customer base, hopefully turning your Web site into a profit-earning resource.

Becoming an Affiliate and Setting Up Your Own Store Front

One way to work with Amazon.com is to join its affiliate or associates program. Doing so will allow you to set up links to Amazon.com that allow you to advertise and sell different Amazon.com products directly from your Web site. For example, if your Web site is dedicated to spreading the word about the importance of global warming, you might want to make your Web site more interesting by selling books that address this subject on your Web site. In doing so, you can provide your visitors with a more complete experience and also provide them with convenient access to current literature on the subject. Best of all, any time a visitor makes a purchase with Amazon.com through a link on your Web site, you get a piece of the action.

To learn about and join Amazon.com's affiliate program, visit **www.amazon.com** and click on the Join Associates link located at the bottom of the page.

Sell Your Products via Amazon.com's Marketplace

If you create and sell books, CDs, or DVDs through your Web site, you should seriously consider signing up with Amazon.com's Advantage program. This program allows authors, musicians, and video content providers to list and sell their products alongside similar Amazon.com items.

To sell products through this program, you must be able to provide Amazon.com with a scanable ISBN/EAN/UPC barcode on every item. As of the writing of the sixth edition of this book, Amazon.com charged a one-time fee of $29.95 to join its Advantage program. Any items you list with Amazon.com gain instant access to millions of customers. Your products are displayed right along with other Amazon.com products. Amazon.com lets you specify your product's description. Amazon.com manages all your sales and sends you payments as your items sell.

If you brand your products with information about your Web site, you can invite visits directly to your site, where you can encourage additional purchases, this time directly from you. To learn more about Amazon.com's Advantage program, visit **www.amazon.com/advantage**.

Attracting the Masses with Giveaways, Contests, Sweepstakes, and More

Traditional marketers have used giveaways, contests, and sweepstakes for years to make their sponsors stand out from the crowd. The simple truth is that we all love the chance to win something for nothing, and whenever we have the opportunity to enter a contest or giveaway, we usually go for the gusto. Web advertisers have pushed traditional giveaways and contests onto the World Wide Web, where the quest for freebies can truly bring the masses to the sponsor's Web site.

Can't Get 'Em Any Other Way? Give It Away!

Giving things away is a great way to build traffic to your Web site. Whether you want to pass out bumper stickers or trips to Europe, people will want to enter your giveaway. Beyond outright giveaways are contests and sweepstakes that ask the participants to answer questions or enter a creative work, such as a poem or a jingle for a commercial.

Giveaways, contests, and sweepstakes promoted on the Web are often direct tie-ins to similar promotions running in print media. If your organization is already planning a giveaway or contest, advertising it on the Web can bring your message to an eager audience of millions.

Universal Studios (**www.universalstudios.com**) is a company that understands the promotional power of giveaways. Universal Studios (whose sweepstakes have been referenced in six editions of this book) follows the pointers offered in this book and understands how to promote contests that tie-in with company products (see Figure 4.23).

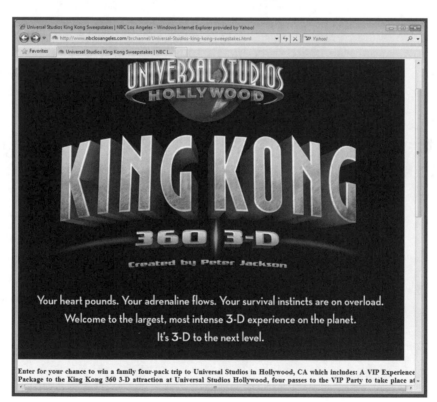

Figure 4.23

Universal Studios understands the promotional power of giveaways. They sponsor new giveaways all the time.

If you have the clout of a major corporation behind you, promotional tie-ins between your Web site and a giveaway or contest running in the print media will work well. But even if you are not part of a major corporation, you can benefit tremendously from running a contest or sweepstakes at your Web site.

Although many traditional promotional campaigns center around give-aways, contests, and sweepstakes, savvy marketers know that the interactive and dynamic nature of the Web opens doors and removes the traditional boundaries and restrictions of print media. On the Web, your giveaway can become part of an interactive trivia quiz with questions that change dynamically each time the page is visited. You can even create an interactive treasure hunt with clues scattered throughout your Web site.

The Web allows you to conduct other types of promotions as well, such as online games that give something away to participants with the best scores. With an online game, contestants get to have fun while trying to win prizes. Online games can range from simple puzzles and teasers to actual video games programmed in Java or another programming language.

Using a giveaway, contest, or sweepstakes to increase traffic at your Web site is a good idea, but it's definitely not the only reason to give things away. By using a giveaway, contest, or sweepstakes, you can also:

- ☑ Build awareness for your products and services.
- ☑ Familiarize readers with other areas of your Web site.
- ☑ Build a profile of your readers based on a survey or questionnaire that is part of the submission form.

Later in this session, you'll learn about different types of giveaways and contests that you might want to use in your promotional efforts. These include:

- ☑ Free-for-all giveaways and sweepstakes.
- ☑ Contests for artists, writers, and other creative people.
- ☑ Trivia quizzes, games, puzzles, and teasers.

Although giveaways and contests are great for increasing your Web traffic, the actual amount of traffic increase you see at your Web site will depend on what you are giving away and how well you promote the giveaway. Keep in mind that they key to success isn't so much *what* you give away, but *how* you give it away. If your hook is great, your giveaway or contest will attract the masses. To help you promote your giveaway or contest, this book will introduce you to Web sites that specialize in freebies, giveaways, and contests. After all, people need to find your giveaway or contest in order to participate.

Free Samples

One point to keep in mind when giving stuff away is that you do not have to give away a full copy of your product to satisfy people's never-ending appetite for free stuff. Many times free samples will do quite nicely. Giving away free samples can save you money while still giving you the opportunity to show your visitors how good your product is. Of course, if giving away free samples means mailing visitors your products, you may need to require visitors to pay postage and handling. Otherwise, giving away free samples may be cost prohibitive.

If, however, you are selling software programs, your sample might be a smaller demo version of your product, which you can distribute via e-mail (giving you the opportunity to further promote your Web site). Likewise, if your product is an online service, you might provide a week of free access to your online service.

Give Away the Junk in Your Closet

What if you don't have any expensive prizes or free samples to give away? One really good source of free stuff that you may want to consider is to use the things that you no longer want or need that are currently taking up space in your closets, attic, and garage. Just because these things no longer hold any value for you does not mean that others won't anxiously want to get their hands on them. Be creative!

Free Articles

If you have a knack for writing, you may want to consider using this skill as another means of driving traffic to your Web site. By writing short articles on subjects that are of interest to your target audience and providing free access to copies of those articles on your Web site, you can bring in droves of readers. Once you have written your articles, you might let everybody know about them by posting an entry in a newsgroup. When visitors show up at your Web pages to get copies of your articles, you can take the opportunity to prompt them to join your mailing list and encourage them to bookmark and visit the rest of your Web site.

Free Advertising on Your Web Site

Another freebie you can give away that will cost you absolutely nothing is free advertising on your Web site. You might, for example, offer a day or week of free advertising. You can bet that people will show up to make sure that their advertising has been posted on their assigned day or week, and their friends may show up as well.

Free T-shirts and Bumper Stickers

If you can afford it, you might want to consider giving away free t-shirts or bumper stickers with your URL on it. This way, your contest and sweepstakes winners will turn into walking and driving billboards, advertising your Web site wherever they go.

Creating your own custom t-shirt or bumper sticker is easier than you might think. You can even do it online. For example, the following Web sites will be happy to you help you create your own custom t-shirt with prices starting at less than $10:

- **http://www.vistaprint.com**
- **http://www.uberprints.com**

Likewise, the following Web sites specialize in the creation of custom bumper stickers. Prices vary, depending on how many you purchase, ranging from one bumper sticker for $3.00 to 100 bumper stickers for $100:

- **http://www.buildasign.com/bumper-stickers**
- **http://www.printmything.com**

What to Watch Out For: The Legalities

Although nothing builds traffic like a good giveaway or contest, there are many things you should consider before you get started. Your primary concern should be the legal ramifications of publishing your giveaway or contest on the Web.

By putting your contest on the Web, you make it available to participants throughout the world, which might make your contest subject to certain laws. Every country has its own laws, and these laws often vary by region within the country as well. For example, each state in the U.S. has its own rules regarding giveaways and contests.

Before you publish your contest or distribute any information related to your contest, you should check applicable federal, state, and local laws regarding contests and giveaways. The best places to research global laws are the Law Library of Congress (**http://www.loc.gov/law/index.php**) and the Guide to Law Online (**http://www.loc.gov/law/help/guide.php**).

Disclaimers for Age and Residency

Because of the extreme diversity of international laws, most organizations that run contests and giveaways restrict their promotions to specific countries. When you restrict your contest to a specific country or countries, you should post a clear disclaimer along with any contest information. The purpose of the disclaimer is to protect your interests and ensure that you don't accidentally violate the laws of another country.

If you've browsed Web sites that run contests or giveaways, you have probably seen a disclaimer that says "U.S. and Canadian residents only" or "U.S. residents only." By restricting a contest to the U.S. and Canada, or the U.S. only, you limit your liability—which is always a good idea.

Another thing to consider is the age of the participants. Because many U.S. states require that participants in contests be at least 18 years old, you should place an age restriction on the contest. You can blend the age restriction right into your original disclaimer, such as "U.S. and Canadian residents 18 and older only" or "U.S. residents 18 and older only."

Granted, verifying a person's age over the Internet is difficult; however, clearly marking the age restriction can only serve your best interest.

Other Disclaimers

Generally, within the U.S. and Canada, your sweepstakes or giveaway should be free, meaning that you shouldn't require entrants to purchase something in order to enter and win. In this way, your sweepstakes or giveaway is truly giving something away for nothing. You should post a clear disclaimer at the contest site notifying readers that no purchase is necessary to enter the contest. An exception is a creative contest, such as an art contest or writing contest, that charges an entry fee.

You should also publish a statement to ensure participants know that local laws apply to the contest and that the contest is void where prohibited. Voiding the contest where prohibited protects you from inadvertently violating the local laws.

Putting the Rules Together

Now that you have made a start on the rules for your contest or giveaway, you should put these rules together in an official form that you can publish on your Web site. In the official rules, you should spell out exactly what you will be giving away and the value of the prizes. If you will be giving away one Sony 19-inch TV valued at $399, specify this exactly.

After you've decided on the rules for your contest or giveaway, you should publish them for the entire world to see. Ideally, you will place a summary of the rules on all the contest pages and make the detailed rules available with a hypertext link.

The following is an example set of rules for a fictitious contest called the Happy Peacock Sweepstakes. As you read it, keep in mind that this is a made-up example that serves only to illustrate some of the points made in this section.

Rules for the Happy Peacock Sweepstakes:

1. No purchase necessary to enter.

2. To enter the sweepstakes, fill out the official entry form at the Happy Peacock Web site. We accept only fully completed entry forms. Only one entry per person is allowed.

3. Sweepstakes begins January 1, 2011, and ends on December 31, 2011. Your entry must be received no later than midnight on December 31, 2011. Winners will be selected in a random drawing.

4. Sweepstakes is open to residents of the United States who are 18 years of age or older. All submissions become the property of Happy Peacock. All federal, state, and local laws and regulations apply. Any taxes due are the responsibility of the winner. Void where prohibited or restricted by law.

5. One first-place prize: Happy Peacock gift set, valued at $299. Ten second-place prizes: Happy Peacock T-shirt, valued at $25 each. Twenty third-place prizes: Happy Peacock coffee mug, valued at $9 each.

6. A list of prize winners will be published at the Happy Peacock Web site within 15 days of the end of the sweepstakes. Happy Peacock reserves the right to substitute a prize of equal or greater value.

 TIP If you need help creating forms, or putting a process in place to collect form results, check out Response-O-Matic at **www.response-o-matic.com**. Response-O-Matic will help you create your forms, collect the data your visitors enter, and send you the results via e-mail—all for free.

Boosting Traffic with Giveaways and Sweepstakes

Giveaways and sweepstakes are great for boosting traffic at your Web site. Every day, thousands of people search the Web looking for the latest giveaways and sweepstakes—and why not? They can win hats, T-shirts, books, jewelry, trips, and much more, simply by filling out a form. Although there is not much difference between a giveaway and a sweepstakes, the term sweepstakes is often used when sponsors and advertisers donate prizes.

Creating a Giveaway or Sweepstakes

When you put together a giveaway or sweepstakes, remember that the prizes themselves are not what attract readers as much as your execution. As a matter of fact, you could give away T-shirts and get more visitors than a site giving away trips to Europe.

Although the organization giving away trips to Europe would argue their case heatedly, the reality is that a well-designed and well-promoted giveaway will be successful regardless of the prizes. Well-designed giveaways and sweepstakes have a professional polish that makes them fun, easy to enter, and visually appealing. Well-promoted giveaways and sweepstakes are announced in all the right places, which includes key pages at your Web site and Web guides that promote freebies.

 NOTE You'll learn all about guides that promote freebies shortly, under the heading "Sites That Promote Your Freebies."

The best giveaways and sweepstakes have a theme that helps sell people on the idea of the giveaway or sweepstakes. If you are giving away trips, it is not just a "trip," but a "passport to adventure." If you are giving away cruises, it is not just a "cruise," but "barefoot strolls along windswept beaches, romantic dinners for two, and quiet, moonlit evenings topside."

After you decide on the type of giveaway or sweepstakes to run, consider the prizes that you will award. As stated earlier, the prizes don't have to be extravagant, but they should be worth the time and effort it takes to enter the contest. Additionally, entering the giveaway or sweepstakes should be as easy as filling out an entry form that asks for contact information, such as name, address, and phone number.

You might also want to add a questionnaire or survey to the entry form. Questionnaires can help you learn more about the type of people who visit your Web site. You can find out whether they use your products and services. You can also learn about visitor preferences, such as their favorite area within your Web site, or their interests.

Looking at an Actual Sweepstakes

A good case study for a well-designed and well-promoted sweepstakes is Frommer's monthly sweepstakes. The sweepstakes ties in with Frommer's travel magazine and books, and is a featured part of Arthur Frommer's Budget Travel Online Web site (see Figure 4.24). The sweepstakes has sponsors who advertise on the contest pages and on the Web site. The sweepstakes serves several purposes:

- The sweepstakes builds traffic to the Web site by inviting visitors to return to the site regularly. Prizes are given away regularly and visitors must return to register each month.

- The sweepstakes highlights sponsors by providing direct links to the Web sites of the sponsors.

- The sweepstakes entry form asks visitors to provide contact information and to answer a questionnaire, which provides valuable geographic and demographic information that the publishers might not be able to otherwise obtain.

- Information entered by visitors is often sold to companies that are interested in reaching this target audience. This sale can provide secondary income for the company.

Figure 4.24

Prizes are what bring visitors, but you might be surprised to learn that a simple T-shirt contest can bring in as many visitors as a $50,000 giveaway. The secret is in the presentation and promotion.

NOTE Never sell information without prior notification. If you plan to sell information gathered through the sweepstakes, you should state this explicitly in the contest rules and in your site's privacy policy.

Frommer's enhances the main sweepstakes entry form by adding input fields that allow visitors to provide the e-mail addresses of up to 6 other people who may be interested in the contest. The entry form also provides subscription fields that allow visitors to sign up for a number of newsletters. All in all, it's a well-rounded effort to invite visitor participation, collect visitor information, and increase Web traffic.

Gaining Readers with Contests

Contests reward people for their talents or creativity. Because contests often require judging and extensive work on the part of the producer, some contests charge a nominal fee, such as $5, to enter. Charging an entry fee for something like a writing contest that offers prestige, publication, and cash rewards to the winners makes sense. Charging an entry fee for a contest that is meant more for fun than to be a career builder doesn't make sense.

Running a Contest

Contests can be just as much fun for you as they are for the participants. Your goal should be to use the contest to build traffic to your Web site. Ideally, your contest will tie in to and promote your business, products, and services. For example, developers of word processing applications might want to sponsor a write-off for the most creative or bizarre advertising gimmick for their product.

The type of contest that you run will depend largely on your interests. If you are interested in comedy, you might want to have a contest that rewards the funniest submissions. If you are interested in graphic design, you might want to have a design contest. If you love poetry, you might want to have a poetry contest.

To keep your contest as hassle-free as possible, you will want to decide on the specific formats that are acceptable for submissions. For a writing or poetry contest, you might want to specify in the rules that all submissions must be saved as standard ASCII text files with a .txt file extension. Similarly, for a design or art contest, you might want to specify that all submissions must be saved in either PNG or JPEG format.

Additionally, any time you ask for creative submissions, you should set limits on the size or length of entries. For a writing contest, you might want to limit entries to 5,000 words. For a design contest, you might want to limit the size of artwork to 1280 × 1024, with a file size of less than 2MB.

After you decide on the type of contest you want to run, you need to think about how you will judge the contest. Most small contests are judged exclusively by the contest developer. Creative contests, such as writing, art, or design contests, are usually voted on by a panel of judges.

Alternatively, you can remove yourself from the judging process entirely by letting visitors to your Web site vote for the best submission. The bottom line is that your judging process should be fair yet manageable using your current resources.

As with giveaways, you can use an entry form to accept submission for the contest, and you might want to add a questionnaire to the entry form as well. Keep in mind that if you run a creative contest, many participants will have their entry in separate text or graphic files. Currently, the easiest way to submit files is as an attachment to an e-mail message. For this reason, you might simply want to supply an e-mail address for submission rather than use an entry form.

 TIP You should state explicitly how many times visitors can enter and how many times they can win. Put this information in the official rules. For example, if visitors can enter only once and win only one prize, state this as a contest rule.

With creative works, you must consider one more thing: U.S. and international copyright law. Creative works are the property of the creator unless the rights are granted or sold. Thus if you plan to publish the winning works at your Web site, you need permission, and you should ask for this permission right in the entry form. The minimum rights that you will want to retain are one-time world-electronic rights to the winning entries. Furthermore, you should state that winning entries will be published at your Web site.

Looking at an Actual Contest

An example of a Web site that uses contests to promote itself and its products is iWon (**www.iwon.com**), shown in Figure 4.25. The Words "I" and "Won" have a wonderful ring that describes the site's theme. The idea behind the site is to attract visitors with the promise of a chance to win great sums of cash. The entire theme of the Web site is built around the contests being offered rather than the products being advertised.

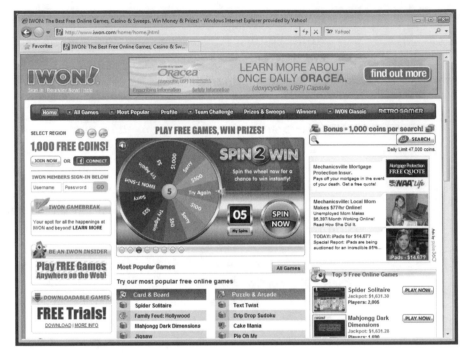

Figure 4.25

A great contest theme can help build traffic and sell your products. Nothing gets a visitor's attention like a chance to win money.

iWon takes the contest site concept to a new level, making it possible for visitors to win huge amounts of money just by visiting the site. Everywhere you look there are graphical and text links trying to lead you to other areas of the Web site. These links and graphics are reminders that the site has more to offer and that the real goal is to sell you something.

Using Games, Puzzles, and Teasers to Attract Visitors

Games, puzzles, and teasers can bring in the masses simply because they are entertaining. People of all ages love to play games that are challenging, fun, or stimulating. Games, puzzles, and teasers are good ways to keep visitors coming back to your Web site again and again. Many game sites take game playing to another level by offering additional incentives, such as prizes. In this way, the game sites make a good thing better by rewarding people for playing. When rewards are involved, you can bet that visitors will come back again and again. Keep in mind that your prize doesn't have to be anything of monetary value. You could simply publish the winner's name prominently on your home page, grant the winner a free home page, or something else that doesn't really cost you anything.

TIP Use your games, puzzles, and teasers as an opportunity to encourage Tell-a-Friend viral marketing by prominently displaying a button or link that opens the visitor's e-mail application and encourages them to send a preformatted message about your product, service, or Web site to a friend or colleague.

Creating a Game, Puzzle, or Teaser

When you think of games, you probably imagine the zippy video games you see in the arcades. You could certainly spend months programming a truly awesome game for your Web site, like the folks at Cartoon Network (**www.cartoonnetwork.com**), as shown in Figure 4.26. However, some of the best games are those that are simple and compulsively playable. Most card games, such as poker or solitaire, aren't popular because of rip-roaring action; they are popular because they are easy to learn yet challenging to play.

One game to consider is a treasure hunt. Treasure hunts are really popular during the holidays, especially at Easter. In a treasure hunt, you hide clues or treasures throughout your Web site and sometimes at participating Web sites. You can display clues or treasures directly on your Web pages using text and graphics. You can also link standardized treasure icons to secret pages at your Web site that describe an item in the treasure hunt.

With a treasure hunt, you need a submission page that lets participants submit a list of all clues or treasures they've collected. Usually, prizes in a treasure hunt are awarded to the participants who find all the treasures first. To ensure fair play, you might want to periodically change the clues and treasures during the hunt.

Figure 4.26

Cartoon Network provides free access to professional-quality online computer games.

A trivia quiz is another game that is a lot of fun and easy to produce. Although trivia quizzes cover any topic, you might want to link the quiz to the theme or topic of your Web site. The best trivia quizzes have at least five challenging questions to which participants can get answers immediately. To keep visitors coming back, you might want to make the trivia quiz a weekly or monthly feature.

If you are giving away prizes on a trivia quiz, you can post answers with a list of winners at a later date. Because many people might know the answers to your trivia questions, you really don't want to award prizes to everyone who submits the right answers. Instead, you might want to award prizes randomly from the list of participants who submitted the right answers.

Another type of game to consider is a puzzle. The best puzzles are word-based brainteasers, such as a crossword puzzle or a word association game.

With a puzzle, you will probably want to reward participants simply for playing and submitting their answers.

A great way to build steady traffic with a puzzle is to change the puzzle often and award prizes randomly to the participants who answer a certain number of puzzles correctly in a given period of time. For example, you can publish a different puzzle every week and award prizes randomly to anyone who gets the answer to four different puzzles in a particular month.

Finding Free Online Games to Add to Your Web Pages

There are a number of Web sites where you can go to find free games that you can add to your Web site. For example, you'll find a free version of a JavaScript-based hangman game at **hangman.bappy.com**. Figure 4.27 shows how the game will look when a visitor starts it from your Web site.

Figure 4.27

Just copy and paste the free code into one of your Web pages, and you are ready to host a free game of hangman on your Web site.

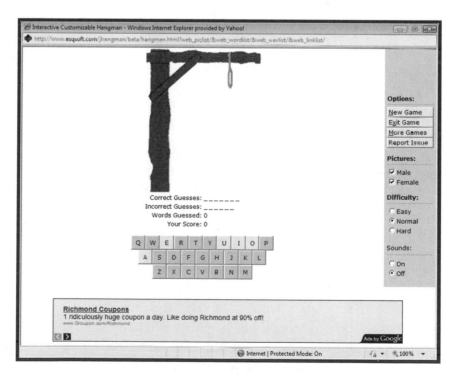

Another site where you can find an assortment of free JavaScript games is **javascript.internet.com**. All you have to do is add the free JavaScript code to your Web pages to get these games up and running.

Looking at an Actual Treasure Hunt

Museum Mania (**www.museummania.com**) features a number of online treasure hunts (see Figure 4.28). The goal of the treasure hunt is to follow a set of clues located at the links embedded in your questions. Once you find the items referenced in the clues, you can submit an entry to see how well you did.

Figure 4.28

A well-designed treasure hunt can be a terrific promotional vehicle for your Web site.

Before visitors submit their answers to any of the many treasure hunts, they are asked to submit information about themselves, including their name, age, school, and city. Museum Mania is able to use this information to track detailed statistics related to the contest participants. These statistics are used to determine the effectiveness of the Web site's effort to interest young people in learning more about history.

Sites That Promote Your Freebies

You need to promote your giveaway, contest, or sweepstakes to make it successful. Although your promotion efforts should definitely begin at key areas within your Web site, you should also promote the contest through guides and directories that specialize in freebies.

In this section, you will find a brief review of some of the most popular contest directories. When you submit your freebie to a contest directory, be sure to provide the URL to the main contest page and a brief description of the contest. The contest description should specify when the contest ends as well as any age and residency requirements.

Promoting Your Freebie at TheFreeSite.com

TheFreeSite.com (**www.thefreesite.com**) is an extensive guide to just about everything that is free on the Web. Features in the catalog include free games, services, samples, screen savers, newsletters, and so on (see Figure 4.29).

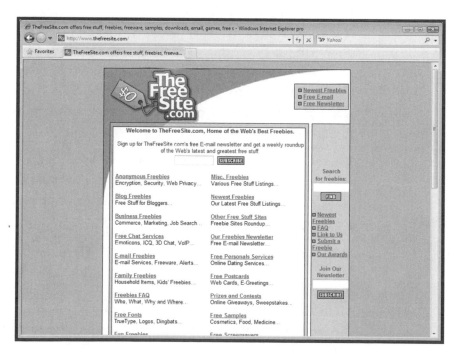

Figure 4.29

TheFreeSite.com is a growing resource for contests, giveaways, and sweepstakes.

Before you submit a listing to TheFreeSite.com, you should wander through the site to familiarize yourself with the various categories. Listings are displayed with a title and a detailed description that includes any relevant information about a particular freebie.

To submit your freebie, visit the Web site and click on the Submit a Freebie link. You'll be required to add a link to TheFreeSite.com on your own Web site. Be sure to include the URL to your freebie page, a description for the contest, the contest's start and end dates, and any other requirements.

Other Places to Promote Your Freebies

With thousands of organizations giving away freebies, it's no surprise there are dozens of Web guides to free stuff. Other freebie guides that you might want to submit a listing to include Free-n-Cool, ContestGuide, FreebieList, and 1FreeStuffSite.

Free-n-Cool (**www.free-n-cool.com**) is a guide to everything on the Web that is free and—per the judgment of the site's creators—cool. The guide is divided into several key sections, including New Totally Free Stuff, New Almost-Free Stuff, New Contests and Giveaways, and New Cool Sites (see Figure 4.30). To promote your contest or giveaway, check out the New Totally Free Stuff and New Almost-Free Stuff sections. The distinction here is between outright giveaways and contests that award prizes to participants.

You can submit your freebie to Free-n-Cool by sending e-mail to **linkrequest @free-n-cool.com**. If you want to increase your chances of getting listed or being more prominently listed, add a link on your page to Free-n-Cool.

ContestGuide.com (**www.contestguide.com**) is a fairly comprehensive guide to contests. This site has a unique focus in that it organizes listings according to how often you can enter a contest (see Figure 4.31). It has listings for contests that let you enter one time only, daily, weekly, and monthly. You can submit a listing to ContestGuide by filling out the submission form at **www.contestguide.com/webmasters.html**.

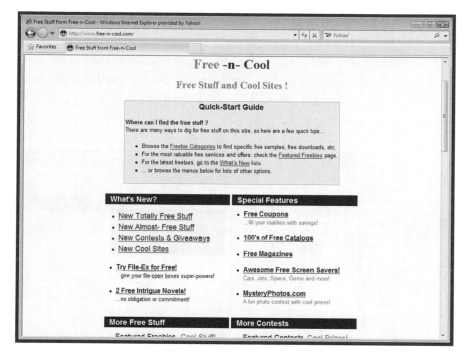

Figure 4.30

Free-n-Cool is a guide to what's free and cool on the Web.

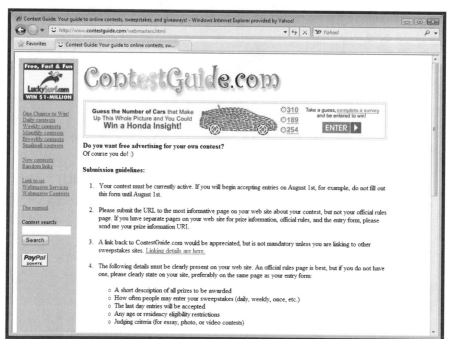

Figure 4.31

Most of the listings in ContestGuide are organized according to how often you can enter the contest.

Another great contest guide is FreebieList (**www.freebielist.com**), shown in Figure 4.32. You can browse by category to find where your freebie best fits. You must add a link to **www.freebielist.com** on your Web site, and then fill out the form at **http://www.freebielist.com/info/add-webmasters.** Be sure to include your site's title, URL, and a description of your freebie and your Web site.

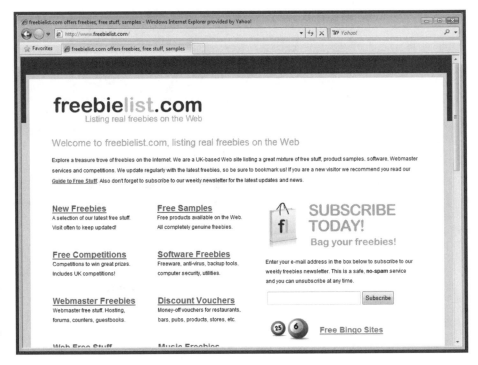

Figure 4.32

FreebieList offers a wide variety for Web surfers and is a good source to promote your giveaways.

One last freebie Web site for you to check out is 1 Free Stuff Site (**www.1freestuffsite.com**). This directory, shown in Figure 4.33, includes free stuff and samples. To add your freebie, you need to first add a link to the 1 Free Stuff Site. Next, drill down into the category where you want your freebie listed, and then click on Add Link.

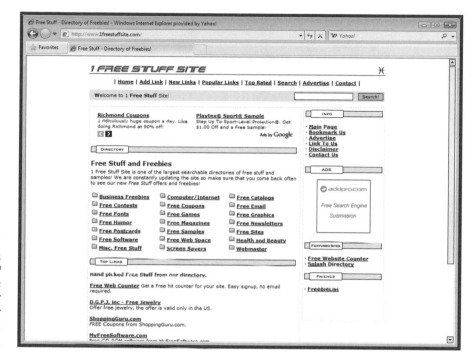

Figure 4.33

1 Free Stuff Site makes it easy for you to get your freebie listed in its directory.

Other Ideas for Attracting the Masses

Just in case you don't feel that you have enough ideas on your list to help your Web site attract more attention, here are a few more. These ideas are targeted at adding more content to your Web pages in order to encourage repeat traffic.

Providing a Tip of the Day

One idea that you can use to keep your visitors coming back over and over again is to create a Tip of the Day (or week). If your tips offer really useful information, your visitors will return to learn more. In addition, by offering tips, you position yourself as a subject matter expert on whatever topic you are covering. For example, the folks at WUGNET (**www.wugnet.com**) encourage repeat traffic by providing a computing tip of the day, as shown in Figure 4.34.

Figure 4.34

Adding a Tip of the Day to your Web site shows expertise and helps to build repeat traffic.

Of course, you'll need to set aside enough time and effort to really make your Tip of the Day worth coming back to. If you are willing to put forth the effort, your tips may help you build up a steady following.

Adding External Content to Your Web Pages

For whatever reason, people like to participate in short surveys or polls that cover topics of interest to them. For example, at **www.vote.com**, you will find a new political poll each day. People who are interested in politics and current events enjoy going to Vote.com just to express their opinions on a given survey question and to see how their opinions stack up with other people's opinions.

Your poll doesn't have to be very long. A single well-formed true/false or multiple choice question will do just fine. For example, take a look at Figure 4.35, which shows a typical poll posted each day on **www.foxnews.com**.

Figure 4.35

A good poll consists of one well-formed question that is of interest to your target audience.

If you want help in the formation and presentation of your polls, check out Free Online Surveys (**www.freeonlinesurveys.com**), as shown in Figure 4.36. Here you'll find everything you need to put a poll (for up to 50 respondents) on your Web site and to provide instant results. If the popularity of your poll rises, you'll be able to pay a fee and accommodate larger audiences.

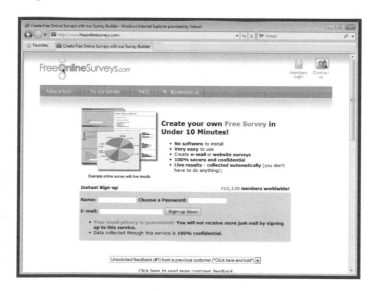

Figure 4.36

Free Online Surveys.com provides a service that you can use to set up and manage small polls.

Setting Up a Survey

Coming up with fresh content every day may represent more of an effort than you have time to commit to. If this is the case, then you should investigate opportunities for posting other people's content on your Web site. Newspapers have been doing this for years, with columns like Dear Abby and comics like the Family Circle. You can travel to any major city in the U.S. and pick up a newspaper and expect to find both of these resources.

Well, you can do the same thing on your Web site. For example, let's say that you want to add a little lighthearted humor. You could certainly sit down once a day and draw your own funny cartoon. But what do you do when you don't have the time or cannot come up with a funny new idea? The answer might be to sign up at Etoon.com (**www.etoon.com**) for the free daily cartoon service, as shown in Figure 4.37.

All you have to do to get up and running is fill in a form at **http://www.etoon.com/cartoon-store/free-cartoons.php**. You'll receive an e-mail with a little HTML to add to one of your Web pages, and you'll be ready to go.

Figure 4.37

Spice up your Web site by adding content that changes every day.

Generating Repeat Visits with a What's New Page

Sometimes people will return to your Web site after having been away for a while just to see what's new and different. However, if your main page has not changed since their last visit, these folks may assume that nothing else has changed and click on their browser's Back button, leaving as quickly as they arrived. One way of avoiding the loss of this type of visitor is to add and prominently display a link to a What's New page.

Your What's New page does not have to be anything too fancy. It could be something as simple as a short series of links to recently updated Web pages at your site along with a brief description of what has changed. The important thing is to let visitors know that you have new information and content for them to look at. You might also want to post dates beside each entry on your What's New page so that your visitors can quickly ascertain if anything has changed since their last visit.

Keep Your Visitors Informed with a Calendar of Events

Another great tool for generating return visits is to post a calendar on your Web site that informs your visitors of upcoming events. This way, they know that if they return in the future on a date specified, that something new will be waiting for them. This might be the release of a new product or a new set of Web pages covering a particular subject of interest. Regardless, the point is to give your visitors a reason for returning.

While you can certainly create and post your own calendar pages on your Web site, an easy way to do so with minimal effort is to look for and take advantage of free calendaring services. One such service is the online calendar service provided by Bravenet (**www.bravenet.com**), shown in Figure 4.38. This free service lets you create calendars with daily, weekly, or monthly views. It lets you post messages and, if you want, will also post entries representing major holidays. You can even set up calendars on which your visitors can post entries.

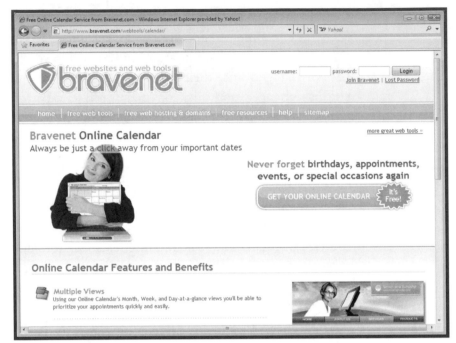

Figure 4.38

Singing up for a free calendar service provided by Bravenet.

To take advantage of the calendar service provided by Bravenet, you will need to sign up for a free Bravenet account and then fill out a simple form, specifying a calendar title and the URL to which your visitors should be directed when they click on the calendar's built-in Return to Home Page link. Once you have finished filling out the form, you'll be given some HTML statements to copy and paste onto one of your Web pages. Once created, you can customize the appearance of your calendar by adding graphics in order to make the calendar look like it is a part of your Web site.

Reward Loyal Visitors with a Members Only Area

As your Web site begins to catch on and gain a following, you will begin to get repeat visitors. One way to keep those visitors coming back is to create a members only area and restrict access to just those visitors who register or who meet certain criteria, such as spending a certain amount of money in a given month.

One way to set up a members only area is to password protect the main page for the area of your Web site that you want to restrict access to, and then assign passwords to visitors who register for access to the pages (via a form or by e-mail). Begin by checking with your Web host to see if a password protect service is provided as part of your service agreement. If one is not, then check out **www.bravenet.com/webtools/passwd**. This free service lets you password protect any Web page by embedding a little HTML that is provided to you. You have full control over the number of accounts that you want to be able to access your password-protected page. You can even view visitor statistics that show you who is accessing your page and how many times they have done so.

Setting Up Your Own Affiliate Program

One way to increase your Web traffic is to solicit others to help bring traffic to your site. You can do this by setting up your own affiliate program. Affiliate programs have been around on the Web since 1996 when Amazon.com started offering a commission-based sales program (see Figure 4.39).

Figure 4.39

Amazon.com runs one of the Web's oldest and most successful affiliate programs.

In addition to helping you sell your products or services, an affiliate program can help to strengthen your search engine ranking because of the links that each of your affiliates will place on their Web pages back to your site. There are many different types of affiliate programs out there. Some, like Amazon.com's, are commission based. Others, such as eBay, pay a flat fee whenever an affiliate brings in a new customer or a returning customer that makes a bid or purchase (see Figure 4.40).

Figure 4.40

Some affiliate programs, like eBay's, pay flat fees.

Other affiliate programs are click-through based, like Google's AdSense program (see Figure 4.41). In this program, Google displays text- and graphic-based content on affiliate Web pages that are deliberately matched up to provide complementary content to the subject covered on affiliate Web pages.

Figure 4.41

Google's AdSense
program pays
affiliates whenever
a visitor clicks on
the text or graphic
advertisement
placed on the
affiliate's Web
pages.

To create your own affiliate program, you will need to create a process for accepting and processing new affiliate applications, come up with eye-catching graphics and links, and develop a system for making payments based on results. To set up something like this from scratch can be a daunting task. Fortunately, there are a number of online affiliate program services that can help you get your affiliate program going. One such Web site is AffiliateShop (**www.affiliateshop.com**), shown in Figure 4.42. This service won't be free, though. At the time that the sixth edition of this book was written, AffiliateShop was charging a $45 monthly service fee. For this fee you get the HTML you need to add to your Web page, along with all kinds of other goodies, like ad tracking, support for an unlimited number of affiliates, and support for a tiered commission system.

Figure 4.42

AffiliateShop
provides a
complete set of
services to get your
affiliate program up
and running.

Sponsoring a Web Site Launch

No matter how long your Web site has been around, it's never too late to spruce it up a little bit and re-launch it. There's no better way to get the ball rolling than to host your own Web site launch. To make your launch successful, you need to spread the word. Not only this, but you need to coordinate your various Web site invitations/announcements so that they all take effect in plenty of time to notify everyone. This means getting your information posted on What's New? sites, updating your banners, sending out your newsletters, posting your invitations in newsgroups, updating your Facebook page, and getting your email campaign all going at the same time.

Your Web site launch shouldn't be too different from the types of launches that you see businesses and stores do all the time. For example, you might want to set up a contest or give something away to the first 10 people who register.

Once you've got everything all set up, don't rush through the experience. There is no reason why your grand opening can't last more than a day or two. In fact, you might want to run the event for a week or even a month.

Free Banner Advertising: No Joke

If you have browsed the Web, you have probably seen hundreds of banners. The banner is the most frequently used advertising method on the Web. A typical banner ad is placed at the top or bottom of a Web page so that it can catch the viewer's eye and possibly prompt the viewer to click on it. Most advertisers pay thousands of dollars to display a banner ad. Why pay thousands of dollars, though, when you can advertise for free? By becoming a member of a banner exchange, you can advertise at thousands of member Web sites without spending a dime—no joke.

What the Heck Is a Banner Exchange?

Ever since the first one sprang onto the scene in 1996, banner exchanges have spread like wildfire. Most banner exchanges have a broad focus that allows just about any type of banner advertising. There are also specialty banner exchanges that focus on specific communities of interest, such as travel Web sites.

You can think of a banner exchange as a cooperative advertising program in which participants work together to advertise each other's Web sites, products, or services using banner advertising. The amount of free advertising you receive is directly related to the amount of advertising you give to other participants.

Although cooperative advertising isn't exactly a new concept, it is definitely a breakthrough for anyone who wants to get his or her Web site noticed. Because most banner exchanges have a network of thousands of participants, you can use the exchange to promote your Web site, products, and services to a massive and extremely diverse audience.

How Do Banner Exchanges Work?

The wonderful thing about banner exchanges is that the exchange is responsible for managing the network. To accomplish this, most exchanges have a banner management system that tracks when and where banners are displayed throughout the network. Every time you display the banner of another member, you receive a credit. Based on these credits, the management system ensures that your banner is displayed at other sites in the network.

If you had to manually edit your Web pages to change banners, the banner exchange wouldn't be of much use. Fortunately, the banner management system is responsible for rotating the banners as well. To enable automatic banner rotation, exchange members are given a section of HTML code that allows the management system to dynamically update banners when the page is loaded. The code snippet also includes an account number that allows the management system to track where and when a banner is displayed and to give credit appropriately.

An added benefit of the banner exchange is the ability to track and view the performance statistics for your banner. Depending on the banner exchange, your performance statistics can range from up-to-the-minute accounting to weekly account summaries. Either way, the stats usually tell you how many times your banner was displayed as well as how many times someone clicked on your banner. Generally, you will need to visit the banner exchange to view the stats.

In Web lingo, the word *impression* describes the instances in which your banner is displayed. The number of times that someone clicks on your banner is called the *click through*. When you divide the total click through by the total impressions, you come up with a *click-through ratio*. Some banner exchanges use the click-through ratio to determine the effectiveness of your banner advertising.

To get a better understanding of click-through ratios, consider the following examples:

- Joe's home page displays a banner ad at the top of the page. Last week 5,000 people visited Joe's home page and 150 clicked on the banner ad. Joe's click-through ratio was 3% (150 / 5000 = .03).

- Ziggy's White Pages display banner ads at the top and bottom of every page. Last week 25,000 people visited the site and there were a total of 100,000 page views (with 200,000 total impressions). Banners were clicked on 5,000 times. Ziggy's click-through rate for all ads was 2.5% (5,000 / 200,000 = .025).

Exchanging Your Banner

Before you can participate in a banner exchange, you must become a member, which usually involves filling out detailed contact information on yourself, your Web site, and your business. You are also asked questions about the type of material you publish at your Web site and the types of sites that can be promoted at your site. Although most banner exchanges unanimously prohibit promoting explicit or offensive Web sites, a rating system usually is in place that covers everything from kids-only sites to sites for mature audiences.

The purpose of the rating system is to protect the interests of the exchange members. After all, if your Web site is for kids, you don't want someone to display a banner that is directed at adults. By the same token, you might not want to display advertising for kids at your adult-oriented Web site.

After you complete the membership process, you will be given a section of HTML code that you can add to any pages at your Web site. The purpose of this code is to display the banner advertising of other exchange members. Your unique account number for the exchange is a part of the HTML code. For this reason, you should copy the code that the exchange gives you and paste it directly into your Web pages without making any changes.

Because you receive a credit each time someone views a banner advertisement at your Web site, your first instinct might be to add the banner code to every page at your Web site. Instead, consider limiting your banner placement in well-visited areas of your Web site and primarily on top-level pages. You shouldn't inundate visitors with advertising or make them wait for banners to load on every page.

NOTE Banner exchanges have many checks and balances in place to ensure that the exchange system is fair. For example, exchanges typically prohibit the use of more than one banner from a single exchange on a single page. In most cases, however, nothing stops you from putting banners from other exchanges on a single page.

After you receive the banner code, the next step is to submit your banner to the exchange. Most exchanges have a form that you can use to submit your banner. Otherwise, you might have to send your banner to the exchange as an e-mail attachment.

Creating a Banner Advertisement

The banner exchange process starts with creating a banner to be displayed at other Web sites. Your banner doesn't have to be designed by a professional but should entice people to read it and click on it. Catchy graphics can attract the viewer's eye as much as the information. Including useful information is also key to a successful banner, especially when the file size of your banner is limited by the banner exchange.

TIP If you want to work with multiple banner exchanges, you should note the limits of file and image sizes for each. Then you should design your banner with these limits in mind. By resizing your banner to fit the requirements of each exchange, you can use the same banner repeatedly.

Selecting a Banner Exchange

No two banner exchanges are the same. When you select a banner exchange, you need to look past the gilded doorways that say you can promote your Web site for free. Instead, look into the heart of the exchange's management system.

Banner exchanges use what is called an *exchange ratio* to indicate the display-to-credit ratio offered by the exchange. The most common exchange ratio is 2 to 1. If an exchange has a 2 to 1 ratio, this means that for every two times that someone views a banner on your Web site, your banner will be displayed at a member site one time.

A quick check of the math tells you that, at an exchange ratio of 2 to 1, half of the impressions are going somewhere other than to banner exchange members. Here is where sponsorship comes into the picture. To make up for the costs of running the exchange, most banner exchanges sell the additional space to sponsors. With the average banner exchange racking up millions of impressions every day, a 2 to 1 exchange ratio has a pretty hefty profit margin.

Beyond the exchange ratio, you should look at the features of the exchange's banner management system. Everything that you do at an exchange should be handled through a password-protected account. Standard features of the account should be to view your current statistics, modify your account profile, and submit a banner. What's more, you should be able to access any of these features directly at the exchange's Web site, and the management system should handle updates automatically.

Some exchanges offer additional features, such as *targeting*. With targeting you can select the specific categories of Web sites that will display your banner and, often, the categories of banners displayed at your own Web site. In this way, your banner is seen only by audiences that you select, which includes audiences that are interested in products, services, or information similar to what you offer at your Web site.

Finally, you should look at the total membership of the exchange and the throughput of the exchange's Web connection. *Throughput* refers to the transfer rate between the server and the client computers. Together, the number of members and the throughput can suggest an average throughput, which in turn tells you how long your visitors will wait for banner ads to display. For example, a banner exchange with 25,000 member sites and a T1 connection to the Web is probably overloaded. As a result, visitors to your Web site might experience longer-than-normal delays while the banner loads.

Without getting into specific measurement criteria, one way to check the performance of a banner exchange is simply to visit pages of current members and see how long banners take to load. To get a solid assessment, you should check on several different days and at different times of day. Keep in mind that peak usage times are typically during the week and specifically at midday.

Banner Exchanges for the Masses

Now that you know the ins and outs of banner swapping, you are ready to take the next step and join the exchanges of your choice. To help you on your way, this section lists some of the most popular banner exchanges.

Exchanging Banners with LinkBuddies

LinkBuddies (**www.linkbuddies.com**) manages an exchange service consisting of more than 50,000 member sites (see Figure 4.43). It supports targeted advertising with over 150 categories. Although targeted advertising is one of the key reasons for the success of LinkBuddies, the exchange has many other features that make it a winner.

LinkBuddies offers a 2 to 1 exchange ratio to its members. When other member banners are not displayed, the exchange displays its own banner as well as the banners of paid sponsors. LinkBuddies provides detailed reporting, including hourly, daily, and monthly data.

Figure 4.43

LinkBuddies allows you to target ads to specific audiences.

Exchanging Banners with Exchange-it!

Exchange-it! (**www.exchange-it.com**) provides an effective banner exchange service with a 2 to 1 exchange ratio (see Figure 4.44). Exchange-it! lets you target your advertising by choosing from more than 300 different categories and provides daily and weekly banner advertisement statistics.

Other Banner Exchanges

LinkBuddies and Exchange-it! are just a couple of a growing number of banner exchange Web sites. A few other free banner exchange services that you might want to look into include:

- ☐ **NEObanners: www.neobanners.com**
- ☐ **Click4Click: www.click4click.com**
- ☐ **BuildTrafficX: www.buildtrafficx.com**
- ☐ **The Banner Exchange: www.thebannerexchange.net**

Figure 4.44

Exchange-it!
provides an easy-
to-use banner
exchange service.

Analyzing Off-Page Factors

The major search engines have had plenty of time to figure out various
ways of dealing with spamming techniques employed by less than scrupu-
lous Web site publishers. Part of the arsenal employed by search engines
is *off-page* ranking analysis.

What makes off-page factors attractive to search engines is that Web site
publishers have very little ability to manipulate them. One of the major
off-page factors is *link analysis*. Using link analysis, search engines gauge
a Web page's relevance by examining both the number of links to the Web
page and the quality of those links. Quality, in this context, refers to the
ranking of the Web pages that provide the links. The higher ranked a
Web page is, the higher the quality of its link.

Another off-page analysis tool employed by search engines is *click-through
analysis*. In click-through analysis, the search engine counts the number
of times that Web surfers click on a link when presented with it (com-
pared to links for competing Web sites).

Building a Strong Ranking through Links

Increasing the ranking of your Web page should be a major goal of your Web site promotion plans. One way to do this is to contact other Web sites and ask them to trade links with your Web site. To come up with a list of sites to contact, open up your Web browser, visit one of your preferred search engines, and then do a search using your keywords and keyword phrases. Make a list of the top Web sites that appear in the results.

Getting links from quality Web sites is one of the keys to improving your own Web site's ranking. So rather than trying to get every Tom, Dick, and Harry to trade links with you, focus on the top sites that show up in your search engine results. Since many of the sites that will appear in your search results may be direct competitors, they may not take you up on your offer to exchange links. However, if you are lucky, some Web sites will agree (in order to try and increase their own ranking).

Of course, just because you find other Web site owners who say that they will exchange links with you, that doesn't mean that they will hold up their end of the bargain. So, from time to time you will want to check on these Web sites and send an e-mail to their owners if you don't see a link to your Web site. Alternatively, you might want to check out Link Checker Pro (**www.link-checker-pro.com**). Link Checker Pro is a software program that you can download, install, and then configure to automate the process of checking on the status of all your reciprocal links.

Avoiding Link Farms

Be careful to make sure that in your enthusiasm to improve your Web page's rankings you don't get caught up in a *link farm* scam. A link farm is a large group of Web pages created for the sole purpose of trying to trick search engines into increasing the Web page's ranking. While it is perfectly legitimate to exchange links with other Web sites (which is one of the basic principles that makes the Web work), it is not at all proper to set up Web pages just so you can establish links with them to your real Web site.

Increasing Your Traffic with Web Rings

One of the problems with looking for information on the Web by performing keyword searches using search engines is that the results usually include superfluous and unrelated links. You must sift through any superfluous results to get to the Web sites that actually contain the type of information that is being looked for.

Directories offer an alternative to search engines. One particular and popular type of directory that more and more Web surfers are turning to is *Web rings*. A Web ring is a free service that organizes related Web sites into groups based on common subject matter.

What makes Web rings popular is that, once a site in the ring is found that contains the type of information a Web surfer likes, there is a really good chance that the rest of the Web sites in the ring will also be exactly what the Web surfer is looking for.

How Do Web Rings Work?

Web rings are organized into major categories, each of which contains any number of subcategories. Drill down far enough, and you will find individual Web rings. Each Web ring is started by an individual owner. It is up to the owner to accept or reject requests by Web site owners to join the Web ring. Each Web site in the Web ring contains navigational controls for moving around in the ring, as demonstrated in Figure 4.45.

A central Web ring server controls Web ring navigation. This server prevents dead ends from breaking the ring by automatically forwarding a Web surfer on to the next available Web site in a ring.

Working with the Major Web Rings

There are currently two major Web rings:

- **WebRing: http://dir.webring.com/rw**
- **RingSurf: www.ringsurf.com**

Figure 4.45

Each Web site has navigational controls for moving forward and backward in the ring and for randomly accessing Web sites in the ring.

RingSurf and WebRing are both 100% free. To join a ring, you just sign up with the hosting Web ring service and fill out a request form. If the Web ring owner approves, you will be sent a little HTML along with instructions on what to do with it. If you don't see a ring that covers your topic, you can start up your own ring. However, you'll have to find four other Web sites to join your ring before the hosting Web ring services will add your Web ring to its directory listings.

Post Company Job Openings on Your Web Site

If the Web site that you are promoting belongs to a company, you can increase Web traffic by posting job openings on your Web site. Nothing gets people's attention like the prospect of finding a good-paying job. Once people interested in your line of work learn that your Web site includes job postings, they will keep coming back week after week looking for the perfect job. Better yet, they'll share your Web site with their friends and co-workers. Even if your visitors never find a job with you, they may turn into your best customers and provide you with all kinds of viral marketing referrals.

Short on Time? Try Paid Inclusion

If you are in a hurry to get your Web site noticed and don't have 4 to 6 weeks to wait for the major search engines and directories to get you listed, you can always spend a few dollars and go with paid inclusion services. Every major search engine accepts some sort of paid listing. This means that within 1 to 2 days, your Web site could start appearing in the top results for a search that uses your specified keywords.

Locating Sponsored Links

Google and other search engines like Yahoo! and Ask typically display paid links at the top of the screen and along the right-hand side of their search results, as demonstrated in Figure 4.46. To identify them even further, paid results appearing at the top of the screen are usually displayed with a different background color, whereas paid results on the right-hand side of the screen are separated from the rest of the results by a vertical bar. In addition, both areas usually display a label like "Sponsored Links," "Sponsor Results," or something similar.

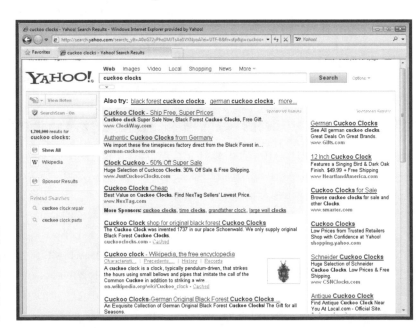

Figure 4.46

Search engines use various techniques to help make their paid listings stand out.

Google AdWords

Google administers its paid listings through its AdWords program (**adwords.google.com**). Paid listings will also appear on some of the sites that retrieve results from Google, including AOL and Ask. This program charges customers a per-click fee, meaning that you only have to pay when somebody actually clicks on your paid link (as opposed to simply seeing it). As of the time that the sixth edition of the book was written, there is a one-time $5 activation fee, and you are required to pay a maximum 10-cent per-click fee. For $50, you ought to be able to get a good 4 to 6 weeks' worth of advertising.

TIP   By the end of this 4 to 6 week period, your free search engine and directory listings should start to appear, and you might then want to stop paying for this service.

Yahoo! Search Marketing

While Google AdWords represents the biggest bang for your advertising dollars, Yahoo! provides an attractive second choice. Yahoo! refers to a paid inclusion as a *sponsored search*. You can sign up for Yahoo!'s program at **advertisingcentral.yahoo.com/smallbusiness/ysm**. Yahoo! requires a $30 initial deposit and there is no monthly spending requirement. Again, just as with Google's AdWords program, you only pay when someone actually clicks on your paid links. And you can count on your listing appearing in the search results of other search engines. For example, in the case of Yahoo!, you could expect to see your listing appear in AltaVista.

Other Paid Inclusion Programs

While Google and Yahoo! may be the two most popular paid inclusion programs, there are plenty of other good programs out there that can help you reach an even larger audience.

These search engines include:

- **Bing: advertising.microsoft.com/home**
- **Ask: sponsoredlistings.ask.com**
- **AOL: advertising.aol.com**

You will find plenty of other paid advertising opportunities with other search engines. In addition, the major metasearch engines also accept paid listings.

Keep 'Em Coming Back

Have you ever visited a Web site that contained some incredibly useful or entertaining content, only to realize a few days later that you have no idea how to get back? Perhaps you can't remember the full URL or the Web site's name. Surely, this is something that has happened to everybody a time or two.

Given that every major Web browser has a bookmarking capability, there is no reason why anyone should ever lose track of an important Web site. Still, it happens all the time, and it is not always the Web surfer's fault. Much of the time this predicament could be averted if only the Web site owner would place a friendly reminder on his or her Web page. This reminder need not be complex; it could be something as simple as a well-placed piece of text that says, "Bookmark this page." Figure 4.47 demonstrates the application of this simple strategy at ComputerHope.com (**www.computerhope.com/startp.htm**).

Wrapping Up and Looking Ahead

Now that you know how to attract the masses to your Web site, it is time to take a look at who's visiting your Web site and how you can improve it, which is exactly what you'll learn in the next session. The first step to understanding your site's visitors is to examine your Web site's statistics.

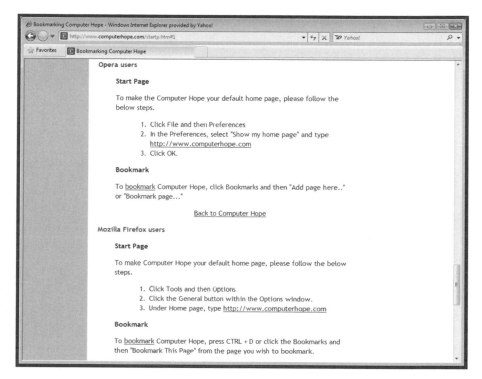

Figure 4.47

Don't just hope
your visitors will
bookmark your
Web pages—ask
them to do it.

Web site statistics provide just about everything you need to determine
who is visiting your site and why. Once you know who's visiting and why
they're visiting, don't forget to keep the pages and links at your site up to
date. Every visitor counts, especially when you are trying to increase
traffic to your Web site. You need to do everything within your power to
build a steady readership. To attract and maintain an audience over the
long haul, you need to maintain your site and provide visitors with lifelines when you move or delete files.

Discovering Who's Visiting Your Web Site and Why

- ➤ Capturing and Analyzing Web Site Statistics
- ➤ Locating Problems with Your Web Site
- ➤ Using Web Site Statistics to Improve Your Web Site
- ➤ Reviewing Your Progress

Your Web site's statistics are the single most important means for discovering what people really think about your Web site, and you might be surprised when you discover which of your resources are bringing in visitors, and which resources aren't. If you're tempted to pay only cursory attention to this section, ask yourself this: What do I really know about the flow of traffic to my Web site? How do I know which pages are drawing visitors and which ones are being skipped? If you make assumptions about your visitors that the stats don't support, then your lack of awareness could cost you dearly.

So settle in with a good cup of coffee or some juice to keep you alert—it's Sunday afternoon and time to roll. By the end of the afternoon, you'll know how to find out who is visiting your site and why. You'll also know how to use your Web site's statistics to begin increasing your Web traffic.

Using Web Stats to Understand Your Site's Visitors

Web site stats tell you much more than which pages at your Web site interest visitors. By tracking stats, you also learn many things about the people who visit your Web site, such as how long they visit, whether they really read the pages that you present or just skip on by, what days of the week are the most popular, what time of day is the best time to make updates, and a whole lot of other things.

For example, Web site statistics typically reveal:

☐ How many people are visiting your Web site each day, week, and month.

☐ The type and versions of browsers being used by your visitors so that you can determine which types of technologies are best deployed.

☐ The IP address of each visitor, allowing you to discover where they come from.

☐ The time and date of each visit, allowing you to determine the best time for making changes to your Web pages.

☐ The keywords visitors are using to locate your Web site so that you can fine-tune your keywords and keyword phrases.

You need to know who is being drawn to your Web site so that you can keep them coming back for more and attract others like them. You need to know about errors and other circumstances that could make your site an obstacle course, which could prevent visitors from coming or staying. You need to get your hands on some useful information so that you can make informed decisions.

Traditional retailers have been tracking information about their customers for a long time, using the information they gather to customize their marketing and advertising plans. Likewise, online retailers and Web sites do their best to track customer habits and to learn as much as possible about the likes and dislikes of the Web surfers who visit their sites. Take Amazon.com for example. Amazon.com places a great deal of emphasis on learning everything it can about each customer's likes and dislikes. By tracking individual habits, Amazon.com is able to create customized Web pages that it thinks each customer will find helpful. Amazon.com displays these custom pages as shown in Figure 5.1.

Jerry's Amazon.com

Figure 5.1

Amazon.com puts a lot of work into tracking customer activities in order to fine-tune its Web site and marketing plans.

As Figure 5.1 shows, Amazon.com has created a customized page to present merchandise that Amazon.com thinks may be of interest to Jerry based on the information that has been collected on him. By tracking visitor activity, Amazon.com is able to fine-tune the way it runs its Web site in order to make it more successful. Similarly, you can begin collecting and tracking user activity on your Web site. One way to do this is by asking visitors to tell you something about themselves when they fill out forms or send you e-mails in order to sign up for your contests, newsletters, sweepstakes, and so on. Web site statistics can be just as valuable to you when it comes to learning more about your visitors. Best of all, Web site statistics allow you to collect data without depending on your visitors to take the time to provide it to you. By collecting and analyzing Web site stats, you empower yourself with information that you can use to make your Web site a better place to visit. This effort will remove your site from the ranks of hit-or-miss Web sites and give it the stamp of professionalism.

Options for Collecting Web Site Statistics

When it comes to collecting and analyzing Web site statistics, you have two options: software based and on demand. With the software-based option, you install an application on your Web server and use it to process the contents of your Web server log files. With the on-demand option, you sign up with a Web-based service that collects and presents your Web traffic data. Perhaps the best, and certainly the most popular, on-demand option is Google Analytics (**www.google.com/analytics**). Which of these two options you decide to go with will depend on a number of different factors.

NOTE Of course, depending on the service provider you are using, your options when it comes to installing custom software may be limited. If your service provider is too restrictive, the on-demand option is probably going to work best for you.

The software-based option works best when you want total control over your Web site's data. This option is viable when you have a talented IT staff capable of running the software. This option requires that you purchase a copy of the software, which involves a one-time cost. With this option, you will also have to make sure that your Web server is capable of accommodating the overhead of running the additional software. Otherwise, you may need to upgrade or replace your Web server.

TIP If you are paying an ISP to host your Web site, you may find that the ISP has already purchased and installed Web site analysis software on the Web server, in which case you may be able to use it for a small additional fee.

On the other hand, if you are comfortable with allowing a third party to collect and process your Web statistics, you may want to go with an on-demand service, especially if you don't have available in-house IT staff to do the job. While this option avoids a potentially hefty one-time cost, it typically requires a monthly service fee. An exception to this is Google Analytics, which is 100-percent free. Google Analytics is also different from many other on-demand service offerings in that it is focused on Web marketers as opposed to Webmasters.

Whether you choose Google Analytics or one of the other on-demand services discussed in this chapter, the primary advantage of on-demand Web monitoring it that it allows you to get up and running almost immediately.

As you will see in the sections that follow, there are plenty of software programs that you can use to analyze your Web server's log files. There is no shortage of on-demand Web services either. In addition to software and on-demand services that perform specialized tasks, there are also companies that have developed versions of their Web site analysis tool that you can either purchase as a stand-alone software program or sign up and use as an on-demand Web service. Two of the best are Webtrends (**www.webtrends.com/Products/Analytics**), as shown in Figure 5.2, and Unica NetInsight (**www.unica.com/products/enterprise-web-analytics.htm**), as shown in Figure 5.3.

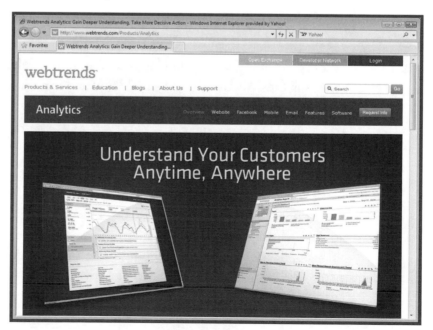

Figure 5.2

Webtrends provides advanced log analysis features that you can use to get a detailed picture of who is visiting your Web site.

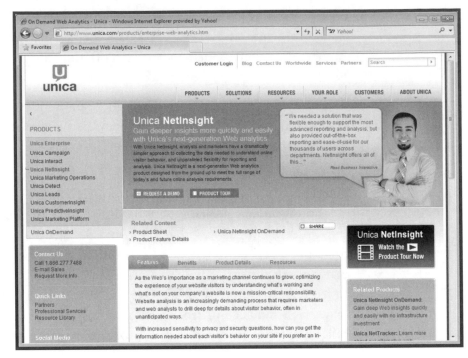

Figure 5.3

Unica NetInsight is a world-class application capable of providing any level of log analysis.

Selecting Your Web Traffic Analysis Tool

Before continuing, you should install a Web traffic analyzer and locate your server log files. Alternately, you should find and register with an on-demand Web service that will collect and present your Web statistics to you.

If you choose to install Web site traffic analysis software on your Web server, you will need to start by getting your hands on the software. In addition to the Web site traffic analysis applications just discussed, you may want to review the list of software presented in the book's Appendix, "Additional Resources on the Web." Here you will find information about a number of other Web site traffic analysis applications. If any of these applications suit your fancy, pick one and then download and install a free trial copy. Then, if after taking a test run you find you like it, purchase a licensed copy.

The list of Web site traffic analysis applications that you will find in the appendix includes:

- ☑ **FastStats**
- ☑ **MozillaTracker**
- ☑ **Surfstats**

If you choose instead to sign up with an on-demand Web service that will collect your Web stats for you, you will have to follow their instructions to set up your pages so that the service can begin collecting your data. In addition to the on-demand Web services just discussed, you may also want to check out these additional online services:

- ☑ **Web Stats Gold: www.webstatsgold.com**
- ☑ **Web-Stat: www.web-stat.com**

The sections that follow provide essential details for making sense of the reports that you'll be able to generate and also provide high-level instruction on how to use the information found on these reports to understand and improve your Web site.

Web Site Stats Are a Necessary Evil

Yes, Web stats truly are a necessary evil. Everyone hates the thought of statistics. However, if you don't track the status of your Web site, you will never truly understand who is visiting and, more importantly, why. The following list shows a few more reasons why you should take the time to track your Web site's stats:

- ☑ To discover popular and unpopular resources.
- ☑ To learn more about the people who visit your site.
- ☑ To learn more about the effectiveness of your banner advertising.
- ☑ To obtain information on search engine usage and referring sites.
- ☑ To determine which browsers and platforms people use when visiting your site.

Before you start having flashbacks of high-school algebra class, you should know that tracking and analyzing Web site stats isn't rocket science. As a matter of fact, tracking and analyzing stats is fairly easy as long as you follow the advice presented in this afternoon's session.

NOTE   If you decide to go with the option of processing your own log files located on your Web server, you'll need to know where they are stored. The location of the Web server log files is defined when a server is installed. The best way to find these files is to ask your service provider or the Webmaster they are stored.

Keep in mind that if you have your own domain, such as **www.yourname.com**, you should have separate log files regardless of whether you actually have your own server or you use someone else's server. If the same server handles multiple domains, the logs probably have a prefix that indicates the domain. Otherwise, you—like anyone using a service provider—will share server logs with everyone else using the server.

Regardless of whether you analyze your own Web site's log files or use an on-demand Web service to collect and process your stats, you can expect to get the same basic information. The following sections provide you with an overview of the types of data and reports that you can expect and provides you with insight on how to analyze this data in order to make improvements to your Web site.

Discovering Popular and Unpopular Resources

By tracking and analyzing stats, you can discover which of the pages at your Web site are visited most often. Although you might think that your top-level home page is the most popular, this isn't always the case. In fact, your analysis might reveal that most people visit some other page at your Web site. This is because the Web allows anyone to visit any page at your Web site, and visitors don't have to start at your home page.

One report that you will want to generate is one that tracks popular Web pages. Depending on which Web traffic analysis tool you use, the name of this report will vary. You should look for a report named something like Most Requested Pages or Most Popular Pages.

Another report that you might want to look for is one that depicts how much traffic each major area of your Web site receives, as shown in Figure 5.4. Using a report like this, you can determine which area of your Web site needs additional attention versus which pages you may wish to further exploit by using viral and permission marketing techniques.

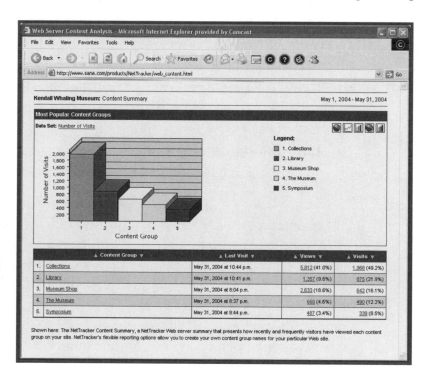

Figure 5.4

Examining a Content Summary report to see which areas within a Web site are being visited most often.

You might also be interested in generating reports that show which Web pages are visited most often and which Web pages receive the least attention. These reports might be called something like the Most Requested Pages and Least Requested Pages reports.

Other types of reports that can tell you about the popularity of your Web pages include:

- **Most Accessed Directories**: Identifies which directories were most frequently accessed. This report is useful when you want to identify popular areas of your Web site.

- **Most Downloaded File Types**: Identifies the most popular type of downloaded file.

- **Most Downloaded Files**: Identifies the executable or document files that are most frequently downloaded.

- **Top Entry Pages**: Identifies which pages were most frequently the first page requested at the site. You can use this report to better understand why people visit your site.

- **Top Exit Pages**: Identifies which pages were most frequently the last page requested at the site. You can use this report to help understand why users leave your site.

- **Top Paths through the Site**: Identifies paths users most frequently take through the site. You can use this report to better understand how users navigate pages at your site.

The main purpose of generating all of these different types of reports is to gain an insight as to how people are visiting your Web site. Using the information presented in these reports, you can determine what content your visitors appreciate most and try to provide more of it. You can also find out which pages your visitors are just skimming through and try to improve them in order to give your visitors a reason to slow down and look around. Finally, by looking for common exit points in your Web site, you can focus your efforts on trying to find ways to redirect your visitors back to other parts of your Web site and increase your overall level of stickiness.

Learn More about the People Who Visit Your Site

By tracking your Web site's stats, you also can learn more about the people who visit, such as where they live, where they work, and how they access your Web site. One of the best ways to learn more about your Web site is to track visitor demographics. For example, you can expect to find reports that identify which countries your visitors are coming from.

Depending on which Web traffic analysis tool you use, you may also find that there are other types of demographic information you might be able to track, such as:

- User profiles by region
- The U.S. state or Canadian province from which users most frequently visit
- The organizations your visitors are most frequently from, such as whether they are from government, military, education, or commercial organizations
- Whether a particular visitor is a new user or is returning for a subsequent visit
- Session information for top users
- The number of visits per user

Find Out When People Visit

Finding out when people visit your Web site is extremely useful, especially if you use this information to plan updates for your Web pages. As Figure 5.5 shows, you can use stats to determine the activity level at your Web site throughout the week. For example, you might discover that Friday is your busiest day of the week in terms of the number of times your pages receive hits or the amount of data that is transferred. At the same time, you might determine that Sunday is the slowest day of the week.

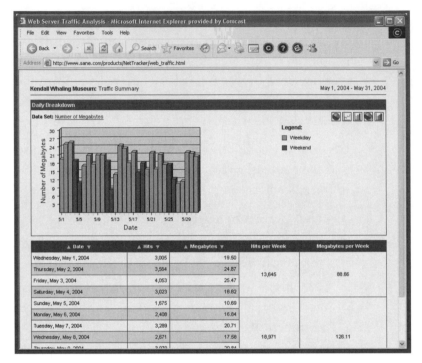

Figure 5.5

Traffic summary
reports can be used
to determine which
days of the week
are the busiest
and which are
the slowest.

Using this information, you could better determine when to post updates
to your Web site and when not to post updates. For example, assuming
that Friday was your busiest day, you might want to post updates on
Sunday in order to provide your biggest audience with the most up-to-
date information.

Other types of activity reports that you might want to look for include:

- **Bandwidth Usage**: Shows the volume of activity according to the
  amount of data transferred.

- **Activity Level by Hour of Day**: Shows the busiest hours of the
  day.

- **Activity Level by Time Interval**: Summarizes activity by week or
  month.

Learn More about On-line Advertising

These days most Web sites have banner ads, and your site is probably no exception. Yet do you know if the banner exchange you are using is telling you the truth about click-through rates? Well, your Web site stats can tell you exactly how many people are viewing banner ads on your site and how many people are clicking on those ads.

Normally, you'll need to tell your analysis software about the specific campaigns you are running. For example, you might have the following three ongoing ad campaigns running:

- ☑ Apple Laptop Giveaway Ad
- ☑ Dell Laptop Giveaway Ad
- ☑ Sony Laptop Giveaway Ad

Assuming that these ad campaigns are linked to specific banners, each time a particular banner ad is displayed or clicked on, information would be recorded. Again, depending on which Web traffic analysis tool you are working with, reports will be named differently. Regardless, you should be able to find reports based on banner ads viewed and banner ads clicked. You should also be able to analyze data showing the ratio of ad views to ad clicks (e.g., the click-through rate).

You can use this valuable information to determine which of your advertising efforts is the most successful and which efforts are not working out. You can then use it to help you make the best use of your limited time, effort, and dollars. As an example, check out Figure 5.6, which shows an example of a Campaign Summary report.

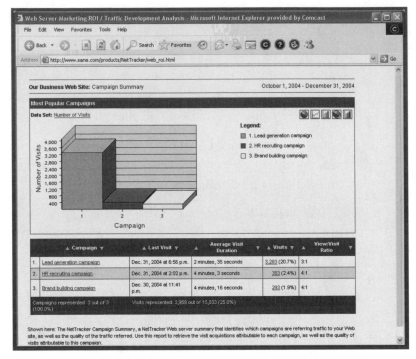

Figure 5.6

By tracking your sales campaigns, you can learn how to best spend your time, effort, and money.

Obtaining Information about Referring Sites, Search Engines, and More

The analysis of your Web site statistics can tell you exactly how users got to your Web site. A key report you'll want to obtain is a Referrer report (or Referring Site report). The report tells you how visitors find their way to your site. This report will show you the search engines and directories from which most of your visitors are coming. In addition, you may see an entry for No Referrer, which indentifies the number of visitors who enter your Web site by directly entering the URL of one of your Web pages into their browser.

The referrer information can also be used to obtain information on which search engines are used to find your Web site. This information will provide you with a list of the top search engines being used as well as the keywords or keyword phrases entered as search parameters.

Determining the Browsers and Platforms Being Used

Often, Web sites are designed with specific types of users in mind. These users probably fit a specific demographic or geographic target, and you've probably made some assumptions as to how tech-savvy these users are as well. For example, in your design guidelines, you might have stipulated that the Web site is designed for users with the newest generation of browsers. You might have even taken this a step further by saying that the Web site was designed for users with the most modern browsers and Windows-based operating systems. To validate the technology assumptions that you've made, or to help establish future guidelines, you'll want to track browser and platform usage.

Most Web site tracking software provides reports for tracking browsers by type and version. A Browser by Type report will tell you the types of browsers being used but won't necessarily tell you the browser versions being used. This information is typically provided in a Browser by Version report.

Zeroing In on Visits

Perhaps the *visit* is the most meaningful Web site statistic. A visit is a collection of hits and page views that pertain to a specific person who requests files from your Web site. When you count visits, you are counting the number of people who stopped by your Web site.

NOTE A *hit* is a term that represents a file access. If a Web page contains five graphics, then six hits would be registered. That's one hit for each graphic that is loaded and one hit for the Web page itself. A *page view* is a representation of a Web page that is accessed. By tracking page views you can determine which pages are visited most and which receive the least amount of visits.

Putting Visits Together

Just as there's a big difference between someone shopping at your store 1 time and 50 times, so there is a big difference between someone visiting a Web site 1 time and 50 times. You need to limit the scope of visits to a specific time period, such as all consecutive file requests that are separated by no more than 30 minutes. Following this, you would say that if a person browsed your site for 5 minutes one day and 15 minutes the next day, you'd have two visits. On the other hand, if a person browsed your site for 10 minutes, went away, and then came back 15 minutes later, you'd have a single visit.

Tracking Visits

Tracking software counts visits by limiting the scope of visits to specific time frames. When you track individual visits, you are mostly interested in the summary information, such as:

- ☑ How long did the person visit?
- ☑ What page did the person start on?
- ☑ What areas did the person visit?
- ☑ How long did the person stay in each area?
- ☑ What was the total number of hits for this visitor?
- ☑ What was the total number of page views for this visitor?

For example, let's look at a scenario in which a Web site has had three visits. A summary of the first visit is outlined here:

```
Minimum length of visit:

    12 minutes, 4 seconds

Start page:

    /

Main pages visited and duration:

    /   - 2 minutes 10 seconds

    vpjic.html  - 1 minute, 36 seconds

    vpepc.html  - 5 minutes, 28 seconds
```

```
            joboppframes.html  - 2 minutes, 50 seconds
Total hits:
      97
Total page views:
      27
```

The summary for the second visit is outlined here:

```
Minimum length of visit:
      5 minutes, 40 seconds
Start page:
      /idn/cissue/resmul.htm
Main pages visited and duration:
      /idn/cissue/resmul.htm  - 37 seconds
      idnfp.htm  - 5 minutes 3 seconds
      /idn/bio/biorev.html   - unknown duration
Total hits:
      13
Total page views:
      3
```

The summary for the third visit is outlined here:

```
Minimum length of visit:
      5 minutes, 25 seconds
Start page:
      /idn/cissue/resmul.htm
Main pages visited and duration:
      /idn/cissue/resmul.htm  - 5 minutes 25 seconds
      idnfp.htm  - unknown duration
Total hits:
      5
Total page views:
      2
```

Getting the Big Picture

The big picture takes into account all visits to the Web site during a specific period of time, such as the 15-minute time slice. When you put together the big picture, you must ask yourself many important questions. The answers to these questions will help you understand who is visiting your Web site and why. The main questions that you will want to ask include:

- What was the total number of visitors for this time period?
- What was the length of the average visit?
- What was the average duration of a page view?
- What was the average number of page views per visitor?
- What was the average number of hits per visitor?
- What domain classes and geographic areas are represented?

When you examine your Web site over a period of days or weeks, you will want to ask these additional questions:

- What are the busiest hours of the day?
- What are the busiest days of the week?
- What are the most requested pages?
- What are the most common last pages requested?

To put this in perspective, let's go back to the three visits summarized previously and create the big picture. When you answer the main questions, you come up with stats that look like this:

```
Visitor count:
    3
Duration of analysis:
    15 minutes
Length of the average visit:
    7 minutes, 3 seconds
Average duration of page views per visitor:
    10.67
```

```
Average number of hits per visitor:
     38.3
Domain classes and geographic areas:
     50% Net
     50% Com
```

With these stats in hand, you can now answer the all-important questions concerning who is visiting and why. The list that follows provides descriptions that can help you make sense out of the stats discussed so far. Keep in mind that these are generalities meant to get you started thinking about how you can use these stats to promote your Web site and to make your Web site a better place to visit.

- **Visitor count**: Tells you how many people are visiting. You can use this to gauge the true popularity of your Web site. Whereas a new or low-traffic Web site might get 5 to 100 visitors a day, a popular Web site might get 5,000 to 10,000 visitors a day.

- **Length of the average visit**: This is an indicator of whether people are really reading pages at your Web site or just browsing. It can also be an indicator of whether people like what they see. The longer the average visit, the more information the visitor is finding and reading.

- **Average duration of page view**: This can be an indicator of whether people are reading or just browsing. When you examine this statistic, you also need to keep in mind the length and style of pages that you have at your Web site. Are they highly textual, highly graphical, or both?

- **Average number of views per visitor**: Generally, the more pages people view, the happier they are; and if people are viewing many pages at your Web site, they are finding information that interests them.

- **Average number of hits per visitor**: Over time, you can use this information to estimate the number of visitors.

- ▣ **Domain classes and geographic areas**: This can tell you where people visiting your Web site live and work, which is great information to have if you want to attract advertisers.

- ▣ **Busiest hours of the day**: Tells you the time of day when most people visit your Web site. This statistic can help you plan daily updates, promotion campaigns, and advertising.

- ▣ **Busiest days of the week**: Tells you the day of the week when most people visit your Web site. This statistic can also help you plan weekly updates, promotional campaigns, and advertising.

- ▣ **Most requested pages**: Tells you the pages that visitors find most interesting and/or useful. Can be used to tailor your Web site to visitors' needs and to help you determine which pages should receive most of your attention.

- ▣ **Most commonly requested last pages**: Can help you spot trends and bad pages. If the last page requested has lots of links to external Web sites, this statistic tells you that this is the point from which most visitors are leaving. If the last page requested doesn't have links to external Web sites, you might want to examine the page in question.

You'll find that Web site traffic analyzers can put together all the reports you'll need for the big picture. Once such report is the Visitor Profile Summary report (see Figure 5.7), which focuses on showing which areas of a Web site are visited, the average length of a visit, the number of visits, and the number of repeat visits.

Take a Break

If you haven't created traffic reports for your Web site, you should do so now. Once you generate the reports, ask yourself the questions previously pointed out. The next part of this session covers how to gain visitors who otherwise would have been lost because of bad links at your site or bad references from other sites. But before you dive in, take a break! You deserve it. Grab yourself a cup of coffee or tea.

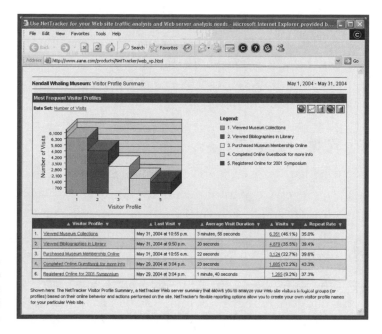

Figure 5.7

Examining a
summary profile
of visitor activity.

Gaining Lost Readers from Error Analysis

After pouring time and resources into your Web site, do you really want
to risk losing people who visit your Web site but don't get to where they
expected? Not really, especially when every visitor is someone who could
help spread the news about your terrific Web site. Don't lose visitors once
they've found a doorway into your slice of cyberspace. Nothing stops
would-be visitors dead in their tracks like an error. They see errors as
brick walls and often race off as quickly as they can click on the mouse.
How many times have you seen the dreaded 404 File Not Found error
message? Did you hang around the Web site that you tried to access, or
did you just click on your browser's Back button and head off in some
other direction?

Errors are often the result of bad links in your Web pages or bad references to your pages from other Web sites. When it comes to finding and
fixing bad links, you have total control and can easily track down the

problems—if you know how. When it comes to bad references to the pages at your Web site, you might think that finding and fixing these problems is beyond your control. However, nothing could be further from the truth. You can fix errors regardless of their source, and you're about to find out how.

Errors: We All Hate Them

We all hate errors, yet we've grown so accustomed to them that they seem like an everyday part of the quest to browse the Web. Stop and think for a moment about your reaction when you encounter a File Not Found error. Your reaction, be it restrained contempt or outright indignation, is mirrored thousands of times every day around the world.

After your initial outrage passes, what is your next reaction? You probably click on your browser's Back button to return to the site that sent you to the wrong address. Or perhaps you enter a new URL into your browser and head off into another direction. Web surfers are seldom persistent enough to puzzle through the error to figure out another way to get at the information using the bad URL. As a result, just about every time your server displays an error, you lose a visitor—maybe forever.

When you are trying to increase traffic at your Web site, the last thing you want to do is lose visitors. Thus one of the keys to increasing and maintaining traffic to your Web site is to reduce errors and help visitors find their way, which is exactly what you're about to learn.

There are three major trouble spots that can cause you to lose potential visitors forever. They are:

- Missing files
- Lost connections
- Server time-outs

All of these trouble spots can be identified and tracked by your Web site traffic analysis tool.

Missing Files

The most common errors are those that relate to files the server can't find. Bad links are a key reason for the File Not Found error. When you create a Web page, you add hypertext links that relate to pages at your Web site as well as other Web sites. Although all your links might work perfectly when you first create your Web site, things change over time. You update your Web pages. You move your pages to different locations. You combine some pages. You delete other pages.

Unfortunately, every time that you move or delete Web pages, you might unwittingly start an avalanche of errors. A visitor who bookmarked one of the Web pages that you moved or deleted can't get to the Web page anymore. Another visitor who created a page showing links to her favorite Web sites now has an invalid link pointing to your Web site. Worse, the search engines with which you registered haven't reindexed your Web site; now hundreds of people who look for resources like yours can't find your pages anymore.

How Can You Fix the Problems?

Use your Web site analysis tool to generate a Page Not Found report. You can then use the report to help you find trouble spots at your Web site. Start by printing the report. Next, compare the file names in the report to the actual files on your Web site. If you find a file that is in the report and available on your Web site, use your browser to retrieve the file from your Web server. Be sure to use the same URL that the user entered. If the file loads without problems, there was probably an intermittent problem with the user's Internet connection, which doesn't necessarily mean that anything is wrong on your Web site. Cross that file off the list and move on to the next one.

If the file doesn't load in your browser, check the file name. Does the file name on the server exactly match the URL you entered? Most servers are case-sensitive, meaning that the mixture of uppercase and lowercase letters must match exactly. When you find a naming problem, you have a bad reference in one of your Web pages that you need to fix. The easiest way to find the problem page—and possibly other pages that contain the bad reference—is to search your Web directories for the bad reference.

For example, a bad reference to a Web page called welcome.htm that should have been referenced as welcome.html could be fixed as follows:

- Change to the directory containing your Web pages. If you have multiple document directories, examine each in turn.
- Search for references to the file name welcome.htm.
- Record the list of file names containing the bad reference.
- Edit the files and correct the bad references.

If you don't have a naming problem, you might have a permission problem. On most Web servers, the directory and the file must have specific permission before visitors can access your files. Generally, the directory needs to be executable, and the file needs to have read access. If you don't know how to check or set file permissions, ask your Internet service provider.

Next, highlight all the files that don't relate to Web pages of other document files, such as references to image files. Most likely, the highlighted list of files points to broken references in your Web pages. Fix these references either by updating the related page or by moving the file to where it is supposed to be.

Now that you've narrowed the list a bit, look for URLs that belong to files that you've moved or deleted. When you find a reference to a file that you moved, jot down the new name of the file. When you find a reference to a file that you deleted, make a note to yourself that the file was deleted.

Because users are looking for these files and you want to build—rather than lose—readership, you will want to redirect these lost visitors to the new location of the resource. Alternatively, you can create a placeholder document with the old URL, telling visitors that the resource is no longer available and then redirecting them to another area of your Web site. The job of the placeholder page would be to direct lost visitors to the resource for which they were looking. This redirection could be done simply by providing instructions explaining that things have changed and providing the visitor with the correct URL. Alternatively, although it involves some pitfalls, you could consider automating the redirection process. For details on how to redirect users to new locations, see the upcoming section titled "Redirecting Lost Readers."

Although the remaining files on your list should pertain to true errors on the part of the user or someone else, you don't want to discard the list just yet. Take a look one more time and ask yourself whether any patterns exist. For example, you might find that a number of visitors are consistently mistyping the name of one of your Web pages. If you think there is a chance that the spelling of your page's name is confusing to some of your visitors, change it.

Lost Connections

Lost connections are often the result of impatient visitors not wanting to wait for your page, its graphics, and other multimedia files to finish loading. Consequently, if you find a page that has lots of lost connections related to it, you might want to change the page so that it either loads more quickly or follows sound design techniques that allow the visitor to use or peruse the page before it finishes loading.

If you have pages with lots of text, graphics, or multimedia, you might want to periodically check for lost connections. To do this, create a Lost Connection report using your Web site traffic analysis tool. For example, Figure 5.8 shows a Page Delivery Summary report, which lists, among other things, information about the number of aborted requests for various Web pages.

Unfortunately, sometimes the connection is lost after the server completely transfers the file but before the client completely processes the data. In this case, you might not be able to determine the cause of the error and should just move on to the next item on the list.

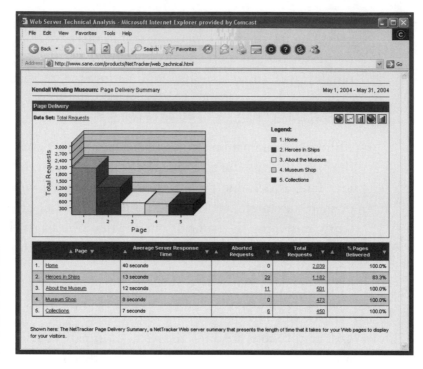

Figure 5.8

Keep an eye on the number of aborted requests. They may indicate technical problems at your Web site.

Time-Outs

Although time-outs are rather rare on Web servers, this section would be incomplete without at least mentioning how to spot them. A time-out is sort of like the server getting impatient with the client and wanting to move on. You probably won't see time-outs unless you have large multimedia or compressed files that are retrieved using the standard Web file transfer protocol, HTTP.

The first step in dealing with time-outs is to generate a Client Error report. If you see time-outs frequently for the same file, you might want to tell your Internet service provider about the problem. Although the service provider should be able to set the time-out ratio higher, the service provider might also tell you that the byte site for the offending files is unreasonably large. In the latter case, you might want to break the large file down into several smaller parts.

Improve Your Web Site with Visitor Feedback

In order to keep visitors coming back to your Web site, it is important that you determine what your visitors think about your Web site and its products and services. There are a number of different ways that you can go about collecting this information, including:

- Blogs
- Guestbooks
- Message forums
- E-mail forms

Setting Up Your Own Blog

As already discussed, a *blog* is an online Web log that allows the blog owner to share her thoughts on a particular subject. Blogs can display text, graphics, and links to other Web pages. Blogs can also be used to collect visitor feedback. There are many different ways to go about setting up your own blog. Your Web service provider may provide you with access to a blogging service. If you have a MySpace account, then you already have a blog. Many other types of social networking sites are also eager to provide you with your own blog. All you have to do is pick one and begin posting to it.

If you have not started your social media optimization campaign yet and don't have a blog, all hope is not lost. You can set up a new blog for free at **www.bravenet.com/webtools/journal/,** as shown in Figure 5.9. This service lets you create a new blog just by answering a few questions. You can specify a title for your blog, select a design theme, and specify whether you want to be notified by e-mail whenever someone posts a comment on your blog.

Figure 5.9

A blog lets you share your thoughts, opinions, and expertise on a subject and solicit visitor comments.

Setting Up a Guestbook

A *guestbook* is a logging system that lets visitors leave comments on what they think about your Web site, products, and services. Guestbooks allow you to display information about visitors, including information about where in the world they are from. Your Web service provider may provide you with access to a guestbook service. If not, you can set up a guestbook using a third-party provider. For example, you can sign up for one such service at **www.bravenet.com/webtools/guestbook/,** as shown in Figure 5.10.

To set up a guestbook using Bravenet's guestbook service, all you have to do is specify a title, pick a theme, and then copy and paste the HTML code that is provided into a page on your Web site. You can even specify whether you want to prevent guestbook messages from being displayed until after you have reviewed and approved them.

Figure 5.10

A guestbook allows you to collect visitor comments and determine where they come from.

Setting Up a Message Forum

A *message forum* is a service that facilitates an online discussion between you and the people that visit your Web site. Your Web service provider may provide you with access to a message forum service. If not, you can set up a message forum using a third-party provider. For example, you can sign up for one such service at **www.bravenet.com/webtools/forum/**, as shown in Figure 5.11.

Bravenet's message forum service lets you select a title and a theme, and then provides you with the HTML code that you can copy and paste onto a page on your Web site. You can even specify whether you want to be notified by e-mail when message postings are made.

Figure 5.11

A message forum provides a medium for you and your Web site visitors to engage in an online conversation.

Collecting and Posting Positive Visitor Feedback

Another way of collecting visitor input that you can use to improve your Web site, products, and services is to employ an e-mail form that allows visitors to send you their thoughts and feedback. Using this feedback, you can continue to tweak and improve your Web site to encourage repeat visits.

One easy way to set up e-mail forms is to take advantage of Bravenet's e-mail forms service (**www.bravenet.com/webtools/emailfwd/**), as shown in Figure 5.12.

Bravenet's e-mail forms service lets you select from predefined forms that specialize in collecting visitor feedback, contest entry, and survey information. Alternatively, you can elect to create your own form from scratch. Once you have designed a form that suits your needs, you can implement your form by copying and pasting the HTML code that is provided onto a page on your Web site.

Figure 5.12

E-mail forms let you collect specific information from your Web site visitors.

Redirecting Lost Readers

As you learned earlier, every time you move or delete a Web page, you can start an avalanche of errors. Anyone who has bookmarked the page that you moved or removed will get an error. Anyone who has created a link to the page from his or her own Web site will be unwittingly directing people to a dead end. Anyone who uses a search engine to find resources might also get a retrieval containing references to the pages that you've moved or removed.

The result is that lots of people who otherwise would have visited your wonderful niche of cyberspace get lost. They hit the proverbial brick wall and run off in some other direction. And they might never return. When a user gets all the way to your Web site through the maze of cyberspace, do you really want to risk losing that user because of something that you can fix?

To remedy this situation, you should create a placeholder document. The key to a placeholder document is that it takes the place of a Web page or other document that you moved or deleted, and then redirects the user to a different location at your Web site. If you have a list of documents that you've moved or deleted, why not create a few placeholder documents right now? Every visitor counts.

TIP The way to avoid brick walls and placeholder documents altogether is to plan out your Web site before your build it. The simplest planning rule is to give each area of your Web site its own directory to start with, and to make the default document for this directory the home page for the area. Unfortunately, in the real world, most Web publishers don't like to plan things out before they dive in, which means they should use placeholder documents to help direct traffic whenever necessary.

Redirection Basics

The technique you use to redirect visitors can be as simple as the one shown in Figure 5.13. Here, you tell visitors that the resource has been moved or deleted. Next, you provide them with the URL of the new resource or an escape route to another location at your Web site. The source for the redirection page is shown in Listing 5.1.

Listing 5.1   *Redirecting the User*

```
<html>


   <head>

     <title>William's Bio and FAQ Pages Have Moved</title>

   </head>


   <body >

     <div align=center>
```

```
<h1>Thanks for visiting!</h1>
<h2>The resource you are looking for has moved to a new home.</h2>
<h2>You will find William's Bio and FAQ at
   <a href="http://www.tvpress.com/writing/">
     http://www.tvpress.com/writing/
   </a>
 </h2>
</div>
</body>

</html>
```

Figure 5.13

A simple but highly effective redirection technique.

When you redirect visitors as shown in Listing 5.1, you come as close as possible to ensuring that 100 percent of your misdirected visitors have the ability to find their way back to your Web page. This technique should work regardless of what type of Web browser visitors may use. This is important because more and more often, visitors may show up at your doorstep using game consoles like the Wii and Playstation 3 and portable wireless hand-held devices like smartphones.

More Redirection Techniques

One problem with the previous redirection solution is that it requires visitors to click on an extra link on their way to your Web pages. For some visitors, this extra effort is enough to drive them away. Another option available for redirecting lost visitors is to automate the redirection process using *client pull* technologies. With client pull, you insert an instruction in the Web page that tells the visitor's browser to retrieve a different Web page. This way, the visitors can get to your Web page without having to make an extra click.

When it comes to client pull technologies, your choices are somewhat limited. Your primary options are the META Refresh tag or a client-side scripting language, such as JavaScript. Unfortunately, as you are about to learn, both of these options have their issues.

The META Refresh Tag

Previous editions of this book taught readers about using the META Refresh tag as an effective means of redirecting lost visitors. However, a lot has changed on the Web in recent years, making this option a questionable choice.

The META Refresh tag is placed in the head section of an HTML page. You use the `http-equiv` attribute of the `<meta>` tag to tell the browser that you want to refresh the browser window. You use the `content` attribute of the `<meta>` tag to tell the browser two things: how long to wait and what document to load.

An example of the `<meta>` tag is:

```
<meta http-equiv="refresh" content="2 url=http://www.tvpress.com/
writing/">
```

Here, the `http-equiv` attribute is assigned the keyword `refresh`, which tells the browser that you want to prepare to refresh the current window. The `content` attribute has two parts separated by a semicolon and a space. The `2` tells the browser to wait 2 seconds before refreshing the browser window. The next part of the `content` attribute tells the browser the URL of the page that you want to load into the refreshed window. The URL must have the full path specified, including `http://`.

Figure 5.14 shows an example of a page that redirects the visitor to a new location at a Web site. As you can see, the page displays an information message explaining what will happen. Just in case the user's browser doesn't support the technology, the appropriate links are placed on the page as well. The markup for the sample page is shown in Listing 5.2.

Figure 5.14

Although this looks similar to the previous redirection technique, the auto-redirect will take the visitor to the new location automatically.

Listing 5.2   *Automating the Redirection Process*

```html
<html>


  <head>

    <title>William's Bio and FAQ Pages Have Moved</title>

    <meta http-equiv="refresh" content="2;
url=http://www.tvpress.com/writing/">

  </head>


  <body>

    <div align=center>

      <h1>Thanks for visiting!</h1>

      <h2>The resource you are looking for has moved to a new
home.</h2>

      <h3>Your browser will automatically be redirected in 10 seconds
to:</h3>

      <a href="http://www.tvpress.com/writing/">

        http://www.tvpress.com/writing/

      </a>

    </div>

  </body>


</html>
```

Unfortunately, this seemingly innocent use of the META Refresh tag can end up getting you into trouble. The reason for this is that some less-than-scrupulous Web site publishers have used a variation of this redirection technique, referred to as *doorway pages*, to try and spam search engines. They do this by creating a number of simple Web pages that are exact copies of one another, except that each Web page is overloaded with a specific keyword phrase and designed to achieve high keyword relevance for a specific search engine.

In many cases, the keyword phrase for which each page has been optimized may have little if anything to do with the content of the Web sites that these Web pages are redirecting visitors to. For example, one of these Web pages may be designed to attract Web servers doing a search on rock music while another is designed to match up against a search for science fiction. Spamming occurs when all these Web pages redirect the Web surfer to a site that has nothing to do with these keyword phrases, as might be the case if the Web site where surfers are being sent was an online discount shop.

Because of misuses like this, many search engines now consider any use of the META Refresh tag as spam. As a result, if you employ this redirection technique in your Web pages, you run the risk of your pages being lowered in rank or even being removed from the search engine's database.

Scripted Client-Side Redirection

A safer option for automatically redirecting Web pages is to use a Web scripting language, such as JavaScript. Currently, none of the major search engines open or inspect the content of externally referenced files. To avoid any possible misinterpretation of your code as being spam, you can place your JavaScript code in an external file and call the external JavaScript from within your Web page. For example, Listing 5.3 shows an example of how to set up a Web page to use an external JavaScript to control Web page redirection.

Listing 5.3   A JavaScript Redirection Example

```html
<html>

  <head>

    <title>William's Bio and FAQ Pages Have Moved</title>

    <script language="JavaScript" src="TestRedirect.js"></script>

  </head>
```

```
<body>

  <div align=center>

    <h1>Thanks for visiting!</h1>

    <h2>The resource you are looking for has moved to a new
home.</h2>

    <h2>You will find William's Bio and FAQ at

      <a href="http://www.tvpress.com/writing/">

        http://www.tvpress.com/writing/

      </a>

    </h2>

  </div>

</body>


</html>
```

Highlighted in bold is a JavaScript statement that tells browsers to open and execute an external JavaScript file named `TestRedirect.js`, which is located in the same directory as was the Web page. The code that resides in this external JavaScript file consists of a single statement as shown here:

```
location.href("http://www.tvpress.com/writing/")
```

This statement loads the specified Web page into the browser, while still leaving an entry for the original URL listed in the browser's history file. The net effect is that the Web surfer should automatically be redirected to the appropriate Web page. However, in the event that the Web surfer's browser does not support JavaScript or has its JavaScript support disabled, the Web surfer will still be able to find his or her way to your Web pages by clicking on the URL link that will be displayed.

Redirection Using Your Web Server

Although these client-side redirection techniques work well, more and more Web servers are starting to support automatic redirection. With automatic server-side redirection, the Web server takes over and maps the old URL to the new one, which makes the redirection completely transparent to the visitor. For example, you could tell the Web server to map all requests for **www.tvpress.com/fun/** to **www.tvpress.com/summer/**.

Most commercial Web servers support URL redirection. You'll find, for example, that Microsoft IIS makes this task fairly easy to accomplish. However, you'll need access to the Web server's administrative tools, which you might not have if you use a service provider.

No More 404 File Not Found Errors

The typical errors servers report are meaningless to most people, and even the people who know what the status codes mean probably would much rather have a helpful pointer than an error that says 404 File Not Found. Fortunately, there are ways to fix it so that the nondescriptive and meaningless errors reported by servers go the way of the dinosaur.

When the Web server software was installed, the technician who set up the server defined specific parameters that told the server how to report errors and which error documents to display. Because the default error documents are rarely replaced, chances are good that visitors to your Web site see the standard non-descript error messages.

You can confirm this by entering an invalid URL that refers to your Web site, such as:

http://www.myserver.com/nothingatall.html

For example, take a look at Figure 5.15, which shows how the 404 File Not Found error is typically displayed. As you can see, it's not particularly friendly or helpful to lost Web surfers.

If your server reports a vague error message, don't worry; this can be changed by defining new error documents. On most servers, regardless of operating system, you can define the documents to retrieve when an error occurs. For example, with Microsoft IIS, you can tell the server the name and location of the page you want to load when a certain error occurs.

With the thought of eliminating forever the dreaded 404 File Not Found error, take a chance and talk to the head technician or Webmaster who works for your Internet service provider. The question to ask is, "Can you help me set up unique error documents for my domain, or, at the very least, is it possible to create some informative error messages for everyone

Figure 5.15

A generic 404 File Not Found error message.

who uses the Web server?" For example, take a look at Figure 5.16, which shows how the folks at **www.oracle.com** have enhanced their 404 File Not Found Error message. The new message not only apologizes to visitors, but it also provides navigation that gives their would-be visitors alternative paths into the Web site.

Taking Advantage of Free URL Analyzers

Of course, the best possible way to handle a 404 File Not Found error is to correct it. To do this you must know where the errors are occurring. One way to make this determination is to visit each of your Web pages and to test the validity of each link by clicking on it. If your Web site is fairly small, this shouldn't be a problem. But if your Web site has grown to more than a handful of Web pages, this exercise can quickly become tiresome.

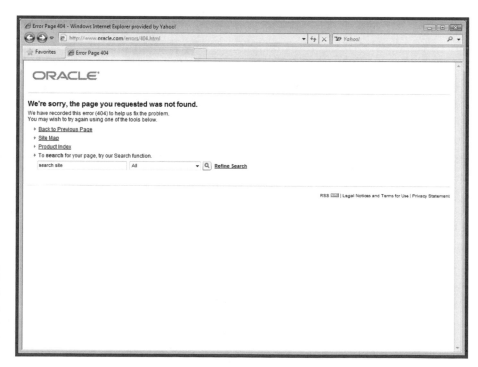

Figure 5.16

The Oracle Web site provides its visitors with alternative navigation links and a Search field.

So the question is, "Are there free tools available on the Internet to help automate this task?" The answer, as you no doubt now expect, is yes. For starters, check out Link Valet (**www.htmlhelp.com/tools/valet**), as shown in Figure 5.17. Link Valet begins by spidering your Web site. Once it is done, it can present its findings in either a summary or a full report. In addition to reporting on your 404 File Not Found errors, it will also point out any links that are being redirected.

Another validation option that you may want to consider is REL Link Checker Lite, which is available as a freeware application that you can download from **www.relsoftware.com/rlc/** and install on your computer, as shown in Figure 5.18.

REL Link Checker Lite is designed to spider Web sites that contain 1,000 or fewer links. If your Web site contains more links than this, you might want to look into trying a free trial of Web Link Validator (available at **www.relsoftware.com/wlv/**).

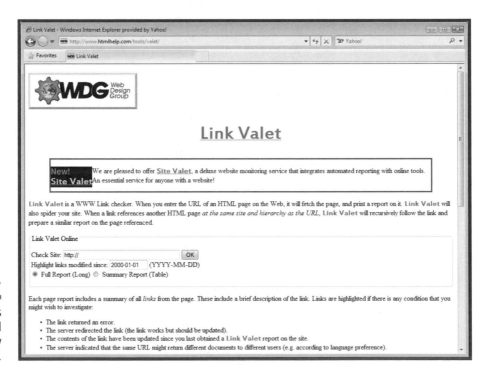

Figure 5.17

Link Valet reports on link errors and will also identify any redirect links.

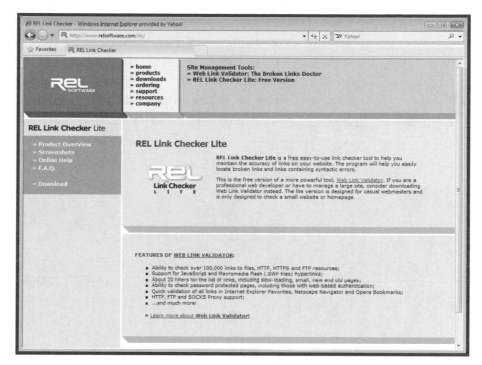

Figure 5.18

LinkValet reports on link errors and will also identify any redirect links.

A Few Last Words on Errors

Errors arc showstoppers. Don't let your visitors think that your Web site is gone. Every visitor counts, especially when you are trying to increase traffic to your site. But the reason for fixing trouble spots goes well beyond preventing the loss of wayward visitors. To attract and maintain an audience over the long haul, you need to maintain your site and provide visitors with lifelines when you move or delete files.

Finally You Know What to Do—So What's Next?

Right about now, you are probably wondering why this book keeps saying that you can use the Web site reports to make your Web site a better place to visit as well as to increase your Web traffic. After all, the title of the book is *Increase Your Web Traffic In a Weekend* not *Make Your Web Site a Better Place to Visit.*

The simple truth is that the long-term success of your Web site is based upon understanding your Web site's good points and bad points. By understanding your site's good points, you learn how to market your Web site to the world. By understanding your Web site's bad points, you learn what you need to do to fix any problems. If you don't fix the problems at your Web site, you might lose visitors just as fast as you find new ones.

The following steps will make your Web site a better place to visit:

- Direct users to popular areas
- Clean up unused pages
- Avoid dead-ends
- Fix errors

After you take a close look at your Web site, you can move on to the next step, which is to find your niche in cyberspace and formulate a plan that uses your niche to market your Web site to the world.

Web Site Analyzers

Now, given that you have most likely made all sorts of modifications to your Web pages, this might also be a good time to take a few minutes to get a third party's opinion on the overall construction of your Web pages. There are any number of Web sites that provide Web page analysis. For example, there is the Web Page Analyzer (**www.websiteoptimization.com/services/analyze/**), shown in Figure 5.19.

The Web Page Analyzer will evaluate your Web page's size, composition, and download time. To use this free service, enter your URL and click on the Submit Query button.

Directing Users to Popular Areas

Every road sign you can add to the Web makes cyberspace just a little bit more enjoyable, so why not create a few road signs that direct visitors to popular areas at your Web site? Your road signs don't need to be extravagant. You can use plain-old text to create links to other pages at your Web site.

Figure 5.19

The Web Page Analyzer provides an extensive analysis of your Web pages.

Obviously, you don't want to tell visitors about every single Web page you've published. Instead, you want to direct visitors to the popular areas of your Web site by creating links to the top-level page within the specific areas you want to promote. The idea here is that people visiting your sports information page, for example, might also be interested in your sports equipment page. However, they can't get to the sports equipment page if you don't tell them it exists.

Say that your Web site's statistics show that seven pages at the Web site get the most traffic. The URLs for the hypothetical pages are:

- **http://www.verycooldays.com/**—Your main home page.
- **http://www.verycooldays.com/summer/**—A page that promotes summertime activities.
- **http://www.verycooldays.com/summer/water-skiing.html**—A page within the summertime activities area that covers water-skiing.

- **http://www.verycooldays.com/surfing.html**—A page within the summertime activities area that covers surfing.
- **http://www.verycooldays.com/equipment/**—A page that discusses where you can look on the Web to get the best bargains in sports equipment.
- **http://www.verycooldays.com/equipment/forsale.html**—A page that lets people post ads to sell their sports equipment.
- **http://www.verycooldays.com/equipment/tips.html**—A page that provides tips for getting the best value for your money when you buy sports equipment.

When you examine the seven most visited pages, you might see that three specific areas of the Web site are getting the most traffic:

- The main home page
- The summertime activities area
- The sports equipment area

The home page is the place to toot your horn about the main areas at your Web site, but you also need to do so on all of the top-level pages within the Web site. Although you might think that most visitors start on the site's home page, this isn't always true. In fact, most people probably start their visit on some other page. For this reason, you should tell anyone visiting the summertime activities area that you have this wonderful sports equipment area, and vice versa.

By promoting both areas, you increase page views at your site and let visitors know that your site really does have a lot to offer. On the Web page at **http://www.verycooldays.com/summer/**, you could add a clear road sign that directs visitors to the sports equipment area, such as:

```
Sports Equipment

    *   Find the best bargains on the Web

    *   Get money-saving tips

    *   Post your own for sale ad
```

Then, on the Web page at **http://www.verycooldays.com/equipment/**, you add another road sign that directs visitors to the summertime activities area. The markup for the road sign is as follows:

```
Fun in the Sun

Interested in summer-time sports like scuba diving,

water skiing, and surfing? Why not stop by

our Fun in the Sun headquarters?
```

Cleaning Up Unused Pages

After studying your Web site to see how you can direct traffic to popular areas, you should take a hard look at pages that rarely get visitors. Although your first impulse might be to delete these pages or stop updating these pages, this might not be the right solution. Rather than remove or neglect these pages, you should ensure that other pages at your Web site have clear road signs that tell people what these pages are all about. You might also want to consider combining the information on this page with information on another page.

Say that your site's stats show that two pages at the Web site rarely receive visitors. The URLs for these pages are:

- **http://www.verycooldays.com/summer/background.html**— A background page for the summertime activities area.

- **http://www.verycooldays.com/summer/scuba/deepwater.html**— A page that promotes deep-water scuba driving.

After examining the background page, you might discover that you can summarize the information and place it on the top-level Web page for the summertime activities area. In this way, visitors to this area of the Web site get a quick summary without having to visit the background page. By adding the information to the top-level Web page, you make the area a better place to visit.

Next, you look at the page that promotes deep-water scuba diving. Your scuba diving pages are divided into three categories: fresh water, salt water, and deep water. Although the fresh-water and salt-water scuba pages attract lots of visitors, the deep-water page is rarely visited. The problem here might be organization; perhaps your top-level page needs to explain that deep water refers to deep-sea scuba diving with submersibles and that you also feature video from a Galapagos undersea expedition.

Avoiding Dead Ends

Dead ends are showstoppers. All your Web pages should end with links that lead back to a main page, the previous page, or the next page in a series of pages. Links at the bottom of a Web page are subtle reminders that the Web site has more to offer. By adding links to the bottom of your Web pages, you make navigating your Web site easier, thereby helping to retain your Web traffic. Remember, if Web surfers visit your sports-related Web site, they are interested in sports; why not help them find the information they are looking for?

Links at the bottom of a Web page can be as basic as

```
Back to Fun in the Sun
```

Or you can use mini-menus that tell visitors about other areas of your Web site, such as

```
Our Home Page  |  Fun in the Sun  |  Sports Equipment
```

Another form of dead end is a page that causes the visitor to lose interest in your Web site. For example, a page full of errors or inconsistencies might make visitors think the rest of your Web site isn't worth visiting. For this reason, you might want to look for pages that are often the last page people visit and see if they need updating.

Understanding Your Niche

After you use a Web site analyzer to track your site's stats, you should have a better understanding of what attracts visitors to your Web site. Understanding your niche and using it to your advantage are the keys to success when you try to promote your Web site to the world. By taking the time to learn exactly why people visit your Web site, you save yourself a barrel full of heartaches.

Before they started tracking their stats, the creators of **www.verycooldays. com** thought that the underwater video sequences they published online were the main events at their Web site. As it turned out, the Web pages covering deep-sea scuba diving were the least visited. Although you could say that the problem was poor organization, it turns out that the Web site had lots of other things to offer visitors.

Although the creators of the Web site started out building a resource for scuba divers, they ended up with a Web site that covered many different water sports, including water skiing and surfing. They also created a wonderful guide to buying sports equipment online. Looking back, they saw their niche covered two different areas:

- Resources for anyone who loved water sports
- Resources for buying and selling sports equipment online

Unfortunately, the site's banners and logos promoted the site as "a great place for anyone who loves scuba diving." Worse, the developers of the site used this same slogan whenever they had an opportunity to promote the Web site. When they registered with search engines, they hyped their great scuba-diving center and forgot the other areas. When they traded links with other sites, they asked the other Web site publishers to be sure to tell people about the site's scuba-diving resources. Even though they did indeed attract visitors who were interested in scuba diving, they missed out on many other opportunities to increase the traffic to other areas of their Web site.

As you can see, the creators of **www.verycooldays.com** should have taken the time to put together a better picture of their Web site before they started promoting their site only as a great place for anyone who loves scuba diving.

A better description of their Web site would have been this:

> A terrific site for anyone who loves water sports! We have tons of resources covering scuba diving, water skiing, surfing, and many other water sports. We also have a great guide to sites that sell sports equipment. Our buying tips might save you a bundle.

The creators of **www.verycooldays.com** could also create separate descriptions for each popular area at the Web site. This would allow them to promote the Web site as a whole and each area separately. For example, the next time they register with a search engine, they could use the combined description and then register each area separately as well.

Before you continue, create descriptive blurbs for your Web site. Start by identifying the most popular areas, then use the subjects that these cover to come up with a brief description that identifies your Web site's niche. Afterward, create separate descriptions for each popular area at your Web site.

Reviewing Your Progress and Planning More for Next Weekend

Wow, the weekend is over already! Hopefully, after reading the sessions and following along, you have a great start on the long-term improvement of your Web site's traffic.

What Have You Done This Weekend?

The first step to putting the motion in promotion is to register your Web site in all the right places. Because search engines are the primary means of getting your site noticed, this book offered you an extensive look at how search engines work and how you can optimize your Web pages for indexing. Although there are hundreds of search engines, it is not practical or worthwhile to submit your Web site to every single one of them. Instead, make the most of your time and resources by registering with the major search engines.

But registering with the major search engines is only the beginning of the promotion process. Next you need to look at Web directories. Just as there are hundreds of search engines, there are hundreds of Web directories as well. As with search engines, you should focus your efforts on the major Web directories. Afterward, you should look to business search engines and Yellow Pages directories. These business-oriented search and directory sites are great places to tout your products, services, and commercial Web site.

Because you also want your Web site to be accessible to people for specific types of information, the next step is to register with industry- and category-specific directories. Beyond these directories, you'll find specialty directories. Whether your site covers home decorating or famous poets, there are specialty directories that will want your listing.

Awards can make all the difference in the world when it comes to increasing traffic to your Web site. Not just any old award will do, though. The best awards are those that are long lasting and meaningful. Still, when all is said and done, the popularity of the award site is the most important factor in determining whether the award will help increase the level of traffic at your Web site. The busier the award site, the better the chances that the site's award will increase traffic to your Web site.

Social networking should play a key role in your Web marketing plan. Web sites like Facebook and MySpace can help you to develop new contacts. Sites like YouTube and Flickr can be used to further garner attention. Social Networking sites are among the most popular places on the Internet. By investing a little time and effort participating in social communities, you can drive high-quality traffic back to your Web site.

One way to spread the word quickly about your Web site is through a registration service that allows you to register with multiple search engines and directories. Although registration services are useful for registering multiple URLs with directories, you get the most out of your Web site's listing by registering your site with individual search engines and directories.

In the final parts of the book, you saw many additional ways to increase your Web traffic, such as e-mail and freebies. Believe it or not, e-mail is a terrific way to promote your Web site. When you promote your Web site through e-mail, you can use the direct, person-to-person method as well as newsgroups and mailing lists. Beyond e-mail, you can steal the thunder of traditional marketers by using giveaways, contests, and sweepstakes. Because everyone loves the chance to win something for nothing, freebies can truly bring the masses to your Web site.

You also learned different ways to compete in the big leagues with banner advertising. The banner is the most heavily used advertising method on the Web. Although most advertisers pay thousands of dollars to display a banner ad, you can advertise through a banner exchange network without spending a dime.

You want visitors to remain at your site, and you want them to return. These are two of the biggest reasons not only to promote your Web site, but also to improve it. After people have found the doorway into your slice of cyberspace, you want to give them every reason to stay. Nothing stops visitors dead in their tracks like an error. Errors are often the result of bad links in your Web pages or bad references to your Web pages from other Web sites. Using Web traffic analyzers you can fix errors regardless of their source.

After you gather stats for your Web site and know who is visiting your site and why, the next step is to put the stats to work. Not only can you use the stats to make your Web site a better place to visit, you can use them to find your niche in the wonderful world of cyberspace. Enhancing your Web site based on what the stats tell you and using your site's niche to your advantage are key ingredients that will help you attract the masses.

Keeping Up with the Latest Web Promotion Techniques

The Web is in a constant state of change. In order to stay on top of things, it is important that you stay up to date with the latest developments.

One way of doing this is to keep an eye on what is being discussed in different Web page marketing forums. One such forum is the IM4Newbies Internet Marketing Forum (**www.im4newbies.com/forum/**) as shown in Figure 5.20.

Another forum that you might want to keep an eye on is Digital Point located at **forums.digitalpoint.com**. Here you will find postings on topics relating to Web site promotion.

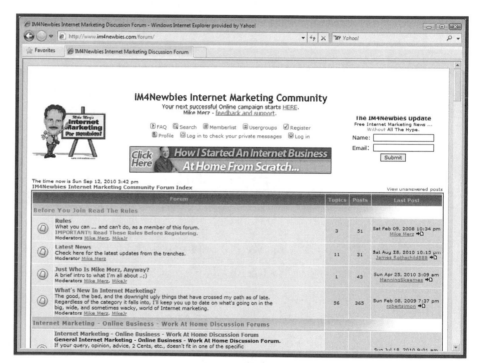

Figure 5.20

Review the discussions occurring at the IM4Newbies Internet Marketing Forum.

Keeping an Eye on Your Competition

Checking out your competition is another indispensable source of information that you can use to help fine-tune your Web site promotion efforts and better meet the needs of your visitors. This means regularly visiting their Web sites and observing what they are doing right and doing wrong.

You want to make sure that your Web site is and remains more interesting, more useful, and more popular than your competitors' sites.

If your competition makes use of message forums and guestbooks, be sure to keep an eye on the feedback they are getting from their visitors and use that to determine what changes you might need to make to your own Web site. The bottom line here is to remain ever diligent in your efforts to ensure that your Web site is the best of its kind. This will keep visitors coming back and will ensure that when new visitors arrive at your Web site what they find is not just a lot of hype.

A Final Note

Just because you've reached the end of this book doesn't mean that your promotion efforts should end. Next weekend, if you have some time, go back and revisit any sessions or topics in the book that you might not have explored as much as you'd like.

After you take another look at the session, use the main topics in this book to outline a long-term promotion plan. Your plan should focus on the items that you will need to periodically address, such as:

- Tracking Web site stats (weekly or monthly)
- Looking for problem areas at your Web site (weekly or monthly)
- Updating your listings in directories if you move the furniture around (only as necessary)
- Resubmitting your site for awards (wait two or three months between submissions)
- Participating in mailing lists and newsgroups (daily or weekly)
- Updating your ad banner (monthly)

That's it. Have some fun this evening. On the other hand, if you're enjoying this creative brainstorming, you might want to keep at it for a while.

Additional Resources on the Web

Throughout the weekend, as you worked your way through this book, you have been introduced to online services and software products that you can use to help increase the traffic coming to your Web site. This appendix provides you with additional information about a number of other software applications that you might want to check out. To help organize this material, the information presented is broken down into the following categories:

- **Site Management Programs.** Applications that can help you manage your Web site more effectively.

- **Site Submission.** Applications that can assist you in getting your Web sites registered with the major search engines and directories.

- **Web Authoring.** Applications that can help you develop your Web pages in a search engine friendly manner.

- **Connectivity.** Applications that can help you make sure you don't lose Web traffic due to problems with slow downloads or poor communications.

For each software application that is covered, you will find information regarding its functionality. You'll also find a description of its purpose, information on whether you can download and try the application as shareware or freeware, and a high-level overview of specific product features.

Site Management Programs

In this section, you are introduced to a number of software applications that you can use to help you manage your Web site effectively.

AccuTagger

Developer Site: http://www.cyberspacehq.com

Product Page: http://www.cyberspacehq.com/products/Accutagger/home.shtm

Product Description: AccuTagger is designed to assist you with the creation and management of your Web page's <META> tags. It helps in the generation of numerous <META> tags, including the Description and Keywords tags.

Distribution: Free Trial Available.

Major features include:

☑ Automated Web page analysis

☑ Built-in spell checking

☑ Best guess <META> tag generation

☑ Automated report generation

FastStats

Developer Site: http://www.mach5.com

Product Page: http://www.mach5.com/products/analyzer/index.php

Product Description: Use FastStats to collect Web site management information from your Web server log files, such as the number of hits your Web site gets each day, the search engines your visitors are using, and the keywords that visitors used to find your Web site. Data can be presented in table or graphic formats. FastStats can also be used to track down bad links and to check on Web server performance.

Distribution: Free 30-day trial.

Major features include:

- ▣ Detailed reporting to assist Web site publishers in analyzing the cost effectiveness of their advertising

- ▣ A graphic hyperlink tree depiction of how visitors move through your Web site

- ▣ Over a dozen reports that measure site sickiness

MozillaTracker

Developer Site: http://www.stefan-pettersson.nu/site/

Product Page: http://www.stefan-pettersson.nu/site/mozillatracker/

Product Description: MozillaTracker is a log analyzer that can be used to report Web site statistics, including the type of browser or operating system your visitors are using. Data can be presented as text or HTML and printed as reports.

Distribution: Freeware.

Major features include:

- ▣ The ability to view data by visitor operating system or browser

- ▣ The ability to sort data alphabetically or by the number of hits

- ▣ The ability to filter data based on browser version or browser titles

NetInsightTracker

Developer Site: http://www.netinsight.unica.com/

Product Page: http:// wwwnetinsight.unica.com/pProducts/ enterprise-web-analytics.htmNetTracker.cfm

Product Description: NetInsightTracker is a log analysis application that provides you with the ability to track usage of one for more Web sites.

It includes a wide collection of built-in reports as well as the ability to generate custom and ad hoc reports. You can use it to track the success of your banner advertisements, examine which keywords visitors are using to find your Web site, and find out which of your pages are being visited the most.

Distribution: Free demo-trial.

Major features include:

- ☑ Built-in and custom reporting with filtering options
- ☑ Trend reports that help you examine traffic over time
- ☑ The ability to examine data collected from logs or from embedded Web page tags

PowerMapper

Developer Site: http://www.electrum.co.uk

Product Page: http://www.electrum.co.uk/products/mapper.htm

Product Description: PowerMapper provides Web site publishers with a tool for creating interactive site maps, which in turn provide simple site navigation and visualization. PowerMapper crawls through a Web site, producing a site map containing thumbnail images of each page, and automatically creates a site map in HTML or GIF format. It also verifies links and detects broken HTML tags.

Distribution: Free 30-day trial.

Major features include:

- ☑ The ability to generate site maps for any Web site
- ☑ The ability to visually examine your Web site's structure
- ☑ The ability to print out your site maps
- ☑ The ability to report on broken links and invalid HTML

Search Engine Commando

Developer Site: http://www.searchenginecommando.com/

Product Page: http://www.searchenginecommando.com/

Product Description: Search Engine Commando provides you with a tool for measuring the progress of your Web site promotion campaign. You can also use it to submit your Web pages to search engines and create ranking reports.

Distribution: Free trial.

Major features include:

- ☐ Supports all the major search engines
- ☐ Works with multiple Web pages and URLs
- ☐ Provides automated scheduling
- ☐ Generates reports showing how well your Web pages rank against your competition

Surfstats Log Analyzer

Developer Site: http://www.surfstats.com

Product Page: http://www.surfstats.com/./ssl_prod.asp

Product Description: Surfstats Log Analyzer provides you with dozens of reports regarding various statistics for your Web site and its visitors. It uses Web server log files to retrieve information that you can use to determine how your Web site promotion campaign is doing over time and to find any errors that may be occurring.

Distribution: Free trial.

Major features include:

- ☐ The ability to view Web site hits and page views
- ☐ The ability to watch specific pages

⊡ The ability to determine which Web pages visitors are using as entry points to your Web sites and which pages are being used as exit points

⊡ The ability to track your banners, determine search engines' referrers, and to tell when visitors are bookmarking your Web pages

TopDog Pro

Developer Site: http://www.topdogsoftware.biz/

Product Page: http://www.topdogsoftware.biz/

Product Description: TopDog is a Web site positioning and ranking application. It queries the top search engines for your Web site and keywords, showing where you and your competitors are positioned. TopDog eliminates the chore of visiting each search engine, typing in your keywords, and analyzing the results. TopDog produces reports on your Web site and on your competitors and alerts users to changes in rank.

Distribution: Free trail available.

Major features include:

⊡ The ability to determine ranking for any specified keywords

⊡ Support for unlimited number of Web sites

⊡ Customizable reporting

⊡ Built-in scheduling

Site Submission

This section presents a collection of software applications that you can use to help you in your efforts to register your Web site with the major search engines and directories and ultimately get your Web sites noticed by as many people as possible.

AddWeb Website Promoter

Developer Site: http://www.cyberspacehq.com/

Product Page: http://www.cyberspacehq.com/products/addweb/

Product Description: AddWeb Website Promoter is designed to increase your Web site traffic by automatically submitting your site to hundreds of Internet search engines and directories. Use its built-in Web site analysis capabilities to make sure that your Web site is as search engine friendly as possible.

Distribution: Free trial available.

Major features include:

- ☐ Web page-ranking analysis
- ☐ Tools for working with <META>, <ALT>, <TITLE> tags, and other HTML specific tags
- ☐ Submission of multiple sites in one run
- ☐ Keyword analysis
- ☐ Link checking

Dynamic Submission

Developer Site: http://www.submission2000.com/

Product Page: http://www.submission2000.com/product.html

Product Description: Dynamic Submission is a Web site search engine submission tool that will help you to register your Web pages with hundreds of search engines. In addition, this product also includes a collection of search engine optimization tools that you can use to analyze and improve the search engine friendliness of your Web pages.

Distribution: Free trial available.

Major features include:

- A keyword library and keyword builder tool
- Link popularity checking
- A <META> tag generator
- URL verification
- Web site rank analysis and reporting

Exploit's Submission Wizard

Developer Site: http://www.exploit.net/

Product Page: http://www.exploit.net/wizard/index.html

Product Description: Submission Wizard is a search engine submission application that helps you to automate the submission of your Web pages to all the major search engines. It also includes filters that help you to weed out search engines that are not relevant to your Web site.

Distribution: Free trail available.

Major features include:

- Built-in filtering based on Web site content
- Support for all major search engines
- Report generation
- Assistance in manually submitting to search engines that are not directly supported
- Automated submission scheduling

SubmitWolf Pro

Developer Site: http://www.trellian.com/

Product Page: http://www.trellian.com/swolf/index.html

Product Description: SubmitWolf Pro is designed to help you promote your Web site. It maintains a database that includes information about all the major search engines and directories and hundreds of automated submission scripts. Just select a search engine and SubmitWolf Pro will download and fill in its submission form and submit it for you.

Distribution: Free trail available.

Major features include:

- Works with all major search engines
- Built-in submission guard protection prevents spamming search engines and directories
- Provides the ability to work with paid submission services

WebPosition

Developer Site: http://www.webposition.com

Product Page: http://www.webposition.com

Product Description: WebPosition is a collection of tools that can assist you in improving your Web site's ranking with the major search engines. It specializes in analyzing competition, Web page optimization and submission, keyword analysis, and rank reporting.

Distribution: Free 30-day trial.

Major features include:

- The ability to establish a baseline for keyword analysis
- The ability to perform keyword research and analysis
- The ability to analyze and make recommendations for improving your Web pages
- The ability to automate the submission of your Web pages to selected search engines

Web Authoring

In this section you will find software applications that will help you to build effective and more search engine friendly Web sites.

HTML Power Tools

Developer Site: http://www.tali.com

Product Page: http://www.tali.com/tools.html

Product Description: HTML Power Tools consists of eight separate tools that you can use to develop your Web site. Use these tools to make sure that your Web pages are as search engine friendly as possible.

Distribution: Free 30-day trial.

Major features include:

- ☑ HTML syntax checking and link validation
- ☑ Built-in HTML spell-checking
- ☑ <META> tag creation and management
- ☑ Search and replace edit features

SiteXpert

Developer Site: http://www.xtreeme.com

Product Page: http://www.xtreeme.com/sitexpert/

Product Description: SiteXpert provides you with the ability to automatically generate your own site maps. No coding is required. Just run SiteXpert and point it to your Web site's main Web page and it will crawl its way through your Web site and generate a site map. Numerous formats are available.

Distribution: Free trial available.

Major features include:

- Automatic Web site crawling

- Built-in link validation

- Cross-browser compatibility

- 11 different site map formats from which to select

Connectivity

This section presents software applications that assist Web site owners by providing tools for checking and verifying Web site connectivity.

Connection Keeper

Developer Site: http://www.gammadyne.com/

Product Page: http://www.gammadyne.com/conkeep.htm

Product Description: Connection Keeper is a software application that you can use to prevent your Internet connection from going inactive. Web site publishers can use it to monitor their Web sites and verify that Web pages are downloading correctly.

Distribution: Freeware.

Major features include:

- Minimal use of system resources or bandwidth

- The ability to control the time interval used to ensure an active Internet connection

- The ability to monitor Web site availability

- Instant popup or e-mail notification messages when problems are detected

Magic NetTrace

Developer Site: http://www.tialsoft.com

Product Page: http://www.tialsoft.com/mnettrace

Product Description: Magic NetTrace is an IP tracer tool that you can use to track down and identify the source of connection problems.

Distribution: Free trail.

Major features include:

- ☑ Multithreaded tracking of all routes for fast results

- ☑ The ability to print or copy test results

- ☑ Multi-language support

MySpeed Server

Developer Site: http://www.myspeed.com

Product Page: http://www.myspeed.com

Product Description: MySpeed is a Java applet that provides you with the ability to provide your visitors with a tool for testing speed and quality of service with your Web site. MySpeed easily installs on your Web server and does not require any client-side code.

Distribution: Online demo available.

Major features include:

- ☑ The ability to perform upload and download speed tests

- ☑ The ability to perform continuous connection speed tests

- ☑ The ability to rate quality of service for your Web site

- ☑ Built-in reporting

VisualRoute

Developer Site: http://www.visualroute.com/

Product Page: http://www.visualroute.com/

Product Description: VisualRoute is a traceroute application that you can use to analyze connectivity problems. The program offers a map of the world, which you can use to view the routes that your IP packets take as your compute over the Internet. VisualRoute is fast, allowing you to track all hops in parallel, making it work quicker than conventional traceroute programs.

Distribution: 15-day trial available.

Major features include:

- The ability to trace connection problems between a remote user and your Web server

- The ability to allow visitors to test their connectivity with your Web server

- Graphical representation of connections and connectivity issues

GLOSSARY

A

advertisement. On the Internet, an advertisement typically consists of paid and free banners as well as search engines and directory Web site listings.

affiliate. A member of a sales program in which the member receives payment for delivering customers to the Web site of the sponsoring affiliate program.

affiliate program. On the Internet, an affiliate program is an agreement between a sponsoring Web site and member Web site in which member Web sites are paid for bringing visitors to the sponsoring Web site.

ALT Tag. An HTML tag that is used as a means of displaying text in place of graphics in browsers that do not support graphics. The ALT tag also provides an opportunity for Web publishers to reinforce keyword and keyword phrase relevance.

animated GIF. An animated image that uses the GIF89aa format.

ASCII (American Standard Code for Information Interchange). A standard encoding system for text.

ASCII file. A standard text file.

attachment. A file added to an e-mail message.

autoresponder. A computer program that automatically answer e-mails that are sent to it.

award. On the Internet, an award is an honor assigned to a Web site for excellence, exceptional presentation, or good content.

B

bandwidth. The amount of data that can be sent through a given communications circuit.

banner. *See banner advertisement.*

banner advertisement. An image used for advertising on the Web; the typical banner ad is a GIF image at 468 × 60 pixels.

banner exchange. A Web service in which member Web sites display other Web site's banners in exchange for displaying their own banner.

banner exchange ratio. The display-to-credit ratio offered by an exchange. The most common exchange is 2 to 1. If an exchange has a 2 to 1 exchange ratio, this means that for every two times that someone views a banner on your Web site, your banner will be displayed one time at a member site.

blog. An interactive Web site that allows visitors to read and post messages relating to a particular subject.

bookmark. A reference to a Web site stored by a browser.

browse. To window-shop on the Internet, wandering from Web site to Web site. See also *surfing*.

browser. A software application that is used to access and surf the World Wide Web.

bulletin board. An online system that allows Web surfers to post and advertise information.

C

case insensitive. A term used to describe software that treats uppercase and lowercase letters as equivalent.

case sensitive. A term used to describe software that treats uppercase and lowercase letters as distinct.

CGI (Common Gateway Interface). Defines how scripts communicate with Web servers.

CGI scripts. Programs that connect to a Web server and other applications. Also known as gateway scripts. See *CGI*.

click through. A count of the number of times that visitors click on a banner.

click-through ratio. The total number of clicks on a banner divided by the total number of impressions.

clickable image. An image that can be clicked on to access a link to a specified target resource, such as a Web page.

client. A computer that requests the services of another computer (or server).

cool site. A Web site that has been awarded a status of "cool" by a Cool Site of the Day Web site.

comments. Hidden text embedded inside HTML pages, which is used by Web page programmers to document the contents of the Web page. Comments also provide an opportunity for Web publishers to reinforce keyword and keyword phrase relevance.

commercial online service. A commercial service, such as America Online (AOL), that connects people to the Internet. Most commercial services provide additional content and features for their users; these features generally distinguish a commercial service from an Internet service provider.

connection. A link between two computers for the purpose of communication.

contest. A marketing tool used to draw traffic to the sponsoring Web site with the promise of a chance to win a prize.

copyright. The legal ownership of a given product or idea.

counter. A program used to track hits or page views.

crawler. See *indexer*.

cybermall. The online equivalent of a modern shopping mall that allows Web surfers to shop and purchase items from multiple online stores. Cybermalls allow Web surfers to pay once for all purchased products, greatly simplifying the surfer's shopping experience.

D

database. A repository used to store and retrieve data. In the case of search engines, a database is used to store and retrieve information about Web sites crawled or spidered on the Internet.

dead link. A pointer to a URL on the Web that is no longer valid. Dead links are typically identified by the appearance of a 404- - File Not Found error message.

Description attribute. A Meta tag parameter that is used to specify a brief description for a Web page.

direct mailing. An e-mail message sent directly to an individual Internet e-mail address.

directory. On the Web, a service that provides a description of Web sites as well as links to the Web sites. Generally, you can browse a directory by category or search by keyword.

domain. The part of an address that identifies a Web site, such as tvpress.com.

download. To retrieve a file from a remote computer and store a copy of the file on your computer.

E

editor. A program used to edit a file.

e-mail (electronic mail). A service that provides the ability to send and receive messages on a network.

e-mail address. Used to identify the senders and recipients of an e-mail message. Created by combining a user name with a computer name, such as william@tvpress.com.

e-mail signature. Text that you can append into the end of your e-mail messages automatically.

exchange ratio. Generally pertains to the exchange ratio for banner ads; see also *banner exchange ratio*.

exclusion list. A list that identifies Web pages that should not be indexed by a search engine.

eZine. A periodic publication that is posted online or distributed via e-mail.

F

FAQs (Frequently Asked Questions). A list of frequently asked questions and their answers. Newsgroups, mailing lists, and other fun sites on the Web often publish a list of FAQs you can read.

frames. An HTML construct that defines a section or area within a FRAMESET as well as the content that is to be loaded into that section or area.

FRAMESET. An HTML construct that provides the ability to map out and represent the available space within a browser window.

freebie. Something given away by a Web site to its visitors with no strings attached.

G

game. A computer program that allows one or more players to compete against each other or a computer opponent.

GIF (Graphics Interchange Format). A compressed file format for images. The most widely used graphics format in Web pages.

.gif. A file extension used for GIF images.

giveaway. An organized effort to attract visitors to a Web site by offering to give visitors a freebie of some type.

graphic. An image displayed on a Web page, such as a picture, drawing, or other type of rendering.

guestbook. A Web site system that permits visitors to post public comments.

guide. See *Web guide*.

H

hierarchy. Within newsgroups, the naming structure that helps computers track the various discussion groups.

hit. The number of file accesses at a Web site. Every file that is accessed to display a Web page, including each graphic, in a browser is considered a hit.

home page. The main page for a person's or an organization's Web site. Your personal home page is the page you see when you start your browser.

host. A computer that handles requests from clients.

hostname. The name of a host computer, such as tvpress.com.

.htm. A file extension used for Web pages.

.html. A file extension used for Web pages.

HTML (Hypertext Markup Language). A text-based computer language used to create Web pages.

HTTP (Hypertext Transfer Protocol). The protocol used to distribute information on the World Wide Web.

human-powered directory. See *directory*.

hybrid sites. A search Web site that combines qualities of both search engines and directories in order to provide visitors with results.

I

image. A name used to refer to a graphic.

image map. An image with multiple hot spots that link to different resources on the Internet; acts as a graphical menu of sorts.

image search service. A search service that allows surfers to search for images and displays those images along with links back to the Web sites where those pictures reside.

impression. Describes the instances in which a banner is displayed.

indexer. For search engines, a utility that creates an index for all the pages at a Web site.

interface. Describes the mechanisms you can use to work with computer programs or the method by which programs communicate with each other.

Internet. A massive networked computing community or the system by which computers around the world communicate with each other.

Internet protocol address. A unique numeric identifier for a networked computer.

IP (Internet Protocol). A standard convention for passing information over the Internet; defines how data is packed and sent over a network.

IP address. See *Internet protocol address*.

ISP (Internet Service Provider). A company that provides access to the Internet.

J

Java. A programming language used on the Internet to deliver dynamic content to Web browsers.

JPEG. A standard for still-image compression that was developed by the Joint Photographic Experts Group.

.jpeg. A file extension used for JPEG images.

.jpg. A file extension used for JPEG images.

K

keyword. A word or phrase specifying words that represent information presented on a Web page.

keyword attribute. A Meta tag parameter that is used to specify keywords associated with the content of a Web page.

keyword list. A list of words or phrases that help identify the topic(s) covered on a Web site.

keyword loading. A spamming technique used to trick search engines into granting higher keyword ranking by repeating the same keyword and keyword phrases over and over again.

L

legal issues. Concerns that govern and restrict the actions and content of Web sites. Legal issues include local, state, national, and international laws and regulations.

link. An element that points to a resource on the Internet and provides the method for accessing that resource.

link farms. A spamming technique used to trick search engines into granting a high ranking to a Web site by making a Web site seem more popular than it really it is.

This is achieved by creating Web pages for the sole purpose of linking to a specific Web site.

list. A collection of links to Web sites.

log file. See *server log file*.

log file analysis. The process of examining the contents of a log file in order to extract data that is then used to create information that can be used to gauge visitor characteristics and behavior.

M

mailing list. A discussion group handled through a standard mail program, or a special type of e-mail address for distributing messages to a group of subscribers.

marketing campaign. An organized Web site promotion effort.

Meta information. Data that is included in a Web page header but is hidden from the reader; generally contains instructions or special notes for Web clients.

Meta search engine. A search site that retrieves results by simultaneously querying multiple search engines and directories.

Meta tag. An HTML tag that provides the ability to specify information that search engines can use when creating listings for Web pages.

MetaCrawler. See *Meta search engine*.

metro guide. A Web guide to a metropolitan area. See also *Web guide*.

moderated discussion. A discussion that has a moderator. Usually, all messages submitted to a moderated discussion are checked by the moderator before they are distributed or posted. See also *moderator*.

moderated mailing list. A mailing list that has a moderator.

moderated newsgroup. A newsgroup that has a moderator.

moderator. A person who manages a discussion and ensures it stays on track.

MySpace. A social networking service that allows members to share information and to post photos and other electric data.

N

NCSA (National Center for Supercomputing Applications). Part of the University of Illinois, and the place where the original graphics-capable browser, called Mosaic, was developed.

network. A group of computers that are all connected in order to facilitate data sharing and communications.

news. Shorthand for newsgroups. See also *newsgroup*.

news server. A computer that stores discussion groups.

newsgroup. An electronic discussion group through which you can post and read messages.

newsreader. A program for reading and posting messages to newsgroups.

NOFRAME tag. An HTML tag that provides the ability to display content shown on browsers that do not support HTML frames.

O

off-page factors. Techniques used to help search engines determine a Web page's ranking using data collected from a source other than the Web page itself.

P

page. A document on a Web server.

page title. A descriptive statement defined in an HTML `<TITLE>` tag.

page view. A request for a Web page, which is normally in HTML format.

paid inclusion. Payment to a search engine made in exchange for an immediate listing in the search engine's database.

password. A security keyword used to protect your Internet accounts.

permission marketing. A process in which visitors are formally asked for permission to send them e-mail related to specific products and services.

poll. A small survey that gives individuals the opportunity to express their opinion on a specific issue or topic.

privacy policy. A formal statement regarding the operations of a Web site and the manner in which the Web site uses the information that it collects about visitors.

protocol. A set of rules for communicating on a network.

R

Really simple syndication (rss). A Web feed that notifies users of changes to blogs, articles, videos, and other Web resources and provides automated access to that content.

reciprocal link. A link placed on a Web site in exchange for a link back to the first site owner's Web site.

redirection. See *server redirection*.

registration. See *search-engine registration*.

registration service. An organization that registers your Web site with multiple search engines and directories.

reindex. The process a search engine goes through when it returns to a Web site in order to validate its content or discover new links.

relevancy. For search engines, a term that is used to identify how strongly a Web site relates to the entered keyword query string.

repeat traffic generator. Any marketing technique that results in visitors returning back to a Web site. Examples of repeat traffic generators include games, online advice columns, and a Tip of the Day.

resource. A general term for a file on the Internet.

robots.txt. A file on your Web server that tells search engines which files should not be indexed.

S

scripts. A collection of programming statements written in a language such as JavaScript that executes within a visitor's browser.

search. The process of looking for Web sites by performing keyword searches using a Web search engine.

search engine. A Web service that assists Web surfers in finding Web sites on the Internet based on keyword searches.

search-engine registration. The process of applying for a listing at a Web search engine.

server. A computer that handles requests and provides resources.

server log file. A file stored on a Web server that is used to record events affecting Web pages.

server redirection. A technique used to point users at a new location.

shopping search engine. A specialized type of search engine designed to assist Web surfers in finding and comparing products sold on the Internet.

signature. See *e-mail signature*.

signature file. A text file used to store an e-mail signature.

social bookmarking. Web sites that allow users to organize, store, comment on, and share bookmarks to interesting Web sites and content.

social media marketing. A term used to describe the Web promotion practices that focus on attracting users through social media channels.

social networking site. A virtual community that allows people with common interests to meet online and to share information.

social news. Web sites that allow visitors to submit and vote on news stories, Web sites, and other Web resources like images and video.

social review sites. Web sites that facilitate consumer review of just about any purchasable item.

spam. An unsolicited message that tries to sell a product or service.

spammer. Someone who distributes unsolicited commercial messages.

spider. See *indexer*.

standard. The widely accepted way to handle a process or technology; usually set by standards organizations.

statistics. Information compiled from a variety of resources, such as server logs.

stats. See *statistics*.

status code. A three-digit number that indicates the status of an HTTP request. The code 404 indicates that a file was not found.

stickiness. A term used to refer to the ability of a Web site to keep visitors interested enough to stick around and visit the site for a while.

surfing. To browse pages on the Web.

sweepstakes. A special type of contest in which prizes are donated by a 3rd party in order to advertise or promote either the 3rd party or its products.

T

T1. A type of digital communications line or the standard for distributing data at 1.44 million bits per second.

targeting. The selection of categories used when determining the appropriate Web sites where banners and other types of ads are to be placed.

thread. A unique subject or topic in a discussion group.

throughput. The measurement of the transfer rate between a server and client computers.

TITLE tag. An HTML tag that is used to specify a name or description for a Web page. The <TITLE> tag provides an opportunity for Web publishers to reinforce keyword and keyword phrase relevance.

top-level page. Another way to refer to a Web site's home page.

tracking software. A software application or Web service that tracks Web statistics and turns them into information that Web site owners can use to analyze the overall performance and success of their Web site.

treasure hunt. A special type of contest in which the hosting Web site hides clues throughout its Web site and challenges visitors to find those clues.

.txt. A file extension for plain ASCII text files.

U

upload. To transfer data from your computer to another computer.

URL (Uniform Resource Locator). Provides a uniform way of identifying resources on a Web server. Also referred to as a Web address or location. A typical URL looks like this:
http://www.tvpress.com/

URL Analyzer. A software application or Web service that examines all of the links located on a Web site and reports on any that are no longer functional.

V

viewer. A program (helper application) for viewing files.

viral marketing. A marketing tool that leverages visitor opinion by encouraging visitors to pass on information provided by the Web sites to friends and colleagues.

virtual launch. The act of promoting the opening or re-opening of a Web site for the purpose of attracting attention and bringing visitors to the Web site.

visit. The set of requests made by a single user in a single session; a collection of hits and page views that pertain to a specific person who requested files from your Web site during a specified time frame.

visitor. A person browsing a Web site.

W

Web 2.0. A second generation of Web development technologies that facilities the development of interactive Web sites in which visitors communicate, collaborate, and share information with one another.

Web address. The URL or location of a resource on the Web.

Web client. An application used to access Web-based technologies, such as a Web browser.

Web guide. A guide to the Web that tries to help you find the best Web sites.

Web master. The person responsible for administering a Web site or Web server.

Web page. A document on a Web server that is displayed when a Web surfer types its URL into a browser.

Web ring. A collection of related Web sites that are set up so that they point to one another under the direction of a central server that manages the ring.

Web server. A computer on the Internet that stores Web pages and allows browsers to access them.

Web site. A collection of Web pages on a Web server.

Web site statistics. A collection of data representing activities that have occurred on a Web server or for a specified Web site.

Web site template. A pre-defined outline used as the basis for rapidly building new Web sites based on its design and layout.

Web traffic analysis. The process of examining Web site statistics in order to extrapolate useful information that can be used to study visitor activity and assist in making decisions on how to improve the Web site.

What's New? directories. A special type of directory that is dedicated to storing and providing information about new Web sites on the Internet.

White Pages. A directory for finding e-mail addresses, phone numbers, and street addresses.

Wiki. A collaborative online Web site that can be edited by anyone who wants to contribute.

WikiPedia. The best known and most commonly used Wiki Web site.

World Wide Web. A hypertext-based system for distributing information and resources. Also known as the *Web*, *WWW*, or *W3*.

Y

Yellow Pages. A directory for finding businesses on the Web and in the real world.

INDEX

Y